To Malcolm   with best

Alan .

Elsie Chamberlain

Gender, Theology and Spirituality

Series Editor: Lisa Isherwood, University of Winchester

Gender, Theology and Spirituality explores the notion that theology and spirituality are gendered activities. It offers the opportunity for analysis of that situation as well as provides space for alternative readings. In addition it questions the notion of gender itself and in so doing pushes the theological boundaries to more materialist and radical readings. The series opens the theological and spiritual floodgates through an honest engagement with embodied knowing and critical praxis.

Published

Resurrecting Erotic Transgression: Subjecting Ambiguity in Theology
Anita Monro

Patriarchs, Prophets and Other Villains
Edited by Lisa Isherwood

Women and Reiki: Energetic/Holistic Healing in Practice
Judith Macpherson

Unconventional Wisdom
June Boyce-Tillman

Numen, Old Men: Contemporary Masculine Spiritualities and the Problem of Patriarchy
Joseph Gelfer

Ritual Making Women: Shaping Rites for Changing Lives
Jan Berry

Sex and Uncertainty in the Body of Christ: Intersex Conditions and Christian Theology
Susannah Cornwall

Being the Body of Christ: Towards a Twenty-first Century Homosexual Theology for the Anglican Church
Chris Mounsey

Elsie Chamberlain: The Independent Life of a Woman Minister
Alan Argent

Elsie Chamberlain
The Independent Life of a Woman Minister

Grace Amid Storms

Alan Argent

Published by Equinox Publishing Ltd
UK: Unit S3, Kelham House, 3 Lancaster Street, Sheffield, S3 8AF
USA: ISD, 70 Enterprise Drive, Bristol, CT 06010

www.equinoxpub.com

First published 2013

British Library Cataloguing-in-Publication Data

A catalogue record for this book is available from the British Library.

ISBN 978 1 84553 931 3   (hardback)

Library of Congress Cataloging-in-Publication Data

Argent, Alan.
   Elsie Chamberlain : the independent life of a woman minister/ Alan Argent.
      p. cm. — (Gender, theology, and spirituality)
   Includes bibliographical references (p.   ) and index.
   ISBN 978-1-84553-931-3 (hb)
   1. Chamberlain, Elsie, 1910–1991. 2. Congregational Union of England and Wales —
Clergy — Biography. 3. Women clergy — England — Biography. I. Title.
   BX7260.C44A74 2012
   285.8092 — dc23
   [B]
                                2011019752

Typeset by S.J.I. Services, New Delhi
Printed and bound in the UK by MPG Books Group

'For thou hast been a strength to the poor, a strength to the needy in distress, a refuge from the storm, a shadow from the heat, when the blast of the terrible ones is as a storm against the wall.' Isaiah 25:4

'God resists the proud and gives grace to the humble.' 1 Peter 5:5

CONTENTS

LIST OF ILLUSTRATIONS

ACKNOWLEDGEMENTS

This book would not have been possible without the help and encouragement of many people, none of whom are responsible for any remaining flaws or omissions, yet debts should be acknowledged. My wife, Jane Giscombe, has been a constant source of hope and support. However this work originated in a suggestion several years ago from the All People Together Board of the Congregational Federation, and particular thanks are owed to Margaret Morris and to Janet Wootton. That initiative from the board led to a series of articles in the then *Congregational History Circle Magazine* and thanks are due to the editorial committee of the Circle (now the Congregational History Society) for permission to publish material which first appeared in an earlier form in successive issues of that magazine.

I am also conscious of the kindness of many who have read and corrected errors. These must include members of Elsie Chamberlain's family, especially Janette Williams and Geoffrey A. Chamberlain. Those who supplied information and assistance with details include Graham M. Adams, Revd Ray Avent, Revd Edmund Banyard, Tony Benn PC, Revd Irene Blayney, Revd Eric Burton, Revd Owen Butler, John Carpenter, Mrs Jan and Revd Vincent Carrington, Dr Richard Cleaves, Revd Anthony Coates, Timothy Cornford, Revd Robert Courtney, Revd Christopher Damp, Mrs A. Forbes, Prof. John Hibbs, the Ven F. House, Dr Elaine Kaye, Mrs Ruth Lawrence, Mrs Avril and Revd Roy Lowes, Revd Elaine Marsh, Revd Deborah Martin, Jonathan Morgan, Revd Elisabeth Neale, Mrs Val and Revd Colin Price, Revd Edwin Robertson, Revd Geoffrey Roper, Joyce Sampson, Mrs Millicent Slack, Mrs B. Smith, Revd Rachel Storr, Joan Taylor, Mrs Annette and Revd Dr John Travell, and John Wilcox. Some of these friends are no longer living and this work should honour them.

In addition to these, I should mention the members of my church, Trinity Congregational, in Brixton, south London, and also of my former churches, St Helier Congregational Church, Morden, and Dundonald Congregational Church, Wimbledon. Their forbearance and consistent encouragement of my studies have contributed much to my regular forays into church history. Thanks are due to colleagues on the Training Board of the Congregational Federation who have expressed an interest in my work. Prof. Jeff Cox of the University of Iowa has been a friend throughout and has never let me lose heart. I have benefited greatly from the willingness of Peter Young to act as an unpaid research assistant in this, as in other projects, and I must thank him especially.

Prof. Lisa Isherwood of the University of Winchester read the script and, at a crucial stage, gave added momentum to my continuance with this work and much needed advice on publishing. I am grateful also to Norma Beavers who has guided me through the editorial process.

I have consulted the records of Elsie Chamberlain's former churches and I am grateful to their ministers and deacons for enabling me to see their minute books and other archives. In addition, I have of necessity carried out research in several libraries throughout the country. The collections at Dr Williams's Library, London, and its companion, the Congregational Library, have been essential for the completion of this book and I wish to thank their staffs.

Finally, my first wife, Yvonne Ann Evans, was keen to see this research in published form but her unexpected death in 2006 prevented that. She remains an inspiration.

Chapter 1

INTRODUCTION AND EARLY LIFE

In the years of austerity following the Second World War, and set against the lacklustre backcloth of the English churches, Elsie Chamberlain was a glittering star whose brilliance illuminated the most conservative of institutions. Her vibrant personality, her refreshing presence and her reassuring and authoritative voice lifted the hearts and lightened the load. This success was all the more remarkable because she was a woman, at a time when women in the churches were allowed to be seen but were not expected to be heard. Women had begun to raise their hopes given the frequent absence of men during the war years and Elsie's success was also remarkable because she belonged to a relatively small, unfashionable Protestant denomination, which wielded little influence on the world stage and, at least in part because of falling church membership, not much more at home. Her singular and unfussy contribution, blowing away the cobwebs and the dust of ages from the churches, with girlish glee and tireless energy, was a breath of fresh air, gratefully acknowledged by the common man and woman, in and out of the pew, and the intellectual alike.

She was a Congregationalist, both by upbringing and conviction, and she was also a minister. Although Elsie was tall and athletic, with a striking presence, she was hardly a glamorous figure, by later estimations of that term, choosing to dress in a plain and sober style, but nor could she be accounted a frump. She had a university degree but claimed no great academic powers, although she always retained a measure of intellectual curiosity. However her insights and questions perfectly matched those of the ordinary believer, whose feelings, hopes and fears she was able to articulate with apparent ease. Given her sex and her vocation, and the complexity of her private life, she followed no smooth, well worn path to recognition. Rather she encountered intimidating obstacles at every turn in both her personal and public lives. Indeed her record almost suggests that she happened upon the most hazardous and awkward routes to navigate. In the light of such disconcerting experience, her unique achievement and sustained success in different fields, throughout her adult life, become all the more remarkable. However, to those who knew her well, even in relatively old age, Elsie was a force of nature, irresistible and awe-inspiring. One learned not to stand in her way but, even in disagreement, to step back and admire.

If Elsie Chamberlain was confronted by so many obstacles to advancement, offsetting these she had the intrinsic advantages of a strong and supportive family, great self-belief and indomitable strength of character. In addition, she was blessed with exceptional vitality and courage, gifts and graces which she used to good effect in her various roles as Congregational Minister, RAF Chaplain, and Broadcaster. A pioneer in women's work and a consistent champion of equal opportunities for women, she betrayed no gaucheness in her dealings with men and little, if any, embarrassment at being a woman who had invaded and succeeded in a man's world. Her manifest competence made it easier for some to accept the ministry of women and, correspondingly, more difficult for others to oppose it. How could her calling and her prowess be denied? How could her achievements not have been blessed by God?

She was not the first woman to be ordained a Congregational minister but she was the first woman chairman of the Congregational Union of England and Wales, in 1956–57, at a time when women ministers, in the churches as a whole, were still widely regarded as things of curiosity. Her triumph, within Congregationalism, was built upon the achievements of these forerunners (like Constance Coltman and Muriel Paulden, both of whom will receive fuller treatment later), the women ministers of the previous generation, and this she freely recognized. Without deliberately courting controversy, she nevertheless discovered it by falling in love with an Anglican clergyman and, despite objections at the highest ecclesiastical and social levels to their union, by refusing to deny their mutual affection and their right to marry. Although postponed for several years, their marriage did finally take place. Thus she became the first minister of another denomination to marry a beneficed clergyman of the Church of England. By then she had already made headline news when Lord Stansgate, as Minister for Air in the post-1945 Labour government in the United Kingdom, had adamantly resisted the pressure, exerted upon him by the Archbishop of Canterbury, to withdraw her appointment to the RAF. If in both these ways her newsworthy activities and stand for principle brought her in different quarters some ephemeral notoriety and renown, and proved her toughness and durability, her 17 years at the BBC consistently revealed outstanding natural talents in the new world of broadcasting and gave her a sustained national celebrity. This experience, tenacity and fame she brought with her in 1972 when, in her older years, she surprisingly shunned the overtures of the promoters of the United Reformed Church and joined the Congregational Federation which she served loyally, until her death, having, with almost regal disdain, simply ignored the option of retirement.

Elsie Chamberlain was, therefore, a brilliant individualist, both by temperament and circumstance, who had sufficient confidence and adherence to principle to blaze her own way, guided and propelled along it, as she believed, by the Holy Spirit. In so doing she encountered and overcame frustration, opposition and relative isolation. Throughout, her life was informed by a warm and accepting Christian faith, which with ready laughter she communicated easily to others, and by an infectious sense of liberating joy. Yet she combined these with impatience and an irrepressible need to cut through all humbug, thus offending some who resented her scrupulous honesty, her curt dismissal of those with whom she disagreed and, while at the BBC, in her pruning of the draft scripts of occasional broadcasters.

Elsie's upbringing contributed greatly to her character and gave her such self-confidence that she could confront and overcome obstacles which would have intimidated lesser souls. Her happy and supportive family, her involvement in chapel life from early childhood, and her education all played their part in the formation of this outstanding woman.

Early Life

Her father, James Arthur Chamberlain (Jim to his friends and family), had attended the local parish church in north London as a child. There he had been befriended by the choirmaster who spotted his potential as a treble and helped him to gain entry to the Dame Alice Owen School in Islington. In time Jim's voice deepened into a fine tenor, enabling him to sing in church choirs until he was 80 years old, and he communicated his evident love of music to his children. On leaving school Jim found employment with the General Post Office where he worked 'long and unsociable' hours. As a young man he met Annie Maria, the middle daughter of Maria Hayward, a widow who had three girls to care for, and he immediately fell in love. Annie had studied at a Church of England school and had begun training to become a pupil teacher but, finding this exhausting, she had instead joined a firm in the City of London as a bookkeeper.

Jim and Annie married on 25 September 1897 and made their first home in three upstairs rooms in a Victorian house in Grange Road (later called Grange Grove), Islington. The couple's first children were twin boys but, despite Annie's difficult confinement, she unwisely declined a doctor's attentions and also refused to go into hospital for the birth. Sadly, one twin was stillborn. The survivor, Sidney James, was followed two years later by another boy, Ronald Arthur. In 1904, Jim and Annie bought a new home and the young family moved to 30 Canonbury Park North, a large semi-detached, three storeyed house, with Annie's mother and the two unmarried sisters occupying the top floor. In addition, the household included a maid who slept in the attic and who received an annual income of £5 for her labours. Therefore, this was a large, but not untypical, middle-class Edwardian household and it was to grow larger. In 1904, Annie gave birth to a daughter named Irene who proved to be sickly and died in infancy. Concerned for his wife's health, Jim had pleaded with Annie to consult a second doctor but she had a strong will and stubbornly kept faith with the family practitioner. Subsequently she became ill herself at their child's death. In this crisis Maria Hayward, Annie's mother, took control of the domestic arrangements. Six years later, on 3 March 1910, their second daughter, the subject of this study, Elsie Dorothea, was born also at home and she quickly became the centre of attention, receiving the doting care of her brothers, her parents and all the family. Elsie, the treasured baby, was dressed by Annie Chamberlain almost as a doll, with Maria Hayward taking great pains to iron her grand-daughter's ribbons, bows and bonnets.[1]

Islington Chapel

Although both parents were devout Christians, Jim, like many husbands, deferred to his wife when it came to the choice of church for the children who, therefore, regularly accompanied Annie to Islington

---

1. J. Williams, *First Lady of the Pulpit: A Biography of Elsie Chamberlain* (Lewes, Sussex: Book Guild, 1993), pp. 11–15. *Oxford Dictionary of National Biography.*

Chapel, in Upper Street. This chapel traced its origins to 1788, that is to the years of the evangelical revival. In the late seventeenth century at least two dissenting academies had been sited, albeit temporarily, in Islington, which had the obvious advantage of proximity to London. Yet religious Nonconformity had passed through a quieter phase since the seventeenth century and the warm breath of the Spirit had a revitalizing effect here as elsewhere in the late eighteenth century.

The first Islington Chapel had been built in Church (later Gaskin) Street and some of the materials, used as hardcore for its foundations, had come from the ruins of the old St James' Church, then being rebuilt, in nearby Clerkenwell. At that time Islington was a village of perhaps some 5,000 people, set on higher ground a little to the north of the City of London proper. In 1811 the parish of Islington consisted of some 15,000 souls but, in the nineteenth century, the area grew uninterruptedly so that by 1891 the population had swollen to 320,000. By 1814 the original building, which passed through various transformations (until the 1970s when it was demolished), had served its purpose and the foundation stone of a new chapel was laid in Upper Street in November that year by Matthew Wilks (1746-1828), the eccentric and popular minister of Moorfields Tabernacle and Tottenham Court Chapels, who had been one of the founders of the London Missionary Society. This second chapel, built in the classical style, and stuccoed and turreted, was much grander than its predecessor. The chapel opened in September 1815 and with alterations in 1847-48 together with the addition of a basement school in 1853, it served well until it was compulsorily purchased by the Metropolitan Board of Works for road widening in the 1880s.

The chapel, which Annie and the Chamberlain children attended in the early twentieth century, had been erected as recently as 1887-88, on part of the old site. Some 90 years later, having joined the United Reformed Church on its formation in 1972, the chapel closed in 1979 and was sold. It subsequently was converted into a suite of offices and recording studios. It remains a handsome building, on the corner of Upper Street and Gaskin Street, built in Queen Anne style, of red brick with gauged brick and Portland stone dressings and a red tiled roof. In its heyday, when the Chamberlains attended, the building comprised a large galleried chapel, a basement school, and several ancillary rooms. Originally painted for the most part in olive green, with the gallery front in white, the large chapel, designed with two side aisles, was able to hold a thousand worshippers. Beneath the chapel the main schoolroom could be divided into various compartments, by means of low folding screens which, when closed, formed a dado round the walls and which enabled almost 30 classes to be taught simultaneously under the supervision of a solitary superintendent.[2]

Each separate room and class cubicle was named after a famous man or woman, drawn from Christian, mainly Nonconformist, history. Such names included not only well-known figures like Isaac Watts, David Livingstone, Oliver Cromwell and John Milton but also the less celebrated, at least in England, Mary Jones of Bala, the Bible loving Welsh girl, Mrs Ann H. Judson, wife to Adoniram Judson the American Baptist missionary to Burma, Colonel James Gardiner, the converted atheist and profligate and a close friend of Philip Doddridge, who was killed in the Jacobite rebellion of 1745, John Pye-Smith, the accomplished teacher of teachers, Jane Taylor, the writer for children who was herself born in Islington and was the daughter of a Congregational minister, and Tetsy (Elizabeth) Doddridge, Philip's daughter who as a little girl radiated love for everybody but died of consumption one week before her fifth birthday. Of the 29 names used in this way at Islington Chapel, eight were those of women or girls. Elsie was thus aware at an early age of the positive contribution of Nonconformists, and among them some saintly and extraordinary females, to the cause of Christ and to society as a whole. Nor was she encouraged to be narrowly denominational in her understanding of God's people, for the names included several who were not Congregationalists, such as the pioneer Baptist missionary William Carey, the Scottish Presbyterian Samuel Rutherford, the Quaker Elizabeth Fry, and the evangelical Selina, Countess of Huntingdon, who remained faithful to the Church of England. The Congregationalists of Islington Chapel could not be accused of having a blinkered and male-centred view of the people of God and Elsie embraced that breadth and remained true to it all her life.

Annie Chamberlain took the children with her to both the Sunday morning and evening services and the children also went to the afternoon Sunday School. Naturally the Sunday luncheon table

2. Williams, *First Lady of the Pulpit*, p. 13; H. McLachlan *English Education Under the Test Acts* (Manchester: Manchester University Press, 1931), p. 10. P. Temple, *Islington Chapels* (London: Royal Commission on Historical Monuments England, 1992), pp. 4, 11, 72–3, 122, 130–31. L. Dixon, *Seven Score Years and Ten: The Story of Islington Chapel during One Hundred and Fifty Years 1788–1938* (London: E.O. Beck, nd), p. 17.

provided the occasion for family discussions on the merits and demerits of the morning's worship and preaching. After Sunday School, the children were given tea and cake at home and then returned to the chapel with their mother for the evening service.[3]

The Ministers of Islington Chapel

The minister of Islington Chapel 1897–1912, at the beginning of Elsie's life, was Joseph Graham Henderson (1860–1938), a warm and respected man from Newcastle-upon-Tyne, who had trained for the ministry at Cheshunt College and who, like many Congregationalists, was a keen supporter of the London Missionary Society. In the 1930s the Australian Lyall Dixon, then minister of Islington Chapel, looked back on the 1890s nostalgically as 'the dream days' and found it impossible, 40 years on, to walk along the streets of Canonbury 'without visualizing the carriages, the fine horses, the coachmen, the parasols, the silks and satins and top-hats' of that by-gone era. In those 'respectable' late Victorian days, 'solid middle-class families lived in their solidly built and ornate houses in Islington, and trained their large families in orthodox and conservative ways', he wrote. Although 'the fashionable and the elite' tended to pass its doors, but did not enter, when Henderson came to Islington in the summer of 1897, the chapel was not 'an exclusive place' and 'many serious-minded, influential citizens', like Annie Chamberlain, had found in it 'a spiritual home'.

At Islington Chapel Henderson learned that the church members were struggling to repay the heavy debt incurred with their new building. Principally through his own strenuous efforts, the debt was cleared during his pastorate. By ministering to rich and poor alike, he enhanced the chapel's reputation for friendliness. Its only danger at this time, according to Dixon, was that the prevailing 'genial warmth and undisturbed peace' of chapel life might result in 'a drowsy dullness and a monotony' which, he pronounced, could 'prove so terrible in organized religion'. From the vantage point of the late 1930s, when warlike nations threatened world peace for the second

---

3. Dixon, *Seven Score Years and Ten*; Williams, *First Lady of the Pulpit*, p. 13. For many of these see *Oxford Dictionary of National Biography*. For Mrs Judson see, J.D. Knowles, *Memoir of Mrs Ann H. Judson Late Missionary to Burmah* (2nd edn, Boston, MA: Gould, Kendall & Lincoln, 1829). Jane Taylor (1783–1824) wrote 'Twinkle, Twinkle, Little Star'.

time that century, Edwardian Nonconformity must have appeared a succession of halcyon but distant days, an age of innocence when all seemed prosperous and when the weight of destruction to come was naively unforeseen.

Was life at Islington Chapel at this time monotonous and complacent? Although a measure of routine must have developed, as in any church or chapel, complacency was not allowed to dominate. If Dixon as historian detected the danger, as minister he realized that Henderson and his church members had tried to address the needs of their day. Before the First World War, the chapel routinely provided free breakfasts for 200 homeless and needy children on four mornings a week, thus helping those who faced acute distress, when little or no relief was available elsewhere. The sheer 'joy of these early mornings' was remembered years later. The chapel also held a Sunday evening children's service, with over 100 local poor children gathering for worship. Although 'noisy and undisciplined', they 'instantly responded to the affection shown them', he recorded. That particular work still formed part of the chapel's programme in the 1930s when 'on a winter's night some hundred or more' gathered 'eagerly to enjoy the children's hour'. In September 1904, a Boys' Life Brigade Company was launched and it too survived until the 1930s. It aimed 'to build character and lay a sound basis for manhood' and, despite fluctuations in numbers, it was judged to have been consistently successful.

However, the attendance figures for the congregations in the Edwardian age revealed a disappointing and steadily increasing drift away from the chapel and, after 14 years' hard work, in 1912 Henderson, honourably but probably misguidedly accepting responsibility for the decline, resigned the pastorate. In 1899, the first year that the Congregational Union of England and Wales published membership figures for its churches, Islington Chapel had 444 members but in 1913, the year after Henderson's resignation, the chapel returned a membership figure of only 305, amounting to a loss of 139 in 14 years. By later standards 305 members would be an impressive total but in a chapel, with room for a thousand, in the Edwardian age, the minister felt the loss keenly and decided that he should leave.[4]

4. Dixon, *Seven Score Years and Ten*, pp. 55–58, 67–69. *Congregational Year Book 1899* (London: Congregational Union of England and Wales), p. 293; *Congregational Year Book 1913*, p. 281; *Congregational Year Book 1939*, p. 699.

The Impact of the First World War on Islington Chapel

In 1913 Francis Hugh Smith became the minister, serving throughout the First World War. Hugh Smith (1860–1946) had studied for the ministry at the Wesleyan Methodists' college at Richmond in Surrey, leaving in 1885. He had then emigrated to America where he had served as a minister of the Methodist Episcopal Church in New York for 10 years, before returning home and becoming a Congregationalist. He had served Congregational pastorates in Kingswood, Bristol, and in Chingford, Essex, before moving to Islington where he remained until 1919.[5]

During Elsie's infancy, the life of Islington Chapel seemed to continue undisturbed by the impending international crisis, as members discussed relatively mundane matters such as the advisability of using individual communion cups, planned sales of work, and arranged a centenary meeting to mark the erection of their second building, a hundred years earlier. On the eve of war in July 1914, the chapel members were optimistically planning to hold an evangelistic campaign the following February.

However, the onset of war took its toll of the chapel faithful and all made sacrifices. Many young men from the chapel, including Elsie's brother, Sidney, volunteered to serve in the forces, among them a whole group from the Boys' Life Brigade who joined up together in the Royal Army Medical Corps. The memorial, erected after the war, at the chapel would recall 18 men who died in the conflict, including the younger son of their former minister, J.G. Henderson. Hugh Smith found the demands of serving his pastorate during the war years a severe strain and he was required to take 'an enforced rest'. As in all churches, the pastoral 'task of consolation' drained spiritual energies. People in general dreaded the minister's calling upon them lest he be the bearer of bad news. The war affected Islington Chapel in a variety of ways as services were interrupted, meetings postponed, congregations declined and finances were stretched to breaking point. Exhausted by the war, Smith resigned as minister on the day following the armistice in November 1918, with his resignation taking effect from February 1919. In that same year Islington Chapel

---

5. *Congregational Year Book 1947*, p. 474. F.H. Cumbers (ed.) *Richmond College, 1843–1943* (London: Epworth Press, 1944), p. 175. Why Smith changed denominational allegiance is not known.

claimed to have 231 members, marking a loss of 213 in 20 years and of 74 during Smith's wartime ministry.[6]

Life between the Wars at the Chapel

In the aftermath of the war, the chapel's services were led by a serving army chaplain, Rudolph Naish Davies, who, with some difficulty, helped voluntarily in the absence of a full-time minister. Davies (1884–1962) who had trained for the ministry at New College, London, had previously held pastorates at Needham Market, Suffolk, and at Slough, Buckinghamshire. At the end of 1919, Davies' discharge from the army meant that he was able to accept the chapel's formal call to its ministry. He knew that he faced an uphill task, as men and women slowly grasped that they could not return to the pre-war certainties, while the churches themselves were subjected to sweeping criticisms. Dixon reported that in these circumstances Islington Chapel had struggled against the tide. 'Year after year it was the same grim battle, and the same faithful few', he stated. Among these dedicated supporters were Annie Chamberlain and her children who were growing up amid these years of turbulence. Davies resigned towards the end of 1923 and, in the following year, Islington Chapel had 230 members, perhaps not as few as Dixon later implied, and only one less than when Davies had first come to the chapel, indicating that he had succeeded in holding the fellowship together, even if he had not reversed the tendency. Subsequently, for almost three years, the chapel was without a minister.[7] Therefore Elsie in her formative years was probably aware of an air of disillusion, if Dixon's description of the prevailing mood at the church was accurate, but, inheriting aspects of her mother's character, she formed her own views and kept to them if need be, in the face of contrary social trends. She learned when young to make up her own mind and not simply to absorb and reflect the dominant temper.

In 1926, when Elsie was 16 years old, Joseph Shepherd (1880–1929) became Islington Chapel's minister. His brother later wrote that their 'home influence' had made his choosing to become a minister

---

6. Dixon, *Seven Score Years and Ten*, pp. 59–64. *Congregational Year Book 1919*, p. 183.

7. Dixon, *Seven Score Years and Ten*, pp. 65–67. *Congregational Year Book 1924*, p. 197; *Congregational Year Book 1962*, pp. 455–56.

'inevitable' and, as a result, Joseph had trained at Cheshunt College and graduated from Cambridge. He then served two rural churches in Huntingdonshire and, with the enthusiasm and commitment of youth, while there, he opened five village churches and superintended them all. Having moved in 1913 to Hopton Church, Mirfield, Yorkshire, he volunteered to work as an army chaplain during the First World War, and served at Gallipoli and in Egypt. In 1922 he became the minister of Claremont Congregational Church, in Cape Town, South Africa, where he remained until 1925, before returning to England.

In Islington, Shepherd took on a church which had lost heart. Realizing the need to improve morale, he befriended his people and inspired affection. Under his vigorous leadership the chapel overcame many of its problems and special services brought crowds again to its worship. Members of the women's meeting lined the gallery seats on a Sunday evening and he was a welcome visitor on his pastoral rounds. Significantly also, Shepherd who was adept at talking to children, conducted a number of broadcast services. We may wonder if his involvement in early religious broadcasting planted a seed in Elsie's mind. The Chamberlain family may have discussed his interest in the evangelical potential of broadcasting which may itself have fired her imagination.

Despite his multifarious interests and activities, Joseph Shepherd had suffered indifferent health since his war service but none suspected that he was as physically delicate as he proved to be. He became ill in November 1929 and was admitted to hospital where, before his family even knew that he was unwell, he died, aged 49 years. His lifelong 'devotion to duty' was singled out as contributing to his untimely death. The Islington deacons and church members were deeply shocked at the sudden loss of their minister and placed a stained glass window in the chapel in his memory. It appeared that the demands of Islington had proved too much for the diligent Shepherd.

Although we must allow that the mood at Islington Chapel, at Joseph Shepherd's coming, was probably downcast, the membership figures by later estimations, as has been suggested, might not be considered too discouraging. In 1926 Islington Chapel had 190 members and in 1927 this had fallen to 185 but, three years later, the year after Joseph Shepherd's death, the membership had grown to 258. By way of comparison, in that same year, 1930, Islington Chapel's neighbour, the vast Union Chapel, also Congregational, which had long enjoyed a greater social prestige than Islington Chapel, and was situated just a short distance along Upper Street, had 188 members, 70 fewer than Elsie Chamberlain's home church![8]

After Joseph's death, the chapel folk at Islington came to know his younger brother, Robert Shepherd (1883–1953), who appeared to many on initial acquaintance almost 'the exact likeness' of the energetic Joseph. Favourably impressed and revealing a measure of the esteem in which Joseph was held, six months later, the church members chose Robert to succeed his older sibling as their minister. Like Joseph, Robert Shepherd had trained for the ministry at Cheshunt College, Cambridge. He had previously served pastorates at Dogley Lane, Huddersfield, and at Elland, also in Yorkshire, before moving to Islington in 1930. Robert was noted as a 'faithful pastor and a scholarly preacher' who was reluctant to leave Leeds but felt obliged to respond to God's call, as he understood it. Like his older brother, he was attentive to the needs of the young. Unlike Joseph, his more scholarly interests resulted in his writing a book on the New Testament and a history of Providence Congregational Church, Elland.

Robert was a quiet, reticent man, in many ways a contrast to his brother, but like Joseph in being a conscientious and dutiful pastor who was able to guide the Islington fellowship through difficult years. Essential repairs to the chapel, its organ and heating system were carried out during his time there. In particular, Robert Shepherd's work with the young succeeded because he was genuinely interested in their welfare, had an 'infectious enthusiasm' and 'tireless zeal', as well as a 'subtle and penetrating mind'. Clearly his gifts won over the young people of his churches to the cause of Christ and, guided by him, six of the younger church members entered the Congregational ministry, among them Elsie Chamberlain. However, during the Christmas season of 1936, both Shepherd's mother and sister died and, consequent upon this dramatic change in his family circumstances, he felt obliged to resign from Islington Chapel. He was never again to hold pastoral charge. He returned to his home in Buckley, Chester, where he died in July 1953.

8. Dixon, *Seven Score Years and Ten*, pp. 67–70. *Congregational Year Book 1926*, p. 273; *Congregational Year Book 1927*, pp. 247; *Congregational Year Book 1930*, p. 329; *Congregational Year Book 1931*, pp. 245–46.

Elsie was to recall Robert Shepherd's ministry, in her chairman's address to the Congregational Union of England and Wales at Westminster Chapel in 1956. She stated then that his death, three years earlier, had been 'a great blow to those of us who entered the Ministry during his various ministries' because 'he prayed for us every day, and I felt at first that one of my props had gone – until I remembered that he is probably better at praying for us now than he was here.'[9] Elsie was not alone in her high regard of Robert Shepherd who was well thought of in Islington, some 20 years after he had left.

In 1936, Shepherd's last full year at Islington, the chapel returned a figure of 250 members, eight less than when he had arrived there six years earlier. However, only one year later, in 1937, its membership had declined by a full hundred to 150![10] If these figures are taken at face value then a crisis must have occurred at Islington, either prior to, or in the wake of, Shepherd's resignation, causing members to resign wholesale. He may have had a sizeable personal following which evaporated on his leaving, although other factors may have been at play. An alternative explanation might suggest that the membership roll had not been properly maintained in Shepherd's time, during which period Annie Chamberlain, Elsie's mother, was the church secretary. We may not know the exact reasons for this apparent haemorrhage of members but it is inconceivable that Elsie Chamberlain and her family were untouched either by the causes or effects of such a sudden or, more likely, gradual decline.

The Coming of the Second World War

The late 1930s were a time of potential world upheaval, with strutting dictators in Germany, Italy, Spain (after its civil war) and elsewhere, and with the aggressive Japan expanding its empire in the Far East. The Soviet Union, under Stalin, was also far from stable, with its secret police, show trials and the forced migrations of peoples from their homelands. With the benefit of hindsight, we know that Hitler's territorial demands for Nazi Germany, despite the efforts of other powers to appease him, made a Second World War unavoidable.

9. E.D. Chamberlain, *White to Harvest* (London: Independent Press, 1956), p. 13.

10. Dixon, *Seven Score Years and Ten*, pp. 71–74. *Congregational Year Book 1936*, p. 381; *Congregational Year Book 1937*, p. 425; *Congregational Year Book 1954*, p. 521.

Amid this political volatility, London too experienced violent disturbance, with the Nazi sympathizing Blackshirts of Sir Oswald Mosley clashing with their opponents in the poor neighbourhoods of the east end, not far from Elsie's home and Islington Chapel.

Did these threatening political events have an impact upon the chapel's work and fellowship? Probably not directly but they may have contributed to a climate of fear and hopelessness, reinforced by economic changes and unemployment between the wars, which made a steadfast witness to Christ seem less exciting and less adequate. Might such events have added to the loss of confidence resulting in the decline in membership at Islington Chapel in 1937? Again, perhaps not, but these events troubled Elsie's contemporaries, and her fellow members at the chapel were not immune from the uncertainty which threatened the assurance of Christ's presence which the chapel's life and worship aimed to provide. The loss of a much loved minister at this time was a severe blow.

Through the intervention of a friend living in Banstead, who had helped the chapel since Robert Shepherd's leaving, Lyall Douglas Dixon, then a young man ministering, only a few miles from Banstead, to the new Congregational church, which had opened in 1932, on the large London County Council overspill estate of St Helier, at Morden, Surrey, just south of London, agreed to conduct a service at Islington in early 1937. Subsequently he was called to and accepted the ministry of Islington Chapel, becoming its sixth minister during Elsie Chamberlain's young life. He had trained for the ministry in Adelaide and had served his first pastorate in South Australia before coming to Britain. He remained at Islington until 1944 when he returned to his native country. Dixon came to a church of 150 members and, at his leaving, it had 146 members. To his credit the coming of war in 1939, and the crises consequent upon it (the London Blitz, the evacuation of children and others from the capital, young people joining the armed forces etc), resulted in neither a dramatic decline in the numbers of formal church members nor, we may infer, in those attending the chapel's worship. However, having arrested the decline, Dixon was unsurprisingly unable to increase the membership figures.[11]

At his arrival at the chapel, Elsie was a woman of 27 years. In her old age, she recalled Lyall Dixon and his ministry at Islington with

11. Dixon, *Seven Score Years and Ten*, pp. 75–77. *Congregational Year Book 1944*, p. 145.

clarity and spoke well of him. Although we should not discount the good efforts and support of these six ministers who contributed greatly to the life of Islington Chapel, it is evident that the principal Christian influences upon Elsie in her youth and early adulthood came from her home, and probably most powerfully from her mother. Nor should we discount the influence of her two schools, the Church of England involvement at Dame Alice Owen's and the liberal thought and social concern of the Unitarian Channing School. Yet Elsie's faith had been nurtured at this north London chapel, with its work among the poor and disadvantaged, and its outreach to young people. Of course, she had witnessed the decline in church membership which occurred at Islington Chapel, as elsewhere, and, in spite of this, she had remained loyal. Hers had not been an easy passage to mature Christian faith. Yet she had stayed true to her home church, as had her mother and brothers, despite the fluctuations in its fortunes.

Growing Up

When Elsie was a child the Chamberlains enjoyed annual holidays at the seaside, notably at Eastbourne, in East Sussex, close to the South Downs and Beachy Head, and at Chideock, a village in south-west Dorset, between Bridport and Charmouth, and near Lyme Regis. Jim's custom was to cycle ahead to find suitable accommodation for the family, before being re-united with the others. Following her mother in this as in most matters, young Elsie did not favour walking and cycling but the two boys would usually go with their father on short outings.

Normally Annie Chamberlain would read aloud from the Bible during the family's breakfasts, although Elsie later confessed that her attention was invariably upon her food rather than the scriptures. Without question, Annie's character and attitudes were crucial in the upbringing of the children. She was herself intelligent, self-willed and a fervent upholder of her Christian principles, which included strictly abstaining from alcohol. With a maid to clean the house, and Annie's mother willing to cook, wash and iron for the whole family, Annie was particularly fortunate and 'never had to do housework'. However, Annie did the shopping, supervised the meals and taught the children to read and write. Music was always encouraged and Ronald took to the piano and Elsie to the violin and to singing. Elsie, therefore, grew up the youngest member of a busy household in which Christianity was the central concern, a faith characterized more by love than law. Sidney Chamberlain was serving in the Royal Naval Air Service during the 1914–18 war at the time that his sister, Elsie, followed her father and two brothers in attending the historic Dame Alice Owen School near their home.[12]

Schooldays

As a young woman, in the late sixteenth century, Alice Wilkes had narrowly escaped death in the fields of Islington, then a village north of the City of London, when a bowman practicing his archery had carelessly released an arrow which pierced her hat. In 1608, having become Dame Alice Owen and having been widowed three times during the reign of Queen Elizabeth I, she bought tracts of land in Islington on which she erected almshouses, in gratitude for her fortunate escape many years earlier. In 1609, the charity was vested in the Brewers' Company, one of the livery companies of the City of London, of which her first husband had been a member. In 1610, she obtained from the Crown a further patent to establish a free school on the same site and in 1613, one month before her death, the school opened, with 30 boys from Clerkenwell and Islington. In 1840, a new and larger school was erected and the original buildings were demolished. In 1865 there were 120 boys, aged between seven and 14 years, in attendance at the school. Entry to the school was keenly contested, with 44 candidates for 7 Islington places and 16 for 4 Clerkenwell vacancies. In 1878, a new scheme was drawn up and the school was again enlarged to take 300 boys and in 1886 a girls' school was opened.[13] The motto of the girls' school, 'Instead of being made – make yourself', seemed to accord with the self-help philosophy of the Victorians and also with the early twentieth century belief that women needed to be more active and prominent in society. Dame Alice would probably have approved of the strong-minded Elsie who in many ways resembled her school's founder, in her Christian faith, in her works of charity, and in her remembrance for God's blessings.

12. Sidney Chamberlain served in the Royal Naval Air Service. Information supplied by Geoffrey A. Chamberlain, Elsie's nephew.
13. J.S. Cockburn, H.P.F. King, and K.G.T. McDonnell (eds) *Victoria History of the Counties of England: Middlesex, Vol I* (Westminster: Archibald Constable, 1911), pp. 310–11.

In 1919 Elsie's report described her performance in all subjects at school, apart from geometry, arithmetic and, most surprising of all, singing, as good or very good. Jim Chamberlain may have spoken to his daughter on that score. Her general conduct was noted as 'good but talkative'!

In 1920 she moved on to the Channing House School for girls in Highgate, a few miles north of her home. She may have known other girls in her chapel or neighbourhood who went there. Perhaps such friendly contacts felt able to recommend Channing House which was soon to experience a transformation, with a new and enthusiastic young headmistress. Unitarian in ethos, the school had been founded in 1885 by the minister, Robert Spears, and by two wealthy sisters, Emily and Matilda Sharpe, and had been named after the noted American philosopher and Unitarian minister, William Ellery Channing (1780–1842).[14] The fee-paying Channing House School aimed to provide 'an expensive education of a public school type' for its young ladies and most of Elsie's fellow pupils were boarders, placing her among the minority of day girls. The compulsory school uniform consisted of a navy blue tunic, a white blouse, thick black stockings and, in winter, a blue felt hat or, in summer, a panama. On special days the girls wore a green dress. Elsie was always proud to have been a Channing girl and, when older, would make occasional detours in her motor car 'just to look at the place'.

The headmistress from January 1921 until 1952 was Miss Alice Haigh, a Unitarian from Oldham, who had gained a master's degree in history from Manchester University. She was an extrovert who encouraged discussion and welcomed fresh ideas, but rigorously enforced the school rules, and thereby gained a reputation for being both 'outspoken and autocratic'. Miss Haigh taught divinity and religious studies in her own room and, during these lessons, ethical themes were explored, such as personal responsibility, the individual's relation to society, and the proper use of leisure, so as to enable the girls to make mature choices. To her pupils, the 'lame' but 'speedy' Miss Haigh seemed omnipresent, appearing 'to materialize magically and often inconveniently'. Elsie knew well that her headmistress could be a dragon but nevertheless she greatly admired her. In later

14. R. Spears, *Record of Unitarian Worthies* (London: E.T. Whitfield, 1876), pp. 49–53. R. Spears, *Memorable Unitarians Being a Series of Brief Biographical Sketches* (London: British and Foreign Unitarian Association, 1906), pp. 319–26.

life, some would find Elsie herself to be something of a dragon, albeit one with admirable qualities.

Alice Haigh devoted her life to the school and maintained a vigorous correspondence with Channing's old girls. As a young headmistress, during the 1920s, she brought 'colour and charm to the precincts', even spending her holidays redecorating and refurnishing the school's dormitories, assisted by the second mistress, Miss A.M. Daniel, and their colleague, Mrs Robertson. In 1952, on her retirement, Miss Haigh moved to a cottage, in the small, and now land locked, Cinque port of Winchelsea, in east Sussex, which she shared with Miss Daniel and there they welcomed many visiting old girls. Alice Haigh died in August 1970 and her funeral took place in Hastings.[15] She had had an immediate and enduring impact upon Channing School, evidenced in the changes of the 1920s, with new buildings and playing fields, and an increased number of pupils (about 140 in 1925). At this time also a new music room came into use.[16]

In the academic year 1924–1925, Elsie Chamberlain was awarded a scholarship of £10, covering most of that year's school fees. She clearly thrived at Channing and was to become the captain of her form and a prefect and, excelling on the playing field, was vice-captain for netball and games and the hockey team captain. Elsie seriously considered becoming a sports teacher but, having deputised for the Channing games mistress during her last term at the school, she became aware that she would rather not spend her life encouraging little girls to exert themselves physically, often against their wills. In addition at school, she further refined her interest in music and attained certificates for violin playing and singing, as well as for elocution and diction, and poetry reading and matriculation. Yet Elsie also had a developing life outside school.

Life Outside School

As a teenager Elsie's activities, beyond the school gates, were concentrated on the chapel and on her family. She helped her mother at

15. *The Inquirer* (12 September 1970), p. 6. I am grateful to Dr David Wykes for this reference.

16. Spears, *Memorable Unitarians*, pp. 288–89. E.M. Saunders, *A Progress: Channing School 1885–1985* (Saxmundham, Suffolk: John Catt, 1984), pp. 35–37, 81, 110. Williams, *First Lady of the Pulpit*, pp. 10–15.

Islington Chapel with a variety of tasks, such as serving teas, talking to the lonely and looking after young children. Later she summarized her upbringing thus, 'I was brought up in a Christian home and nearly lived in the church'. Her brothers, Sidney and Ronald, both married when she was at Channing so that, while still young, Elsie found herself with two nephews and a niece, all of whom she loved and indulged with various treats, as any doting aunt might do. The Chamberlain family also moved home, a few miles to the north, to Muswell Hill, in consequence of discovering that their house in Canonbury Park North needed significant structural repairs. They settled in the impressively titled Tudor Lodge, in Grand Avenue, London, N.10, an address which signifies that the residents may have entertained upwardly mobile social pretensions.

In 1927 Elsie left school and, although unsure about what career she should follow, she maintained her studies in music and gained a diploma, qualifying her to teach the violin. However, she knew that neither her temperament nor her talents would permit her to become a professional musician and she was aware that she lacked the patience to teach an instrument to beginners. At college she studied dress design part-time and, having qualified, she found paid employment as an assistant designer in an east London clothing factory. When the senior designer left unexpectedly, Elsie was promoted and, at a young age, found herself with considerable responsibility and an enhanced income. In time, however, she tired of dressmaking. As she put it, she enjoyed designing clothes but was wearied by making up the dresses. Elsie later confessed that in her 'young days there was a great deal of petty persecution of the church-goer in office and factory'.[17] This strongly suggests that she had herself been the victim of name calling and jibes, during her time in the clothing industry. Such casual unpleasantness is not easily forgiven nor forgotten.

On her father's retirement from the General Post Office in 1933, he was able to fulfil a long cherished desire to visit South Africa. He had originally hoped that Elsie and her mother would accompany him but Annie Chamberlain was unwilling to travel so far and, conse-quently, Jim bought a car for his wife and daughter as a consolation prize. Elsie, a keen motorist in later life, was taught to drive by her brothers at a time when British drivers were not required by law to take a driving test!

17. Chamberlain, *White to Harvest*, pp. 16–17.

Chapter 2

THE CALL TO THE MINISTRY

As a young woman, Elsie had become involved in almost every aspect of the work of Islington Chapel. Her mother had been elected to serve as the church secretary in 1929, initially to work with the previous office-holder and from 1930, in Robert Shepherd's first year as minister there, as secretary in her own right. At that time the number of women holding such an office in Congregational churches in this country was very low – only nine women, including Annie Chamberlain, were listed in 1930 as church secretaries in the London Congregational Union, out of a total of 251 churches. In that same year only 173 women were recorded as church secretaries in the Congregational Union of England and Wales as a whole, out of a total of approximately 2,700 churches.[1] Strengthening the family link, Elsie's brother, Sidney, and his wife were the secretary and treasurer of the missionary work at the chapel. It was at this time that Robert Shepherd, having detected in her the gifts and the required toughness of mind, urged Elsie to consider the ministry as a calling. She seems to have responded quickly for he was soon teaching her and others the rudiments of Old Testament Hebrew and encouraging her to make initial enquiries about ministerial training.

Her father was not immediately happy about this unexpected course. Striking a cautious note, he expressed reservations about his daughter possibly becoming a Congregational minister because he saw that, although the Congregational Union of England and Wales had admitted women ministers on its roll since 1917, their numbers were small and the pastoral opportunities for such ministers were few. As a dress designer she was well paid and might anticipate a secure future. Was it sensible for her to surrender such security for the precarious life of a woman Congregational minister?

There is no evidence to suggest that Jim's reservations reflected the Church of England's negative stance on the ordination of women,

1. *Congregational Year Book 1931.*

although that stance in the 1930s was by no means confined to the established church. Characteristically Elsie did not share her father's caution. She reasoned that, should even his worse fears be proved correct, she could always return to dress designing. Given the strength of Elsie's convictions, her parents could hardly withhold their support. She resigned from her job and, working as a freelance designer, she aimed to save enough money to finance her forthcoming studies for the ministry.[2]

Constance Coltman (1889–1969), the first woman to be ordained to the Congregational ministry, had stated candidly in 1924 that, in the Free Churches, 'Where women are officially or otherwise exercising pastoral charge, it is usually as leaders of small causes, which are glad to get such help, but can hardly pay a living wage'. An even stronger difficulty, than 'the economic hindrance' to women's ministry, she reckoned, was 'the pressure of public opinion' for undoubtedly much prejudice existed then 'among many of the rank and file'. Jim Chamberlain's fears for his daughter in the mid-1930s were but echoes of those of the first woman Congregational minister in Britain. Constance Coltman's uniquely well-informed view was that, although 'the door to the ministry stands open, or at least ajar; yet it is not surprising that so few women seek to pass through it' but instead 'they shrink from claiming so awful a privilege'.[3] Elsie was not the shrinking kind. She would not hesitate to claim her privilege.

The Ministry of Women

In order to become a minister, Elsie would need training, probably at one of the colleges recognized by the Congregational Union of England and Wales, yet her initial overtures to those colleges were not universally welcomed. Mansfield College, Oxford, had trained Constance Coltman (1889–1969) who had been ordained in 1917 and, since then, it had educated a few more women students. Indeed

2. J. Williams, *First Lady of the Pulpit: A Biography of Elsie Chamberlain* (Lewes, Sussex: Book Guild, 1993), pp. 16–19. Dixon, *Seven Score Years and Ten*, p. 97.

3. C. Coltman 'Post-Reformation: The Free Churches' in A.M. Royden, *The Church and Woman* (London: J. Clarke & Co., 1924) pp. 116, 35. For Constance Coltman, see, *Oxford Dictionary of National Biography* and J. Taylor and C. Binfield (eds), *Who They Were in the Reformed Churches of England and Wales 1901–2000* (Donington: Shaun Tyas for the United Reformed Church History Society, 2007), pp. 40–41.

the Congregational Union of England and Wales had declared its willingness to recognize suitably qualified women ministers as early as 1909, at a time when the issue of women's rights, with campaigning suffragettes and suffragists, was prominent in the country as a whole. Constance and her husband, Claud Coltman (1889–1971), whom she had met as a fellow student at Mansfield College, had had joint ministries as assistants at the King's Weigh House, London, under W.E. Orchard, and as ministers at Kilburn, Cowley Road, Oxford, Wolverton, Buckinghamshire, the Old Independent, Haverhill, and lastly, after the Second World War, again at the King's Weigh House. Constance was elected president of the newly formed Fellowship of Women Ministers in 1927 and was among the founders of the inter-denominational Society for the Ministry of Women in 1930. She retired from the active ministry in 1949 and was an encourager of women ministers all her life, just as Elsie Chamberlain was to be.[4]

Constance Coltman's better known friend in the cause of women's ministry was the influential pioneer (Agnes) Maude Royden (1876–1956) who came almost to personify, in the first half of the twentieth century, the hopes of women with such a vocation. In 1913, the church congress of the Church of England at Southampton had debated a number of themes of relevance to women and 21 speeches to the assembly were made by women. Yet it was generally acknowledged that the outstanding speech of 'that week of speeches' was made by Royden who spoke courageously to the assembled clerics on 'social purity', which for her involved such awkward issues as prostitution, the hypocrisy of double standards of sexual virtue for men and women, and the apparent need for 'harlots' in society. This forthright, articulate woman made an unforgettable impression upon her audience of 2,000 men. It was clear that this Edwardian young lady was a force to be reckoned with. Four years later, Congregationalism somewhat controversially gave this lay Anglican a public platform, when in 1917 she accepted Dr Fort Newton's invitation to become assistant preacher at one of the leading Nonconformist churches in the country, The City Temple, in Holborn, London.[5]

---

4. *Congregational Year Book 1969–70*, pp. 429–30. Taylor and Binfield, *Who They Were*. For Claud Coltman, see, *Congregational Year Book 1972*, p. 353.

5. J.F. Newton, *River of Years* (Philadelphia, PA: J.B. Lippincott & Co., 1946), p. 153. For Royden, see, *Oxford Dictionary of National Biography*.

Although Maude Royden was widely reputed as 'one of the strongest and most influential personalities of all the religious leaders and teachers of the day', her work at The City Temple brought her not only praise but also sharp criticism, especially from many in her own ecclesiastical home, the Church of England. One Sunday in 1917 she officiated at the baptisms of three children at The City Temple which outraged some Anglo-Catholics.[6] She remained at The City Temple until 1920 when she left to found, with Percy Dearmer, the Fellowship services at Kensington Town Hall, which services later moved in 1921 to the Guildhouse, in Eccleston Square, London (occupying a former Congregational church building). In 1924 Maude Royden published, in 'The Living Church' series, *The Church and Woman* which contained a lengthy chapter on the Evangelical and Free Churches by Constance Coltman.[7]

Maude Royden's life, work and publications proved widely influential in the 1920s and 1930s and in the eventual acceptance of the ministry of women within the churches as a whole. Constance Coltman saw Maude as a woman of 'outstanding genius' who, by preaching regularly from 'such a world-famous pulpit' as The City Temple, 'made a deep impression on the public mind and greatly forwarded the cause of women among all denominations, both in this country and abroad'.[8] In 1929 the inter-denominational Society for the Ministry of Women was founded, with Maude Royden as its first president. Although she remained faithful all her life to the Church of England, she enjoyed a consistently high reputation among Congregationalists. Given Elsie's later activities, it is relevant to point out that Miss Royden also became an effective broadcaster on the wireless, blessed as she was with 'a voice of unusual charm and distinctiveness'. Her unique contribution to British life received public recognition when she received the distinction of being appointed a Companion of Honour in 1930.

Like many other women of the day, and men too, Elsie admired Maude Royden for her courage and out-spoken advocacy of the cause

6. F.A. Iremonger, *William Temple Archbishop of Canterbury His life and Letters* (London: Oxford University Press, 1948), p. 236.

7. A.M. Royden *The Church and Woman* (London: J. Clarke & Co., 1924), p. 5. E. Kaye, 'A Turning-Point in the Ministry of Women: the Ordination of the First Woman to the Christian Ministry in September 1917' in W.J. Sheils and D. Wood (eds), *Women in the Church* (Oxford: Basil Blackwell, 1990).

8. Royden, *Church and Woman*, pp. 123–24.

of women, especially in the churches. To her, as to others, Maude Royden was heroic, for she had defied her prejudiced opponents and proved that, given the opportunity, women could be, not only as good as men, but, as Elsie would have put it, better. Through her achievements, intellect, Christian faith and strength of personality, Maude Royden had forced people, of all ranks and stations, to re-think their attitudes to women and she had gained recognition at the highest level for that. Inspired by her and others, Elsie wanted to carry on that work.

Women in Leadership Roles in the Churches

In 1936 the Congregational Union of England and Wales's commission on the ministry of women reported that, since 1917, 17 women had been ordained. *The Congregational Year Book* in 1937 included some 1,965 ministers, on List A of the Congregational Union of England and Wales, so the number of women ministers was less than 1 percent, in numerical terms, an insignificant amount. As Constance Coltman had stated in the 1920s, these women had gained the status of minister but they were not accorded an equivalence of treatment from the churches and often found themselves serving fellowships in positions which had been previously turned down by men. Elsie's desire to train for the ministry, and her father's caution, should be seen in this context.

The report also noted that, of the 2,700 or so Congregational churches, 200 then had secretaries who were women, including, of course, Islington Chapel where Annie Chamberlain filled that voluntary position.[9] The number of women church secretaries was marginally greater than it had been six years earlier, which may reflect a greater willingness to recognize the capabilities of women or, less happily, the fact that fewer men attended the churches and, of those who did, many were unwilling or unable to assume responsibility.

9. O. Chadwick, *Hensley Henson: A Study in the Friction between Church and State* (Oxford: Clarendon Press, 1983), pp. 117–18. E. Kaye, *Mansfield College, Oxford: Its Origin, History and Significance* (Oxford: Oxford University Press, 1996), pp. 161–62, 181–82; 'Constance Coltman – A Forgotten Pioneer' in *Journal of the United Reformed Church History Society* IV, no. 2 (May 1988). *Who Was Who, 1951–1960* (London: A. & C. Black, 1961). R.T. Jones, *Congregationalism in England, 1662–1962* (London: Independent Press, 1962), p. 409. For (Agnes) Maude Royden, see, *Oxford Dictionary of National Biography* (Oxford: Oxford University Press, 2004).

Albeit reluctantly, the potential of women as lay leaders was coming to be identified in the churches. The true potential of women ministers was yet to be grasped.

The principal of New College, London, from 1933, Sydney Cave (1883–1953), was unwilling to accept women students in training for the ministry, because he feared the formidable obstacles that they would confront on leaving college. He preferred all women students at New College to have a private income, thus releasing them, on completion of their studies, from financial reliance on a call to a pastorate, and from desperation should such a call not be forthcoming. Cave discouraged Elsie from applying to New College also because he felt inhibited from reprimanding women in the way that students sometimes needed. Nathaniel Micklem (1888–1976), the principal of Mansfield College, Oxford, differed from Cave. He granted Elsie an interview, declaring himself happy to accept her as a student for the Congregational ministry, once she had become a university graduate. However, between 1932 and 1953, the years of Micklem's principalship, only four of the students at Mansfield College, who took courses lasting two or more years, were women. Even his predecessor as principal, W.B. Selbie, had trained five women students.[10] The situation within Congregationalism was not significantly improving for aspirant women ministers.

King's College, London

Encouraged by Micklem's positive attitude, Elsie entered King's College, London, in 1936 to study for a degree in theology. King's College was then overwhelmingly Anglican in ethos, being used by the Church of England to train ordinands, and having at its centre a chapel in which the Church of England services were sung daily. Elsie found herself among a tiny minority of women studying theology but she stood out even more for her adherence to Congregationalism. She was one of only three women taking the degree, the others being a Methodist and an Anglican. During her time at King's, the college had an average of 225 theology students per annum, only 76 of whom were studying for the Bachelor of Divinity Degree, while

10. Kaye, *Mansfield College*, p. 229. Williams, *First Lady of the Pulpit*, p. 20. E. Kaye, J. Lees and K. Thorpe, *Daughters of Dissent* (London: United Reformed Church, 2004), p. 60. *Oxford Dictionary of National Biography*.

the remainder were studying for a diploma. The number of full-time women students in the theology department varied from eight to 13, although there were about 20 female occasional students also, among whom was Margaret Wedgwood Benn (later Viscountess Stansgate). Elsie and Margaret were drawn to each other from the outset and quickly became friends. In her second year Elsie was awarded an exhibition or scholarship, on the production of a certificate of good conduct and of satisfactory progress, signed by the college dean. In her third and final year she was awarded a bursary.[11]

Throughout Elsie's time as an undergraduate the theological department at King's could boast some notable scholars. The dean of King's College, London 1932–1945 was Revd Richard Hanson (1880–1963) who upheld the traditions established by his friend and predecessor, the well-known and much respected Dr W.R. Matthews (1881–1973). Matthews, who had graduated himself from King's in 1907, had been a lecturer in philosophy at the college 1908–1918 and had been college dean and professor of the philosophy of religion 1918–1932. He served also as chaplain to the king 1923–1931 and in 1931 had become the dean of Exeter. Three years later in 1934, he returned to London as dean of St Paul's and he often attended functions at King's College, including informal theological discussions. Matthews was a prolific writer, publishing books, articles, reviews and sermons. He did much to establish and enhance the reputation for scholarship and piety of the department, which the 26 year-old Elsie Chamberlain joined in 1936.

At King's Matthews had aimed at a breadth of theological views, alongside sound scholarship and 'true religion', and the departmental teaching staff under Hanson, who had himself taught at King's since 1919, continued to reflect this tolerance. Among her lecturers at King's were W.O.E. Oesterley (1866–1950), the Professor of Hebrew and Old Testament Exegesis 1926–36, whose impressive works on the Old Testament were eagerly read by his students, and Herbert Maurice Relton, the Professor of Biblical and Historical Theology since 1931, who specialized in Christian doctrine and was acclaimed as 'a brilliant lecturer'. Clement Rogers (1866–1949), who taught pastoral and liturgical theology, and who spoke on Christian Evidences every Sunday afternoon for many years at Speaker's Corner in Hyde Park, was also popular. His little volumes, entitled *Question Time in Hyde*

11. Information supplied by the archivist of King's College, London.

Park, were in Dean Matthews' opinion, 'a mine of sensible and well-informed answers to popular objections to the Christian faith'. His teaching, and especially his practical example, probably had a lasting impression on Elsie who was never afraid to take the gospel outside the institutional church. Among the younger members of King's teaching staff, Eric Jay (1907–89) stood out. He taught theology there 1934–1947 and, among his later publications, was *New Testament Greek: An Introductory Grammar*[12] which was to be used by successive generations of students.[13]

One of Elsie's fellow students at King's was John Leslie St Clair Garrington, an Anglican of high church views, who had felt a call to the ministry when only seven years old, as Elsie herself boasted in later years. Before he began training for the priesthood of the Church of England, he had worked in his father's tailoring business in Aberystwyth and then in journalism. He had also developed an enduring interest in psychology. Garrington entered King's in 1933 and three years later, in Elsie's first year, was the president of the theological students. The two first met when Elsie attempted improperly to place notices for the women students on the men's notice board. The resulting confrontation eventually led to a compromise and, although they felt no initial attraction, each recognized the mettle of the other. Given time, this mutual respect grew to warm regard and eventually romance blossomed. They became engaged to be married, even before Elsie had graduated as a Bachelor of Divinity in 1939, with an undistinguished pass degree.

John had left two years earlier, having become an Associate of King's College. He was ordained a deacon in St Paul's Cathedral in 1937 and served as a curate at St Martin's Church, Kensal Rise, in north London. Living in Willesden, only a few miles from Elsie's

12. E. Jay, *New Testament Greek: An Introductory Grammar* (London: SPCK, 1958).

13. G. Huelin, *King's College, London 1828–1978* (London: King's College, University of London, 1978), pp. 167, 168–69, 170, 172, 236. F.J.C. Hearnshaw, *The Centenary History of King's College, London, 1828–1928* (London: Harrap, 1929), p. 471. W.R. Matthews, *Memories and Meanings* (London: Hodder & Stoughton, 1969), pp. 99–100. For Matthews, see, *Oxford Dictionary of National Biography,* for Oesterley and Rogers, see, *Who Was Who, 1941–1950;* for Hanson see, *Who Was Who, 1961–1970,* for Jay see, *Who Was Who, 1981–1990.* Those studying for the Associate of King's College were required to cover many of the subjects studied for the Bachelor of Divinity but at diploma rather than at degree level.

home in Muswell Hill, he did his best to continue their courtship. Yet some hard decisions were called for. Neither Elsie nor John had excelled academically at King's, although they had entered fully into the opportunities provided for the students of the day, but both were practically minded and keen to put their energies to work in a local church. However, although Garrington had completed his training for the ministry and had already spent two years in parish work in London, Elsie had only acquired a degree, qualifying her to begin her studies for the ministry at Mansfield College, Oxford. Would she then follow her original plan and set off for the glittering spires in the autumn of 1939?

Chapter 3

ELSIE BEGINS HER MINISTRY, 1939

In her last year at King's, immediately prior to sitting her final examinations, Elsie had attended a conference, at which the Revd Muriel
Paulden, herself a Congregational minister, had given a memorable
address. She was immediately drawn to Miss Paulden and to her
commitment and vision of selfless ministry. Preparing for her finals,
as she then was, Elsie must have known that her natural strengths did
not lie in academic study. Muriel Paulden's vision seemed to offer
Elsie an exciting future and perhaps an alternative route to ministry
from that of further study at Oxford. After her examinations, in the
summer of 1939, she knew even more that her gifts were not those of
the scholarly minister or university lecturer which Mansfield College,
especially under Micklem, was increasingly producing.[1] She would
not prosper in the rarefied atmosphere which Mansfield could offer
and, even in Oxford, she would stand out as a woman training for
the Christian ministry. Had King's, London, sufficiently satisfied
her appetite for theological learning so that a move to Mansfield,
or to any other of the colleges serving the Congregational Union of
England and Wales, would now be unwelcome?

In the summer of 1939 far greater problems than those of Elsie's
ministerial training were presenting themselves to the world. The
coming of war against Germany had long been predicted and the
expected conflict broke out, only three months after she had graduated
from King's College, in September 1939, absorbing the attention of
church leaders, almost as much as politicians, and affecting all walks
of life. What implications would this hold for Elsie's future?

In mid-1939 Elsie's curiosity increasingly lay in other directions
than those of the colleges and she wanted to learn more from Miss
Paulden who had trained for missionary work during 1915–1919 at

---

1. During Micklem's principalship, of the 106 students at Mansfield College,
Oxford, whose courses lasted for at least two years, 21 became teachers in
higher education. E. Kaye, *Mansfield College, Oxford: Its Origin, History and
Significance* (Oxford: Oxford University Press, 1996), p. 229.

Carey Hall, where the Baptists, Presbyterians and Congregationalists then trained their women missionaries together, and which was one of the Selly Oak Colleges in Birmingham. However for 20 years Miss Paulden had been serving as a Congregational minister in Liverpool. To the down-to-earth and impetuous Elsie, keen to cut her teeth where the churches were engaging with society's rawest needs, Muriel Paulden's work must have seemed more attractive than the rigorous study which Mansfield College would demand from her.[2] Surely, she must have reasoned, she would learn more of how to be a woman minister within the Congregational Union of England and Wales from an experienced woman minister than from the poetic, erudite and charming aesthete, Nathaniel Micklem, and the male teaching staff of Mansfield College. Muriel Paulden's work in Liverpool must also have struck a familiar chord, reminding Elsie of Islington Chapel's efforts, including those of her mother and herself, to assist the poor children of the neighbourhood, and of what had first inspired her to want to be a Congregational minister. Was not Muriel Paulden also the kind of strong, pioneering woman who had always attracted Elsie? If Elsie were given a free choice at that time between academic study at Mansfield College and practical, pastoral work in Liverpool then, without hesitation, she would have opted for the latter.

Muriel Paulden

Muriel Olympia Paulden (1892–1975) had hoped to serve as a missionary in south India with the London Missionary Society but, failing her medical test because of a slight hunchback, she had instead become an assistant tutor in Old Testament studies and ran the social work courses at Carey Hall. In 1919 she moved to Liverpool to become superintendent of the Berkley Street training centre where she established training courses for Sunday school teachers, youth workers and others. The centre opened formally in March 1920 and two years later she reopened and became the minister of Berkley Street Congregational Church. In doing so, Muriel Paulden became

2. J. Williams, *First Lady of the Pulpit: A Biography of Elsie Chamberlain* (Lewes, Sussex: Book Guild, 1993), pp. 21–22. D. Watson, *Angel of Jesus: Muriel Paulden of Liverpool 8* (Wimborne, Dorset: D. Watson, 1994), pp. 14–19. King's College, London archives. For Paulden see also, J. Taylor and C. Binfield (eds), *Who They Were in the Reformed Churches of England and Wales 1901–2000* (Donington: Shaun Tyas for the United Reformed Church History Society, 2007), pp. 175–76.

the first woman minister in Lancashire and many years later, having become well-known and respected in the county, she was elected chairman of the Lancashire Congregational Union in 1945. Her ministry at Berkley Street, Liverpool continued until her eventual retirement in 1960, some 41 years after her move to the city and 38 years after she had become the minister of the church. In 1923, one year after the church was reopened, she had written of her plans for Berkley Street when describing how a 'downtown' church could be used for regular worship while also serving as a 'social institute'. In that year the Berkley Street centre was already proving its worth to Liverpool, with approximately 100 students regularly availing themselves of its educational services.

During the 1920s and 30s the training centre developed into a night school providing tuition in biblical studies, Christian worship, social study, the principles of education, youth and children's work, and related subjects. The year's educational work consisted of three terms, each of 11 weeks, while the students were mainly, but not exclusively, drawn from the churches of Liverpool and its neighbourhood. The course of study at the centre lasted for four years in all and Miss Paulden was to be assisted in her work there by a number of junior colleagues, mostly women. By 1945 over 2,000 students from Lancashire and Cheshire had completed some training at Berkley Street, some of whom later went on, after further studies, to become ministers and teachers. Muriel Paulden's unique work was later to be described as 'novel and pioneering'.[3]

In 1939 the eager Elsie Chamberlain learned that Muriel Paulden needed an assistant to work at her church in Liverpool and she enquired about the position. Consequently Miss Paulden visited the Chamberlain family, at their Muswell Hill home, which resulted in Elsie's travelling north to preach at Berkley Street. Following this, after the necessary meetings with church members and officeholders, Elsie was offered the vacancy. However, obvious complications arose. It was all well and good for Muriel Paulden and Elsie to come to a mutually beneficial, private arrangement, which appeared to cater

3. Watson, *Angel of Jesus*, pp. 16, 18, 20, 21. *United Reformed Church Year Book 1976* (London: United Reformed Church, 1976), pp. 305–306. W.G. Robinson, *A History of The Lancashire Congregational Union 1806–1956* (Manchester: Lancashire Congregational Union, 1955), pp. 149, 174. M.O. Paulden, 'How to Use a Down-town Church', *Congregational Quarterly* I (1923): 91.

for Berkley Street's needs and had the formal support of the church
there, but had serious thought been given to Elsie's call to become a
minister? Elsie may have been jeopardizing her future, although she
may have intended to spend only a year or so in Liverpool, before
attending a college to train for the ministry. Of course, Muriel Paulden
may have suspected that the practical training which she could offer
would be acceptable to the Congregational Union of England and
Wales in wartime, as proved to be the case. Indeed, a greater contrast
with the scholarly training at Mansfield College could hardly have
been imagined.

Progress to the Ministry

At this stage, in the summer of 1939, Elsie had not specifically
undertaken any formal training purposely designed for the
Congregational Union of England and Wales's ministry but, rather,
following the advice of Nathaniel Micklem, she had completed an
academic course of study in theology, intended to be only preparatory
to her becoming a full-time student at a ministerial training college.
However, if she were to go to Liverpool, as she wished to do, it is
unclear whether she intended her studies at Mansfield College,
Oxford, to be postponed or abandoned altogether. It is unlikely
that a woman of Elsie's determination would give up all thought of
being accredited as a minister, even in exchange for the attractive
prospect of service in a rundown district of Liverpool. Yet without
adequate training, either at Mansfield or at one of the other colleges,
recognized by the Congregational Union of England and Wales, how
could she hope to be received on to its roll of ministers? Her sense of
vocation needed the wider recognition of the Congregational Union
of England and Wales which would necessitate some formal training.
In addition, even if she were to become a Congregational minister she
knew that, as a woman, she would face many obstacles in the course
of her work. Surely she should avoid adding to those obstacles, by
not receiving the best possible and most widely accepted form of
ministerial training, as indeed other women were then doing and
had already done?

On the other hand, Muriel Paulden both taught and organized
practical training for church work and she herself had been ordained
after her studies for missionary work at Carey Hall. Miss Paulden may
have had grounds for thinking that the practical training of Berkley

Street might offer a way forward for Elsie. At that stage Elsie did have a theology degree and she could expect to receive on-the-job training of a kind in Liverpool, while all the traditional colleges were still oriented towards training men, although women students were not so rare that they were necessarily made to feel uncomfortable.[4]

In the summer of 1939, with the threat of war growing ominously, the wise and experienced general secretary of the Congregational Union of England and Wales, Sidney Berry (1881–1961), like other denominational officials, knew that the churches faced uncertain years ahead. Indeed he may have foreseen the interruption of the work of the theological colleges, as was to occur at Oxford when, on 24 August – St Bartholomew's Day – that year, Nathaniel Micklem received a telegram announcing that the Mansfield College buildings were to be requisitioned for government work on the following day, an ironic date for Congregationalists to receive an eviction order! Such factors may have weighed on the minds of those deciding Elsie's fate, and specifically her education for the ministry.[5]

The patrician Berry, always prudent and approachable, who had been secretary of the Congregational Union of England and Wales since 1923, interviewed Elsie in his commodious office at Memorial Hall in Farringdon Road, London, where they discussed her future. Having listened to Elsie's pleas and arguments and, understanding her frustration and that her mind was essentially matter-of-fact rather than reflective, he decided to advocate her cause before the appropriate committee. Berry was also the chairman of the Mansfield College council, which office he held during the period 1921–1947, and he knew well the atmosphere of the college, what Micklem expected of his students and what demands would be placed upon Elsie there.[6] Muriel Paulden's reputation as a successful educator surely helped Berry in his presentation of Elsie's position to the committee members. None could doubt Miss Paulden's sincere desire to educate the people of the church, nor that she had a special interest in the training of women ministers.

---

4. Williams, *First Lady of the Pulpit*, p. 22.

5. St Bartholomew's Day in 1662 was the date by which ministers were required to conform to the Restoration Church settlement or face ejection from their livings. Those who refused to conform were clearly Nonconformists. Kaye, *Mansfield College*, p. 211.

6. Kaye, *Mansfield College*, p. 319.

Muriel Paulden's deeply felt concern for the training of women resulted, immediately after the Second World War, in 1945, in her founding St Paul's House in Liverpool, to provide special training, exclusively for women students called to the work of home missionaries and to other full-time service in the churches in this country. At that time Miss Paulden understood that the theological colleges were reluctant to accept women students for the ministry. The training provided by St Paul's House was to be 'intensely practical' and not 'overloaded' with academic theology, exactly the pattern of experience-based grounding which attracted Elsie Chamberlain and which she found at Berkley Street. One former student recalled Muriel Paulden as 'No angel. Rather pioneer, rebel, a great teacher, a great Christian'. Elsie stated that Muriel Paulden had 'showed her how to bring the Bible alive' and that 'she never forgot the lessons'. Certainly she could have expected very different lessons at Mansfield College!

Miss Paulden was to gain enthusiastic support for the projected St Paul's House from the Merseyside churches and the Lancashire Congregational Union, but rather less backing from the Congregational Union of England and Wales. Yet the Congregational Union of England and Wales Reconstruction Fund (set up during the war to repair its ravages) did provide some support, as did some churches in the USA. She was herself to be the warden of St Paul's House (1945-1957), local ministers were used as tutors and the principal of Lancashire Independent College acted as its chairman. On completion of the course, of two or three years, a student was commissioned as a home missionary in a small church in an area of some need, for three years or so. There she took full pastoral charge which included preaching and the administration of the sacraments, although such home missionaries were not duly accorded the status of Congregational Union of England and Wales' ministers. By the early 1960s St Paul's House had come to be regarded as 'one of the historic acts of modern Congregationalism', although that favourable judgment did not save it from closure in 1965 when it was felt that women students should attend the traditional ministerial training colleges.[7]

7. Williams, *First Lady of the Pulpit*, pp. 22-23. Robinson, *A History of The Lancashire Congregational Union*, pp. 149-50, 182. E. Kaye, J. Lees and K. Thorpe, *Daughters of Dissent* (London: United Reformed Church, 2004), pp. 63-64, 183-84. *The Independent*, 20 April 1991. E. Routley, *The Story of Congregationalism* (London: Independent Press, 1961), p. 99. Taylor and Binfield, *Who They Were*, pp. 175-76. The Reconstruction Fund raised £550,000. R.T. Jones, *Congregationalism*

To her relief, Dr Berry informed Elsie that her work in Liverpool would be considered part of her preparation for the ministry. Elsie had been granted her wish. Yet since then the question has been asked whether this was entirely proper. Although Elsie as a minister was later to achieve distinction within the Congregational churches, it remains true that her ministerial training was less exacting academically than that of the majority of her colleagues. Some might feel that the rules had been relaxed to make her path smoother. If such a relaxation had occurred because she was a woman, then that would not help women's ministry to be seen as the equal of men's. Yet, even if that was not the case, it might have appeared so to contemporaries and have left the impression that women ministers, like Elsie, were offering only a second class ministry. In truth, the older Elsie retained a somewhat cavalier attitude to the various denominational rule books, especially with regard to ministerial training, rather believing that rules and regulations should be relaxed for those whose talents she had herself spotted, that is usually for her *protégées*. Elsie's own ministry did much to raise the profile of women, especially in the churches but, arguably, the manner of her entry to the Christian ministry did little for that cause.

Berkley Street, Liverpool

Nevertheless, in August 1939 Sidney Chamberlain drove his sister to Berkley Street with her belongings. There she was allocated a study in the church's basement and she assumed responsibility for the running of a nursery school. Only one month later the Second World War broke out and Elsie took rooms in a hostel, to her parents' chagrin. They concluded that their daughter's housing was unacceptable and that she urgently needed their support. As a result they simply upped roots and moved home to be with her. In 1939 Annie Chamberlain was still described as the church secretary of Islington Chapel but one year later the minister, Lyall Dixon, was acting as the secretary himself, which smacks of an emergency measure, introduced to cover the situation caused by the Chamberlains' sudden departure.[8]

in England, 1662–1962 (London: Independent Press, 1962), pp. 397–98. For Muriel Paulden, see also, *United Reformed Church Year Book 1976*, pp. 305–306.

8. *Congregational Year Book 1939* (London: Congregational Union of England and Wales, 1939), p. 419; *Congregational Year Book 1940* (London: Congregational Union of England and Wales, 1940), p. 373. Williams, *First Lady of the Pulpit*, p. 23.

In their response to Elsie's predicament, her parents seem to have been over-protective. Although it may seem curious to suggest this of a young, but not very young, woman with such an independent nature, her parents' actions suggest that they had little confidence in their daughter's ability to cope. Was she really in danger? A hostel in Liverpool in wartime may not have been ideal accommodation but there is no reason to believe that she would have had to stay there for long. Elsie was then 29 years old. Her brothers were married and Elsie was the baby of the family and the only girl. Annie Chamberlain was also to reveal her unwillingness to allow that her daughter had a right to her own choice of friends, when it came to her relationship with John Garrington. Perhaps Elsie should have asserted herself more obviously against her parents' mollycoddling. Of course, she may have been a little intimidated in a strange town, so far from home in wartime and, therefore, have welcomed her parents' reassuring presence.

It would appear that Elsie, always strong in her dealings with others, had little choice but to acquiesce in her immovable mother's decisions. No doubt she did feel safer with her parents, as they knew well. Their move north took them to a flat in a large house in Aigburth where they held a party for the young people of the Berkley Street church. Elsie was to invite many of these young people to join the church choir which she led in singing four part harmony. She became its conductor, displaying her interest in church music which remained a constant of her ministry in its different settings. She was ever an encourager of those with musical gifts. Her work with the Berkley Street children was interrupted by their evacuation from the city, soon after the outbreak of war, which caused the Sunday School to suffer for a time.

Elsie was very involved in the pastoral care of the young people of Berkley Street church, organizing outings and sporting activities, like rounders in Sefton Park on fine evenings. She would cycle around Liverpool on her 'old sit up and beg bike' but, during the Blitz and the blackout, was often escorted to her home by the young people of the church on their own bicycles. They fondly nicknamed her the 'church police' because she would regularly visit their homes on Mondays, if they had been absent from church the previous day. Several senior members of the youth group were shortly to be called up for military service and, in that circumstance, Elsie's support was always welcomed. She left her mark on the folk at Berkley Street where she was greatly admired, as a later minister there recalled. She is remembered as having been always bright and encouraging, and having shown a fine Christian spirit. Her sense of humour was evident, as was also her intolerance of humbug. Witnessing the devastation wreaked by the Luftwaffe's bombs on the city, and being privy to some of the personal tragedies and sufferings caused by the conflict, Elsie's experiences in wartime Liverpool convinced her of the need in all situations to strive for peace.

After the evacuations of the Berkley Street children, Miss Paulden and Elsie visited them in their new homes in the country to reassure their parents and themselves that they were comfortable and well placed. However, by March 1940, most had returned to the city, finding the unfamiliar quiet of the country away from their homes too disturbing. Consequently the schools re-opened and Elsie was busy organizing activities for them at the church.

The Second World War transformed the church's normal weekly routine. Refreshments were served to the soldiers stationed nearby who also used the church's schoolroom for table tennis, billiards and writing letters. Berkley Street's student numbers declined as travel became more difficult. Liverpool was subjected to 50 days and nights of repeated bombing from the Luftwaffe in late 1940, with the result that public shelters and the Mersey Tunnel became very crowded. Many residents of the city had little sleep for weeks on end. Berkley Street was situated just over one mile from the Liverpool docks, a prime target for enemy bombs in 1940 and 1941. Among Elsie's duties was regularly visiting the air-raid shelters to bring comfort and to deliver hot drinks. Muriel Paulden had the wisdom to hire a large house in Llandegla in north Wales for six weeks, to provide holidays for needy families and young adults for a week at a time. In addition during the summers of 1940 and 1941 Elsie helped to run camping activities for Berkley Street's children.[9]

Miss Paulden taught her charges the knowledge of God's constant presence with his people and she opened a prayer room at Berkley Street, by furnishing a disused entrance hall on the premises. Elsie appreciated that her mentor, Muriel Paulden, was a 'remarkable woman' and in her maturity she realized that she owed the older woman a lifelong debt, for teaching her not only how to offer pastoral

9. Watson, *Angel of Jesus*, pp. 39–41. Williams, *First Lady of the Pulpit*, pp. 24–26. Private information supplied by James Jones, Philip Robinson and Alice Platts.

leadership to a church but also how to sustain a high level of personal Christian devotion.[10] Without doubt, Elsie benefited greatly from her time in Liverpool where she was exposed to a different form of Congregational churchmanship from that which she had known hitherto. Moving from the busy inner London suburb of Islington where she had grown up, and from her home in middle-class Muswell Hill, to the northern port of Liverpool, must have been a culture shock. There in Toxteth she discovered that the conscientious minister's response to the social needs of her people and of the community at large was exhausting, physically and emotionally. In addition, Elsie found herself working at the heart of a city which was crucial to the survival of Britain, as a base for both the Royal Navy and for merchant shipping, at the height of the German U-boat threat to the Atlantic trade routes and was, therefore, subject to sustained attack from the air. Destruction of buildings and lives, fear, loss and physical weariness were regular concomitants to daily existence. Coping with emotional stress was part of Elsie's unusual training for the ministry.

In London John Garrington also endured enemy bombing in these years. Alongside his work as curate of St Mary Abbots, Kensington, to which he had moved in 1940, he became an air raid warden, helping to extinguish fires and to free those trapped under the rubble of bombed out buildings. To add to his troubles, his courtship of Elsie was not welcomed by her parents, especially by her mother, who would take, but deliberately forget to relay to Elsie, his telephone messages. Clearly Annie did not approve of this charming Anglican curate as a future son-in-law and her opinion counted for much in the Chamberlain household. Under these strains, in 1941 Elsie broke off her engagement to John. He, showing his spirit, simply refused to accept that as her final decision.

Ordination

However, at this time when her personal and romantic life had taken a turn for the worse, her professional hopes were on the ascendant. Happily that same year she was ordained to the Christian ministry and was admitted to List A of the roll of ministers of the Congregational Union of England and Wales, by resolution of the special committee of the Congregational Union of England and

10. *The Times*, 12 April 1991.

Wales. She was first listed as such in the *Congregational Year Book* in 1941.

This small but important special committee advised the Congregational Union of England and Wales on the recognition of churches and ministers. Both Sidney Berry and Sydney Cave sat on it, as did also the theologian and ecumenist A.E. Garvie, the principal emeritus of Hackney and New College, the historian A.J. Grieve, the principal of Lancashire Independent College since 1922, the layman Sir Arthur Haworth, who was also the treasurer of Mansfield College, Oxford, T.T. James, the secretary of the Lancashire Congregational Union and the moderator of the Lancashire province since the 1920s, and J.D. Jones, twice chairman of the Congregational Union of England and Wales and its honorary secretary – all senior and respected men whose word and wisdom few Congregationalists would dare to challenge. Indeed a more distinguished panel would have been hard to imagine for together they represented the Congregational establishment of the first half of the twentieth century!

Allowing for the fact that Grieve, Haworth and James had close Lancashire links, and would have probably known of Elsie's work in Liverpool, we may assume that a body of opinion on the committee was predisposed in her favour. Even so Berry's word may have carried the greatest weight in their deliberations and certainly the Congregational Union of England and Wales' secretary was to prove a constant friend to Elsie in the troubled years to come. This committee of worthies concluded that Elsie's essentially pastoral training for the ministry, under Muriel Paulden, was sufficient. The stresses of war and the closure for the time being of the colleges where Congregational ministers were trained may have played a part in their decision. She was one of 52 new ministers welcomed by the Congregational Union of England and Wales assembly in the great hall of Memorial Hall, London on 13 May 1941. She was the only woman amongst them.[11]

11. Williams, *First Lady of the Pulpit*, p. 25. *Congregational Year Book 1941*, p. 269; *Congregational Year Book 1942* (London: Congregational Union of England and Wales, 1942), pp. 17, 34. *Congregational Union of England and Wales Spring Assembly – Official Programme* (London: Congregational Union of England and Wales, 1941), pp. 4, 8–10.

Chapter 4

THE RETURN TO LONDON, 1941

Elsie was impatient to be the minister of her own church. She may have entertained hopes that a return to London might enable her on-off romance with John Garrington to be rekindled. Three months after her appearance at the May assembly of the Congregational Union of England and Wales, on 17 August 1941, Elsie Chamberlain preached at Christ Church Congregational Church, Friern Barnet, in north London. The church there had been looking for a minister since its former pastor, Herbert Cecil Pugh (1898–1941), had left to join the RAF as a chaplain in October 1939, one month after the outbreak of war. Pugh had trained at Mansfield College, Oxford (1920–1924) and, after a brief ministry at Camberley, had served as Christ Church's minister since 1927. On 5 July 1941 Pugh was on board a ship, carrying over 1,300 passengers, bound for West Africa, when it was torpedoed in the Atlantic. He learned that several injured airmen were trapped in the damaged hold and, dismissing all protests, insisted that he should be allowed to join them, although he understood that to do so meant his certain death. By acting thus, he disregarded his own safety, believing that his duty as a minister was to be with his men and, 'in the best tradition of the service and of a Christian minister, he gave up his life for others'. In 1947 Pugh was posthumously awarded the George Cross.[1] His death occurred, therefore, only six weeks before Elsie came to preach at Christ Church.

The secretary of the London Congregational Union (1906–1941) and moderator of the London province of the Congregational Union of England and Wales (1935–1941), R.J. Evans, had forwarded a number of names of ministers, each accompanied by a thumbnail character, to the deacons at Friern Barnet but many of these had declined second invitations to preach and several had already sought and found

1. A. Peel, *The Noble Army of Congregational Martyrs* (London: Independent Press, 1948), pp. 77–78. E. Kaye, *Mansfield College, Oxford: Its Origin, History and Significance* (Oxford: Oxford University Press, 1996), p. 213. Christ Church Friern Barnet – ministerial committee records.

alternative positions. In June 1941 Evans stated baldly, as reported to the church members, that he had 'nobody... to meet our needs' and, consequently, the church contemplated making a temporary wartime appointment. The main difficulty was that the church was only offering an annual stipend of £250, without a house, which was £50 less than that recommended by the London Congregational Union at that time. In addition London was, even more than Liverpool, a prime target for bombing from enemy aircraft – a further disincentive, especially to men with families.

On 22 August, five days after Elsie's first visit, a letter from the moderator was read aloud, to the ministerial committee at Friern Barnet, praising Elsie 'very highly'. She was seeking a full charge and, doubtless, a return to London would have been welcome for the not easily intimidated Chamberlain family. The committee unanimously decided to invite her to visit the church again and to preach 'with a view', that is, according to the Congregational pattern, to preach as a formal candidate for the vacant ministerial position. Elsie's letter to the church was considered 'most businesslike'. Her attitude seemed to be at one with the church members in regard to 'Bible study, fellowship and inter-denominational cooperation'. She was described as 'very easy to get on with, a good visitor as well as preacher, and keenly interested in young people's work'. She understood the church's financial position but stated that this would not be a determining factor in her thinking.[2] On 27 September, the proposal to recommend to the church meeting that Revd Elsie Chamberlain should be invited to become the minister was passed unanimously. The church meeting was also unanimous in its support and Elsie's letter of acceptance was read aloud at the services on Sunday, 9 October, 1941. Although others wished to avoid London during the war, Elsie was obviously happy to return to the capital where she was to experience the attacks of the German V1 flying bombs and V2 rockets in 1944 and 1945 which would terrify the population.

Christ Church, Friern Barnet

As might have been expected from their conduct following her move to Liverpool, Elsie's parents chose to return to London with their

2. Christ Church Friern Barnet, church meeting minutes 1938-1950, 3 September 1941. J.H. Taylor *LCU Story 1873-1972* (Southampton: Hobbs the Printers Limited, 1972), pp. 34, 37.

daughter and bought a house for them all near the church in Friern
Barnet. Such a purchase was necessary as the church then lacked a
manse for the minister to occupy. Christ Church, which traces its
foundation to 1884, is situated at the corner of Friern Barnet and
Bellevue Roads. The original lecture hall of 1883–84, where regular
worship was conducted for 26 years, is a red-brick building with
stone dressings in an early English style. It contained committee
rooms, a common room, and a hall able to hold over 300 people. The
church building was erected in 1910, on a north-south axis. It is also
of red-brick with stone dressings, is square and has a low south-west
tower, with battered buttresses, and a spire. It was built to seat 600,
thus doubling the places for those who might attend worship.[3]

Christ Church's first minister had been Benjamin Waugh
(1839–1908), the notable philanthropist and social reformer, who
had founded the National Society for the Prevention of Cruelty to
Children which grew out of his work in London. The church arose,
out of his response to the urgent pleas of a number of young men who
habitually did not attend a place of worship, and by his procuring a
site for a church building at New Southgate, two miles from his home.
There Waugh had overseen the construction of 'an excellent lecture-
hall', as his friend W. Garrett Horder called it. In 1887 Waugh resigned
from his pastoral ministry, in order to concentrate exclusively upon
philanthropic concerns, especially the alleviation of the sufferings
of children.[4] In 1910, to mark the fresh start, implicit in the erection
of the new building for worship, the church changed its name from
New Southgate Congregational Church, which it had been called
since its founding, to Christ Church, Friern Barnet, although in truth
the change of name could not disguise the fact that it remained but
a short distance from New Southgate railway station.[5]

---

3. T.F.T. Baker (ed.), *Victoria History of the Counties of England: Middlesex,
Vol VI* (London: published for the Institute of Historical Research by Oxford
University Press, 1980), p. 32.

4. *The London Congregational Directory* (London: Alexander & Shepheard, 1889),
p. 84. R. Waugh, *The Life of Benjamin Waugh* (London: T. Fisher Unwin, 1913),
pp. 111–12, *Oxford Dictionary of National Biography*. A. Peel, *The Congregational
Two Hundred* (London: Independent Press, 1948), pp. 227–28.

5. *Congregational Year Book 1910* (London: Congregational Union of England
and Wales, 1910), pp. 282; *Congregational Year Book 1911* (London: Congregational
Union of England and Wales, 1911), p. 291.

Therefore, the church to which Elsie was to minister had gained an enviable reputation, in and beyond the local area, for outstanding witness and service, over 60 years. In Waugh and Pugh, its first and its most recent ministers, it had been led by exceptional men who had set an example of Christian concern, personal courage and social action of which any church would be proud. Elsie was entering into a fine inheritance. Some might have been intimidated by following in this succession. Elsie was exhilarated. This was where she had been called and this was her first sole pastorate.

The church was situated, for many years, directly opposite a large hospital set in extensive grounds (Friern Hospital, formerly Colney Hatch Asylum, which closed in 1994) which specialized in treating the mentally ill. The hospital was planned to house 1,000 patients and had been built originally, with extraordinary lavishness, between 1848 and 1851. In 1857–1859 it almost doubled in size and was extended again both in 1896, when its population was over 2,500, and 1908–1913.[6] The buildings of this sombre, Victorian institution remained grand and imposing when Elsie was active in the neighbourhood. During the Second World War, St Bartholomew's Hospital, located at the heart of the City of London proper, was evacuated to the Colney Hatch site. Given these extraordinary pressures, this hospital was very busy during the war years and, throughout her ministry in Friern Barnet, Elsie never lacked subjects for prayer nor requests for the prayers of the church. Patients from and visitors to the hospital routinely sought her advice.[7]

Her induction service at Christ Church was held on 29 November 1941 with R.J. Evans, the moderator of the London county union of the Congregational Union of England and Wales, presiding and with Mr Fletcher Hunt, the secretary of Berkley Street Church, Liverpool, giving the commendation. The charge to the minister and to the church was given by Robert Angel Wakely (1897–1950), the minister of the neighbouring North Finchley Congregational Church 1935–44, who was recalled as 'a true pastor and a fine preacher'. Wakely's friendship and example may have had a positive influence

6. B. Cherry and N. Pevsner, *The Buildings of England London 4: North* (London: Penguin, 1998), pp. 132–33. E. Harwood and A. Saint, *Exploring England's Heritage. London* (London: English Heritage, 1991), pp. 155–56.

7. J. Williams, *First Lady of the Pulpit: A Biography of Elsie Chamberlain* (Lewes, Sussex: Book Guild, 1993), p. 28.

on the young minister. He 'led a simple life' and was noted for 'his children's talks' and for bringing 'the same simplicity, directness and forcefulness into his sermons'. Such a description would have applied equally to the frugal Elsie in later life. Four hundred people attended the induction and were invited to stay for tea, despite the wartime rationing.[8]

Elsie's First Sole Charge

Elsie was to commit her energies to Christ Church, Friern Barnet, and she worked hard there. She spent Easter 1942 in Bangor, in north Wales, where she spoke to a young people's conference, after having arranged for Handel's 'Messiah' to be performed on Good Friday at Christ Church. By April the deacons were convinced that she should take 'a full week's holiday at the earliest opportunity' because they were concerned about her health. She had been overdoing it and, therefore, she planned to be away at Leigh-on-Sea, in Essex but she could not slow down for long and was keen to return by the following Sunday, although the church meeting urged her to take 'all the leave necessary to ensure her full recuperation'. In June 1942 the minister was 'informally congratulated' by the deacons on her first six months at Friern Barnet. Elsie had several ideas of how to improve life at Christ Church. In June 1942, she asked the deacons to join her in the vestry five minutes before the Sunday services for prayers. Her 'demand for an effective local church life and personal spirituality had been nurtured' in Liverpool.[9] In July appreciation was expressed for the minister's work among young people which had resulted in their 'growing interest' in the church. Aware of the large number of children in the area whose fathers were absent from home, serving in the forces, Elsie had set up a children's club, a youth club and an orchestra. That same month she made proposals to raise money towards the Congregational Union of England and Wales' Reconstruction Fund's appeal for £500,000. In September 1942 a 'sacred concert' given by the organist and choir of Hampstead Garden Suburb Free Church raised £8 15s 6d towards church funds.

8. Christ Church Friern Barnet, ministerial committee minutes, 4 May, 22 August, 27 September, 9 November 1941; deacons' meeting minutes 1935–1948, 29 June, 27 July, 23 October 1941. *Congregational Year Book 1951* (London: Congregational Union of England and Wales, 1951), pp. 522–23.

9. *The Guardian*, 15 April 1991.

In 1943, a bookstall for borrowing books was installed in the church. She also set up a canteen, catering for soldiers on leave, their wives and for old people.[10]

Elsie gained a fine reputation at Friern Barnet. She attracted the attention of the popular press in October 1942 when the London newspaper, *The Evening Standard*, commented favourably on her work. She was reported as having said that many 'gifted women' were 'unable to exercise their vocations in their own church', citing in support the writings of Miss Dorothea Edith Belfield, a deaconess in the Church of England since 1933, who was then publishing works on women's ministry through the inter-denominational London Society for the Equal Ministry of Men and Women in the Church. Although Elsie undoubtedly had the common touch, she was never merely a populist. For instance, in 1943 her principles about the consumption of alcohol led her into controversy. She publicly opposed the Red Cross's provision of free beer for repatriated British servicemen (released prisoners of war) and, as a result, was condemned as a killjoy.

In May 1944, Elsie was invited to address the crowds at Speakers' Corner, in Hyde Park, London, as part of the regular Friday evening Free Church Forum, led by Revd Hugh Parry. In speaking there, she was following the example of her teacher at King's College, Clement Rogers. She was reckoned to have been the first woman preacher to occupy such a difficult position and, according to *The Christian World's* report, 'she gave an excellent account of herself'. The occasion must have brought out the best from Elsie, as the report continued, 'For nearly three hours she faced a host of questioners who were undoubtedly impressed by the wit and aptness of her answers'.[11]

The Impact of her Ministry

In February 1943 the church meeting had noted that Christ Church's membership then stood at 166, of whom the greater proportion was

10. Christ Church Friern Barnet, deacons' meeting minutes 1935–1948, 29 December 1941, 23 February, 27 April, 1 June 1942; church meeting minutes 1938–1950, 29 April, 29 June, 1 July, 9 September 1942, 3 February 1943. Williams, *First Lady of the Pulpit*, p. 28.

11. Williams, *First Lady of the Pulpit*, pp. 28–29. S. Fletcher, *Maude Royden: A Life* (Oxford: Basil Blackwell, 1989), p. 252. *The Christian World* (25 May 1944). This Hugh Parry may have been the Parry (1874–1953) who was then minister of Barbican Church, New North Road, London. *Congregational Year Book 1955* (London: Congregational Union of England and Wales, 1955).

active. During the war the Finchley and District Congregational Group was founded and the church meeting minutes proudly record that there was 'an unlimited opportunity for service, under the leadership of our minister. The Front against Evil was the Christians' unending duty and privilege, and the work of the church was needed more than ever to bring in a better world'. Under Elsie, Christ Church discovered a sense of purpose. This was undoubtedly due to her drive and commitment.[12]

Given the former straitened circumstances of the church's finances, it is significant that Elsie, in January 1943, was reluctant to accept a proffered increase in her stipend. She asked that the amount of the proposed increase should be retained in the funds, available if a change in her situation should lead to heavier expenses. One obvious development at Christ Church since her arrival was that many applications to become church members had been received, several of these from women (this would be a feature of her ministry in other churches too). However, Elsie was not satisfied with this development and, in February 1943, she expressed a concern that 'more men should be attracted to the church, and particularly the husbands of new members. In several cases married women were joining the church, but their husbands showed little or no interest', she stated.[13]

The church members realized how dedicated their minister was and again advised her in 1943 to take 'an adequate holiday for her own good'. However her ceaseless activity continued. On 1 September the church meeting was attended, not only by 34 members, but also by 12 prospective members. All were there for the 'shorter studies of Congregational principles' which Elsie intended to run (perhaps adapting an idea from Berkley Street, Liverpool). Such studies bore fruit later that month when ten new members joined the church. In January 1944, Elsie was at last persuaded to accept an increase in her stipend, although she stipulated that she would only take it, if it proved not to be a burden to the church. She arranged that the choir would sing the Messiah on Good Friday for the fifth successive year and Stainer's Crucifixion would be sung on Sunday, 2 April 1944. In

12. Christ Church Friern Barnet, church meeting minutes 1938–1950, 8 October 1942, 13 February 1943.

13. Christ Church Friern Barnet, deacons' meeting minutes 1935–1948, 12 January, 2 February 1943.

March, Elsie had invited the notable Methodist, Leslie Weatherhead, then minister of The City Temple, Holborn, to preach at Christ Church for the anniversary services of the fellowship. On 7 June 1944 the church remained open all day, for any who wished to pray, following the allied invasion of Nazi-occupied Europe on D-Day, the previous day.[14]

Visiting Preachers and Elsie's Desire to Help a Small Church

In July 1944 the deacons reported that their invitation to New Southgate Baptist Church (whose building had been badly damaged by bombs) to worship at Christ Church had been declined. Instead the Baptists had accepted the hospitality of the Society of Friends. Among the ministers preaching in 1944 at Christ Church was Revd Dorothy Wilson (1893–1956) who had trained at Mansfield College, Oxford, and, mainly through ill health, had served a series of short term ministries since 1928, including being an assistant at Carr's Lane Congregational Church, Birmingham 1928–1929 to Leyton Richards and later being an associate to Leslie Weatherhead at The City Temple 1938–1939. She was reckoned to be an 'impressive preacher'. In 1941 she had been living in Liverpool 8 and had, therefore, been a neighbour of Elsie and of Muriel Paulden, for Berkley Street was located in the same postal district. Almost certainly they came to know each other then. Women Congregational ministers were not common and they would have found mutual support from sharing experiences. In June 1939 Dorothy Wilson, when working at The City Temple, had given a broadcast talk on 'Women and the Ministry', a subject of obvious interest to these colleagues. From 1941 to 1943 she had been minister of Muswell Hill Congregational Church, and in 1944 she was living in Highgate, both areas familiar to Elsie from her youth.[15] Dorothy Wilson will appear in the narrative again, at a later stage in Elsie's life.

In August 1944 Christ Church received notice of Elsie's insatiable appetite to offer help wherever she discovered a need. She informed her church members that she had suggested to Danbury

14. Christ Church Friern Barnet, church meeting minutes 1938–1950, 30 June, 1 September, 29 September 1943, 5 January, 19 January, 7 June 1944; deacons' meeting minutes 1935–1948, 28 February 1944.

15. Kaye, *Mansfield College*, p. 182. E. Kaye, J. Lees and K. Thorpe, *Daughters of Dissent* (London: United Reformed Church, 2004), pp. 57, 73–74.

Congregational Church, near Chelmsford in Essex, that she might be able to serve there as minister for one week in each month. The churches at Danbury and neighbouring Little Baddow hoped to call a minister to serve them jointly at some future date. The Congregational church at Danbury had, in fact, been founded in 1936, only eight years previously, and in 1944 it claimed a membership of 41 adults, among whom were two lay preachers. In contrast the church at Little Baddow, was far older, claiming a foundation date of 1661, but it had a comparable membership of 40, of whom one was a lay preacher.

Christ Church members were undoubtedly relieved in September 1944 when Elsie reported that her help for Danbury would not be required after all. The official minutes fail to explain that, in the interim, the ministry of the two Essex churches had been accepted by an experienced man, George William James Cameron-Price (1900–1972), who had trained at Hackney and New College, and had served pastorates at Greenwich 1928–1939 and Alfriston, Sussex 1939–45. He remained at Danbury and Little Baddow until 1954, when he moved to minister at Sudbury, in Suffolk and, from 1969, at Tisbury and Fovant, in Wiltshire.[16] Although Elsie's help was not actually needed, the question lingers whether, with her heart fixed on this course, would her church members at Friern Barnet have been able to prevent her helping these Essex churches, had they tried? She had already offered her help and, once her mind was made up, she was immovable. Elsie's kind but headstrong and eccentric desire to help churches geographically far apart would surface again later in her ministry.[17]

A Living, Vital Force

In 1940 the church at Friern Barnet had decided that, every three years, a review should be held of the ministry and, therefore, in November 1944 Elsie's work was considered. Forty-one members

16. *Congregational Year Book 1944* (London: Congregational Union of England and Wales, 1944), p. 91, *Congregational Year Book 1945* (London: Congregational Union of England and Wales, 1945), pp. 95, 298; *Congregational Year Book 1972* (Congregational Church in England and Wales, 1972), p. 352.

17. Christ Church Friern Barnet, church meeting minutes 1938–1950, 30 August, 27 September 1944. *Congregational Year Book 1941* (London: Congregational Union of England and Wales, 1941), pp. 269, 341; *Congregational Year Book 1944*, p. 367. J. Travell, *Doctor of Souls Leslie D. Weatherhead 1893–1976* (London: Lutterworth Press, 1999), p. 121.

attended a special church meeting – 30 women and 11 men. All comments recorded were favourable to the minister – her 'powers of leadership had led to the work prospering', 'an inspiration to young people', 'inspired leadership of the past three years.... could not be bettered', 'remarkable'. In February 1945, the church members stated that Christ Church is seen as 'a living, vital force in the district'. Also in November 1944, the deacons discussed the desired proportion of men to women deacons, deciding to leave the ratio at the existing three women to seven men.[18]

In November 1972, Elsie's outstanding work at Friern Barnet was somewhat belatedly noted in the general synod of the Church of England. In a debate on the proposed ordination of women, the bishop of Chelmsford, whose diocese had voted overwhelmingly in support of the motion in 1971, drew attention to 'a suburban parish in north London where the down-town end had been dominated by a Congregational Church where the minister was a woman, namely the Revd Elsie Chamberlain, who became in time the president of the Congregational Union'.[19] Probably he expected his listeners to draw from Elsie's success and dynamism the conclusion that women's ministry could be a great blessing both to the churches and to the community at large. By 1972 he might have used other and later aspects of Elsie's work, to illustrate his theme, but surely one strong point was that her ministry was remembered with thanks, almost 30 years later, by many in and around Friern Barnet.

In August 1944, the new moderator of the London Congregational Union, Alan Green, had reported the grave news that 190 of the 210 Congregational churches in the capital had suffered some damage from German bombing. The following month the deacons discussed the needs of the Reconstruction Fund of the Congregational Union of England and Wales, which had been brought to the attention of the churches by its chief commissioner, Alec Glassey. London, of course, was not the only city to suffer extensive damage to its

18. Christ Church Friern Barnet, deacons' meeting minutes 1935–1948, 27 July, 28 August, 27 November 1944; Minutes of special church meeting, 1 November 1944, 3 February 1945.

19. J. Field-Bibb, *Women Towards Priesthood: Ministerial Politics and Feminist Praxis* (Cambridge: Cambridge University Press, 1991), p. 122. Elsie was never the president of the Congregational Union of England and Wales, for no such office existed. She was the chairman of CUEW in 1956–1957 and president of the Congregational Federation 1973–1975.

Congregational churches and their ancillary buildings. The churches of Birmingham, Bristol, Cardiff, Coventry, Liverpool, Manchester, Sheffield, Southampton, Swansea and other towns had suffered also. The Reconstruction Fund had been launched in October 1941 with the hope that £500,000 would be raised in three years.[20] The Christ Church deacons decided that the church should aim to raise £300 and, by the spring of 1945, almost £320 had been collected. Elsie's own efforts toward the total included giving violin lessons at six pence for fifteen minutes tuition.[21]

Another Appointment

By November 1945 change was in the air at Christ Church when Elsie reported that she had been offered the post of Woman Secretary of the London Missionary Society, in succession to Joyce Rutherford who had held that office since 1931. Elsie declared that she had to make 'a difficult decision' but her statement, that she intended to continue the pastorate until a new minister could be found, clearly implied that she was minded to accept the offer. The letter of invitation from the distinguished Dr A.M. Chirgwin, the LMS general secretary 1932–1950, was read aloud to the deacons who all expressed their views. They advised Elsie to be cautious. If the London Missionary Society work was, as she visualized it, then they felt that she should accept the job but if it was merely of a 'secretarial nature' then she should refuse. They were unanimous in maintaining that her going would be 'a heavy loss' to Christ Church. However, Elsie was ambitious and in London she was noticed more than she would have been elsewhere. She was evidently ready to consider opportunities beyond Friern Barnet and such opportunities were becoming available to her.

In January 1946, the minister reported to the deacons that on the very day that she had accepted the offer from the London Missionary Society, she had been asked also to consider an appointment which Lord Stansgate, then Secretary of State for Air, 'had been striving to have made' ie a woman chaplain in the Royal Air Force. Had Elsie been making subtle enquiries of her friends about opportunities

20. R.T. Jones, *Congregationalism in England, 1662–1962* (London: Independent Press, 1962), pp. 397–98.

21. Christ Church Friern Barnet, church meeting minutes 1938–1950, 30 August 1944; deacons' meeting minutes 1935–1948, 25 September 1944, 28 February, 29 October 1945. Williams, *First Lady of the Pulpit*, pp. 27–28.

beyond Christ Church? It is curious that these two offers were made at the same time. Although the minister disclosed that the subject was of the 'strictest confidence', it seemed clear that Elsie had already decided to leave Christ Church, and Lord Stansgate's offer was to a high-profile position which would put Elsie in particular, and the ministry of women in general, in the news. Congregationalists have traditionally been critical of the church's involvement with the state. The records do not reveal that Elsie ever shared this historic suspicion of the state's interest in church affairs. She expressed a hope to the deacons in January 1946 that her successor would have a special regard for the young people of the church and she was sad at leaving such a 'happy ministry'.[22]

Elsie's eventual appointment as the first woman chaplain in the RAF meant that she had to resign, not only from Christ Church, but also from the presidency of the London Women's League of the London Congregational Union, to which office she had been called in 1945. As a result the willing and competent Mrs Grace Rider Smith, who had been president in 1944, and was to be the first woman chairman of the London Congregational Union (in 1956, some ten years after her husband had held this office), and of the Shaftesbury Society, stepped into the breach and became the only woman to serve a third term as president.[23]

Her Legacy to Christ Church

In 1941, when the pastorate at Friern Barnet was vacant, Christ Church had returned a figure of 162 members, with 110 Sunday school children, 14 teachers and no lay preachers. One year later,

22. Christ Church Friern Barnet, deacons' meeting minutes 1935–1948, 26 November 1945, 28 January 1946; Special church meeting 30 January 1946. N. Goodall, *A History of the London Missionary Society 1895–1945* (London: Oxford University Press, 1954), pp. 546, 624.

23. A. Oldfield, *The Story of the London Women's League of the London Congregational Union 1909–1959* (London: Independent Press, 1959), pp. 31, 33, 39. *Congregational Year Book 1946* (London: Congregational Union of England and Wales, 1946), p. 149, *Congregational Year Book 1956* (London: Congregational Union of England and Wales, 1956), p. 194. J.H. Taylor, *LCU Story 1873–1972* (Southampton: Hobbs the Printers Limited, 1972), pp. 41, 47. The Rider Smiths were the only man and wife to be chairmen of the London Congregational Union. The only other woman to have held this office was Eva Spicer in 1972, the last year of the LCU's existence. See, Taylor, *LCU Story*, p. 47.

with Elsie as minister, the members stood at 159, but the children had dropped markedly to 65 and the teachers numbered only 9. In 1943, Elsie was beginning to make her presence felt, as is shown in the figures of 164 members, 123 children and 21 teachers. In 1944, the figures rose again to 169 members, 158 children and 23 teachers while in 1945 the membership had increased to 184. In 1946, the Christ Church membership was 180 whereas one year later, when Elsie had left the church, the church had 184 members although still no lay preachers were recorded. In 1948, now with Colin Campbell as minister, the church had 181 members.[24] It seemed that Elsie had made a positive and lasting impression upon the church in this her first sole ministry. It may be worth noting that she did not apparently 'rock the boat' because the two church secretaries who were serving the church when she arrived were still in office when she left.

She was presented with the parting gift of a cheque for £40 on her last Sunday at Christ Church – 24 March 1946. In June, among the various invitations to preach, one, almost certainly at Elsie's prompting, was sent to Lady Stansgate who was then still a member of the Church of England. She was not regarded as a possible future minister of the church but was willing to preach at both services on 22 September. On 30 June 1946 the newly appointed Squadron Officer Revd E.D. Chamberlain was in Christ Church again to conduct the services. However, only five months later, in November, the church secretary reliably reported that 'from several sources' he had learned that Elsie Chamberlain was to be discharged from the RAF on grounds of ill-health. The obvious question immediately presented itself to several church members, 'Would she be willing to return as Christ Church's minister?' Yet, because exact details were unavailable, it was felt improper to pursue such an enquiry at that stage.[25] Elsie had made such an impact at Friern Barnet that she would have been warmly welcomed back.

24. *Congregational Year Book 1941*, p. 118; *Congregational Year Book 1942* (London: Congregational Union of England and Wales, 1942), p. 124; *Congregational Year Book 1943* (London: Congregational Union of England and Wales, 1943), p. 140; *Congregational Year Book 1944*, p. 142; *Congregational Year Book 1945*, p. 146; *Congregational Year Book 1946*, p. 154; *Congregational Year Book 1947* (London: Congregational Union of England and Wales, 1947), 174; *Congregational Year Book 1948* (London: Congregational Union of England and Wales, 1948), p. 191.

25. Christ Church Friern Barnet, ministerial committee 12 June, 19 July, 22 August, 18 November 1946; special church meeting, 29 May 1946.

Chapter 5

FLYING INTO THE STORMS: CHAPLAIN IN THE
ROYAL AIR FORCE, 1945

Elsie Chamberlain and Margaret Stansgate, then Mrs Wedgwood
Benn, had become firm friends after first meeting as students of
theology at King's College, London, and their friendship was to
persist for the rest of their lives. In the 1930s Margaret, an occasional
student at King's, had developed a particular interest in Hebrew.
After the Labour party's landslide victory in the general election
of 1945, Viscount Stansgate was appointed by Clement Attlee, the
incoming Prime Minister, to be the secretary of state for air, with a
seat in the Cabinet. Margaret Stansgate seized her opportunity to
further the cause of women, on the day when her husband went
to 10 Downing Street to answer Attlee's call, and she broached the
question of women chaplains, which was close to her heart.

During the Second World War she had worked with the chaplains
department, among those women serving in the forces, and she
was confident that she had discovered an 'urgent' and overlooked
need for women chaplains. However, the Church of England had
no women priests at this time and an outraged established church
could be expected to mount sustained and powerful opposition to
any attempt to appoint a woman chaplain. Margaret specifically
recommended Elsie Chamberlain, by name, for such a post before
her husband left to see Attlee that morning. Of course, it is possible
that Elsie had already indicated that she would welcome a move
away from Friern Barnet and that Margaret, having formulated her
strategy, had simply waited for the correct time to put forward her
plan to her husband. Perhaps they had spoken about it before this
time and Margaret was merely reminding William of Elsie's openness
to such an offer.

Viscount and Viscountess Stansgate

William Wedgwood Benn, the first Viscount Stansgate (1877–1960),
was the second son of Sir John Williams Benn, a Liberal member of

parliament and leader of the Progressive Party in, and sometime chairman of, the London County Council, and also a publisher. William's elder brother, Sir Ernest Benn (1875–1954), was a well-known writer, publisher and proponent of the rights of the individual. William was himself 'a lifelong radical nonconformist', having accepted for himself the faith of the Congregationalists in which he had been brought up. As Liberal candidate for his father's former parliamentary constituency, St George's, Tower Hamlets, he was elected to the House of Commons in 1906. During the First World War he had led a colourful but dangerous life, serving in the Gallipoli campaign, bombing the Baghdad railway from the air, being rescued from a sinking aeroplane in the Mediterranean, commanding a party of French guerrillas against the Turks, and fighting as an articled privateer in the Red Sea. After qualifying as a pilot in England, he had worked with the Italians in organizing and taking part in the first parachute landing of a secret agent behind enemy lines. For these wartime services, Wedgwood Benn was decorated by the British, French and Italians. At the cessation of hostilities in 1918, he had returned to his parliamentary work but, as a supporter of Asquith and no friend to Lloyd George, who became the Liberal leader in 1927, his sympathies had moved away from the Liberals and towards the Labour Party which he joined also in 1927, and, as a man of principle, he resigned his seat. In 1929, back in the House of Commons, he had become Secretary of State for India, with a seat in the Cabinet, and he had then also become a privy councillor.

With the decline of the Labour Party's fortunes in the 1930s, Wedgwood Benn was without a seat in the House of Commons from 1931 to 1937. At the outbreak of the Second World War in 1939, the irrepressible Wedgwood Benn, now again in Parliament, and although 62 years old, had enlisted in the Royal Air Force and eventually had risen to the rank of Air Commodore. His son, Tony Benn, later explained, 'He had rejoined the air force because he felt that during the war you had to fight and not be a parliamentarian – he ended up as an air gunner before they caught up with him, because he had been a pilot in the First World War'. As implied, although Wedgwood Benn was not officially authorized to take part in flying operations, it is clear that he did so, being mentioned in dispatches. His eldest son Michael, a Flight Lieutenant, was killed in 1944, dying of injuries received in action.

During the war, Winston Churchill, the Prime Minister, decided that more Labour peers were needed in the House of Lords and, subsequently, in January 1942 William Wedgwood Benn became Viscount Stansgate, a hereditary peerage (at that time no life peerages existed). Well-known for his sincerity, freedom from malice, buoyant spirits and natural modesty, he was described as 'the happy warrior, a man of profound ethical conviction, with a great love for his fellow men'. Rare among politicians, he was said to have 'many admirers and no enemies'.[1] In 1945 this principled parliamentarian happily found himself 'in complete agreement' with his wife over the issue of Elsie's being appointed a woman chaplain.

Margaret Eadie Holmes (1897–1991), herself the daughter of a Liberal MP, Daniel Turner Holmes, who had represented Govan, Lanark 1911–1918, had married William Wedgwood Benn in 1920. As the daughter, daughter-in-law, wife, and mother of Members of Parliament she was herself an active, experienced and natural political campaigner. Among other recollections, she vividly remembered being in the gallery of the House of Commons in 1914 when Winston Churchill, as first Lord of the Admiralty, reported the sinking of a German 'shubmarine'. Her passionate and consistent advocacy for women's causes, especially for the ordination of women, was to lead her into inevitable conflict with successive Archbishops of Canterbury. Influenced by her husband and also by her friendship with Elsie, she herself became a convinced Congregationalist 'quite late in life', in 1948, after the inaugural meetings of the World Council of Churches where 'she was offended by the negative attitude' of the Anglicans to Christians of other denominations.[2]

Viscount Stansgate's Policy

Although encouraged by his wife to make this appointment, Lord Stansgate, having been brought up a Congregationalist, was himself

---

1. *Oxford Dictionary of National Biography.* Tony Benn MP, Lord Carrington, Lord Deedes and Mary Soames, 'Churchill Remembered: Recollections', *Transactions of the Royal Historical Society* (6th series, XI, London: Royal Historical Society, 2001), pp. 393–97. M. Stansgate, *My Exit Visa: An Autobiography* (London: Hutchinson, 1992), p. 233.

2. *Oxford Dictionary of National Biography.* Benn et al., 'Churchill Remembered', p. 394. Stansgate, *My Exit Visa*, pp. 198, 233–34. J. Williams, *First Lady of the Pulpit: A Biography of Elsie Chamberlain* (Lewes, Sussex: Book Guild, 1993), pp. 28–29.

keen to have a woman chaplain in the Royal Air Force but he knew that his proposal amounted to a major assault on the civil and ecclesiastical establishment of the day. Displaying the wisdom of the experienced politician, he wrote to King George VI and Queen Elizabeth to inform them of his plan. Their reply approved his scheme. However, Lord Stansgate correctly anticipated objections to his proposals in 1945, from the hierarchy of the Church of England, and he made a courtesy call upon Archbishop Geoffrey Fisher of Canterbury at Lambeth Palace to acquaint him with his intention to appoint Elsie Chamberlain to this position.

The Church of England had suffered much during the war, not only from enemy air raids which had destroyed many church buildings, halls and schools and, incidentally, had made of Lambeth Palace 'virtually a bomb-shattered wreck', but also from pragmatic decisions which had left many doctrinal questions unanswered.[3] Archbishop Geoffrey Fisher unexpectedly invited his wife, Rosamond, to join him in conversation with the air minister. Although the archbishop was adamant that Elsie's appointment was improper and represented an affront to the established church, Lord Stansgate was not to be deflected. However, finalizing the appointment proved difficult, taking some nine months to complete, and meeting 'intense' opposition at every stage.

Archbishop Geoffrey Fisher

Geoffrey Francis Fisher (1887–1972) had been educated at Marlborough, Exeter College, Oxford, where he gained first class degrees in classical honour moderations (1908), literae humaniores (1910) and theology (1911), and at Wells Theological College. In 1914, aged only 27, he became headmaster of Repton and in 1917 he married. After 18 years at Repton, he was appointed Bishop of Chester in 1932 and, seven years later, moved to become Bishop of London which office he filled with distinction and energy. Arriving in London at the beginning of the Second World War, he established a metropolitan area reconstruction committee which prudently included all the Christian denominations, as well as the Jews. In 1944, the popular William Temple's sudden and unexpected death led to Fisher's elevation to Canterbury in January 1945.

3. W. Purcell, *Fisher of Lambeth: A Portrait from Life* (London: Hodder & Stoughton, 1969), pp. 118, 130, 132.

As archbishop, he was prepared to speak out on contemporary political, social and ethical issues, such as the law on homosexuality, marriage, lotteries and premium bonds (which he vehemently opposed). Notably in November 1946 Fisher was to preach in Cambridge, in the course of which he would issue his famous invitation to the Free Churches to 'take episcopacy into their own system'. Certainly he sought to establish cordial relations with the other church bodies in this country and his interest in ecumenism led to his becoming, in 1946, one of the presidents of the World Council of Churches. Fisher was to be the first Archbishop of Canterbury since 1397 to visit the Pope in Rome, when he called upon the aged and saintly reformer, John XXIII, in 1960. This 'courtesy call', as Fisher modestly called it, was 'nevertheless a historic occasion, a significant breakthrough, and a triumphant conclusion' to his archiepiscopate. He resigned his position in January 1961.

Fisher's wife, Rosamond Chevallier, was, like the archbishop himself, the child of an Anglican parson. Indeed his father, grandfather and great-grandfather had all served the same rural parish in Leicestershire, Higham on the Hill, with an unbroken line of Fishers there from 1772 to 1910. Fisher was the youngest of ten children and had been steeped in conservative Anglican tradition from childhood. He had, therefore, a deep and intimate understanding of the Church of England and of its relations with the State and with English society. In her own right, Rosamond Fisher also appreciated keenly the Church of England's traditions, especially with regard to the ordination of women. She herself was the ninth of 14 children and she had six young sons to care for, all of whom were to achieve some distinction in their chosen fields. In addition, Rosamond Fisher was an enthusiastic supporter of the Mother's Union, serving as its national president. The Fishers enjoyed a mutually supportive marriage and had 'a happy, loving and close-knit family life'.[4]

Having breathed an Anglican air all their lives, they understood and embodied much of the Church of England's traditions and attitudes. Indeed the headmasterly archbishop was determined to uphold the Anglican establishment and would have seen Lord Stansgate's proposal as an assault on that position. The objections which the archbishop and his wife raised to Elsie's becoming a chaplain in the RAF, based, at least in part, on deep-seated Christian

4. *Oxford Dictionary of National Biography.*

convictions, were not to be dismissed as merely old-fashioned and reactionary.

Progress and the Reaction

Yet on her part Margaret Stansgate made light of the Fishers' doctrinal objections to Elsie's appointment – 'purely a matter of Anglican prejudice against women priests, for Elsie was an experienced minister' was her judgment. Applying her down-to-earth common sense and appealing to natural justice, she objected to the absurdity that, although there were 'women doctors who were members of the RAF, like male doctors, ... the chaplains would not have a woman chaplain' – exactly the kind of blunt, straightforward reasoning which characterized Elsie herself. Despite Margaret's theological education, her arguments, as presented here, were essentially political, not so much based on scripture or doctrine as on social progress and equal rights for women. On this issue, therefore, the Fishers and the Stansgates were, in truth, not really addressing each other in terms which the others understood as appropriate.

Fisher's Victorian upbringing and old-fashioned views meant that he had little sympathy for new ways of thinking in post-war Britain. In the late 1950s a number of bishops protested at his conservative leadership and at his inability to welcome change and allow more freedom in worship. In addition, he was opposed to reforming the cathedrals. His refusal to countenance Lord Stansgate's proposal was entirely predictable.

Whatever the theological merits or demerits of their argument, the Stansgates were formidable opponents who were sure to win the day. Elsie was to become a full chaplain in the RAF, although she was officially given the rank of Squadron Officer in the WAAF. On 20 March 1946, Archbishop Fisher, who was a compulsive letter writer, wrote to Lord Stansgate, in response to the announcement of Elsie's appointment in *The Times* that morning. The letter was given the unceremonious title of 'the Archbishop's stinker' by the politician's family. *The Times'* caption read 'Woman Appointed an RAF Chaplain' and simply described Elsie's tasks. 'She will perform the ordinary duties of a Royal Air Force chaplain and be commissioned as a Squadron Officer in the WAAF.' This notice was placed modestly towards the foot of the page in the newspaper, although her photograph was displayed more prominently, but curiously on another page. Although it was given the oxygen of national publicity, the story was not headline news.

Fisher's letter explained his dismay that Elsie's being described as a chaplain 'will certainly bring me enquiries' and, implicitly acknowledging that the decision would not be revoked, he asked for an assurance that she would not 'exercise her ministry or take Services for Church of England personnel'. He praised the Army's markedly different attitude to that of the RAF, implying a severe criticism of the minister for air, Lord Stansgate. He maintained that the army had set an 'admirable example' for, in the army, Elsie could have been appointed to act 'as a Chaplain's Assistant', far more satisfactory to the archbishop and to the Church of England.

The matter was not even then finally settled because the editor of the Royal Air Force Annual chose to list her in his publication, not as a chaplain, but rather as a welfare worker. Lord Stansgate refused to let this deliberate slur pass and he formally rebuked the editor, whose motives he dismissed as 'pure prejudice', words which reveal how totally he shared his wife's view about Anglican motives. He insisted that the printed lists in their entirety should be pulped and that the whole list be reprinted, with Elsie's name placed, as it should have been, among the chaplains. This was duly done.[5]

Maude Royden, by then a veteran campaigner for the advancement of women, was in contact with Lady Stansgate at that time and may have played some small part in supporting her morally and in securing Elsie's appointment in the RAF. Certainly she took an interest and a pleasure in the eventual outcome. Commenting on the affair, she told her sister that 'The Arch [that is Archbishop Fisher] and the Bishop of London are both anti-feminist to an astonishing degree'.[6]

Sister Li Tim Oi

Fisher's attitude to Elsie's appointment as an RAF chaplain, and to women's ministry in general, was not only informed by his entirely responsible concern to promote what he understood as orthodox Christian doctrine but he was especially influenced by the distress,

---

5. *Oxford Dictionary of National Biography*. Stansgate, *My Exit Visa*. Williams, *First Lady of the Pulpit*.

6. S. Fletcher, *Maude Royden: A Life* (Oxford: Basil Blackwell, 1989), p. 282.

felt acutely in Anglican circles, at a singular problem thrown up
by the exigencies of the Second World War. Bishop Ronald Hall
(1895–1975) of Hong Kong had licensed Sister Li Tim Oi (or Florence
Li) in 1942 to take charge of a congregation of 150 at Macau (Macao)
which had been accustomed to receiving holy communion monthly
from Hall's assistant bishop. Macau was cut off from the Chinese
mainland. As no other priest could hope to reach them during the
exceptional circumstances of the Japanese occupation, Hall gave
Sister Li permission to preside at the Lord's Supper, so that the Macau
congregation would not be deprived of the sacrament during the
crisis. In a letter to Archbishop William Temple in June 1943, Hall
stated that, had he been able to reach her physically, he would have
ordained her a priest rather than have permitted her to celebrate the
eucharist, since the latter was 'more contrary to the tradition and
meaning of the ordained ministry than to ordain a woman'. Hall
went so far as to hope that the next Lambeth conference of bishops
(which finally met in 1948) would allow such ordinations where there
was a shortage of priests. Temple realized that the implications of
Hall's letter and actions were 'devastating' but Hall, brushing aside
Temple's advice to be cautious about giving Sister Li the permanent
status of a priest, ordained her in 1944 and licensed her to minister
to the Macau congregation.

Many complaints about Bishop Hall's unprecedented initiative
had been received at Lambeth, just at the point when Geoffrey
Fisher was assuming his duties as the Archbishop of Canterbury.
Fisher regarded this ordination of Li Tim Oi as very irregular and
saw no need to delve further into doctrinal niceties. Yet reluctantly,
he was drawn more deeply into the controversy by the Anglican
communion's refusal to accept Hall's initiative (although the diocese
of Hong Kong was not strictly subject to Canterbury) and the ensuing
dispute took up a great deal of the archbishop's time. In July 1945,
in a long conversation at Lambeth, Fisher advised Hall to suspend
Li from all priestly functions but Hall had a conscientious difficulty
in doing so. The authoritarian Fisher's 'firm line' was echoed in the
regret, expressed by the synod of the Anglican church in China, in
March 1946 at Hall's 'uncanonical action' over Deaconess Li. In April
1946 the Church of England issued a press statement that she had
resigned her priestly ministry and had resumed her former status
and duties as a deaconess. This controversy, by absorbing so much
of Fisher's time, proved 'a worrying preoccupation' for him at the

beginning of his archiepiscopate.[7] The former Bishop of Durham, Hensley Henson (1863–1947), had long opposed the ordination of women and disapproved of Bishop Hall's action, although he could see nothing against it in principle. He was more disturbed that his successor at Durham had licensed deaconesses to preach, for he reasoned that 'if you concede the ministry of the Word, how shall you refuse the ministry of the Sacrament?'[8]

Such a public controversy, over the proper role of women in the Church, and all the ramifications of Bishop Hall's action, prompted by his pastoral concern, must have been at the forefront of Fisher's mind in late 1945 and early 1946, when Lord Stansgate's insistence on Elsie's appointment was made known to him. The minister for air's decision must have seemed to the archbishop like political interference in the affairs of the church which Lord Stansgate did not sufficiently understand. Was he not heaping coals on a fire which Fisher was trying to put out? Was Lord Stansgate opening Pandora's box? Fisher's strict attitude was clearly informed, not only by his own views and ingrained Anglican prejudices, but also by his necessary pastoral care for worldwide Anglicanism and the need to rebuild confidence in particular in the Church of England, after the Second World War. However, the Stansgates were well aware of Li Tim Oi's unique situation. Lady Stansgate later recalled a meeting at her own home, at which 'a very indignant' Bishop Hall spoke of the 'enormous pressure' under which he had laboured at this time. The whole episode proved to be of great significance within the Church of England and the Anglican communion as a whole over the ordination of women. A serious High Churchman himself, the saintly Hall had not primarily been concerned about feminism but rather about providing the people in his care with the means to receive the eucharist.[9]

7. E. Carpenter, *Archbishop Fisher – His Life and Times* (Norwich: Canterbury Press, 1991), pp. 649, 653, 659–63. On 21 January 1984 a service was held in Westminster Abbey to give thanks for 'the long years of her priestly ministry' of Revd Li Tim Oi. Carpenter, *Archbishop Fisher*, p. 667.

8. O. Chadwick, *Hensley Henson: A Study in the Friction between Church and State* (Oxford: Clarendon Press, 1983), pp. 329–30.

9. For Hall see, *Oxford Dictionary of National Biography*. Stansgate, *My Exit Visa*, p. 200.

Elsie in the RAF

Certainly Elsie had a particular advantage in the RAF, in that she had access to the women's quarters which were out of bounds to her male colleagues. She was uniquely placed to understand the problems of women in the services, as Margaret Stansgate had believed, although she also found that male servicemen were prepared to share their concerns, especially about problems at home, with a woman chaplain. Perhaps we should not be surprised that Lady Stansgate judged Elsie to have been 'a very great success as an RAF chaplain'.[10] Initially Elsie had been posted to RAF Cranwell where the officers' training college was located and where she was at first terrified at leading the parade ground prayers. Then, in August 1946, she had moved to St Athan, in south Wales. The Welsh climate is notoriously wet and windy and the RAF base, situated close to the Bristol Channel, exposed its residents to the fierce Atlantic gales which might blow even in summer. At St Athan her normally robust health declined and she was diagnosed as suffering from 'infective arthritis' in September 1946. She took to her bed, unable to walk, and was admitted to hospital.

Had the stress of the preceding 12 or more months taken its toll of, what had always seemed to be, her inexhaustible reserves of good health and vigour? When at Friern Barnet, she had been warned by her deacons in April 1942, and by the church members a year later, to take holidays for her own health's sake. She had reluctantly accepted their advice, but allowed herself only a few days away. They had been worried that, through her dedication and commitment, she would drain her physical resources. It seemed that they had correctly diagnosed her needs and that, under the greater pressures of an RAF chaplain's duties, her energies had finally given way.

Elsie made only slow progress in the first three months of her illness but in November 1946 she was permitted to continue her recovery at home. Her physical condition was the subject of correspondence that month between Geoffrey de Freitas, the Under Secretary of State for Air, and Elsie's older brother, Ronald Chamberlain (1901-1987), who was the Labour MP for Norwood, in Lambeth, south London 1945-1950.[11] This was, of course, exactly the time when the deacons of Christ Church, Friern Barnet, were wondering whether their previous minister might welcome an invitation to return to her

10. Stansgate, *My Exit Visa*, p. 200.
11. *Who Was Who, 1981-1990* (London: A. & C. Black, 1991), p. 130.

former pastorate. With her parents still living in Friern Barnet, the church members were well placed to learn the facts. While Elsie was recuperating at home with her parents, she received a friendly letter from Sidney Berry, the secretary of the Congregational Union of England and Wales, who was himself close to retirement and had spent much of his life dispensing sound advice.

Dr Berry told her to 'take very great care' and expressed his relief on learning that Elsie had returned home, 'out of the hands of RAF medical authorities and all that sort of business'. However, in informal language, he made it clear that he regarded her as still 'a bit of a crock' and confessed that he hoped that she would fail her coming 'medical' examination. He feared that any recurrence of her illness might 'permanently damage her health' but he was 'certain' that there would be 'another big job' for Elsie. This last point he underlined, 'I have no doubt in my mind about that'. Coming from Berry, with his authority and his finger on the pulse of all things Congregational, in England and Wales, and throughout the world, this amounted almost to a promise. He had advocated her cause in the past and there was no reason to believe that he would fail her in the future. He reassured her that she had already 'established the principle which Lord Stansgate was determined to carry through' and, knowing her restless nature and desire to be active, he concluded by urging her 'to keep as patient as you can, and the way to the future will open'.[12]

Life after the RAF

Berry's letter was perfectly designed to lift Elsie's spirits and to make her think of the future. She would have a life beyond the RAF and she had many friends. She need not feel that her service career had been an abject failure, nor that she had failed to make the point which she and the Stansgates had hoped to make, about the ministry of women. The Church of England had been humbled and a blow had been struck at the establishment, by directly challenging the Anglican grip on British institutions. Whether, in truth, the cause of women's ministry in the armed services, and in the country as a whole, had been significantly advanced is questionable. Other women chaplains did not immediately follow her into the forces and the Church of England was no nearer to accepting the equal status

12. Williams, *First Lady of the Pulpit*, pp. 31–36.

of the ministry of women to that of men. Yet, the defiant Elsie could not be blamed for these disappointments. She had tried, as best she could, at some personal cost, to advance the cause to which she was wholly committed.

Nevertheless Elsie's poor health led to her leaving the RAF, after only a brief service career, in July 1947 when she relinquished her commission, on grounds of medical unfitness. She continued to suffer from her illness until 1951, being treated on a special diet of lemon juice, as recommended and administered by her mother (derived from a Swiss doctor's programme). Lemons were strictly rationed in the immediate post-war years and Elsie was fortunate to have a friend, working for an airline, who was able to obtain the fruit for her from abroad. At approximately the same time as Elsie's worrying deterioration in health, in late 1946, as part of a minor reshuffle of the Labour government, Viscount Stansgate was required to resign his office as Secretary of State for Air. He would not hold ministerial office again. Elsie was proud to have served as a chaplain and, for the rest of her life, she would wear her RAF stole for special services.[13]

13. Williams, *First Lady of the Pulpit*, pp. 31–36. *Oxford Dictionary of National Biography*.

Chapter 6

A SEASON OF CLEAR SHINING: MARRIED LIFE

Just three days before her discharge from the forces, Elsie finally married John Garrington. He had contracted scarlet fever in 1939 when they had first expected to marry, at a time when his marriage to Elsie would have been acceptable to the Church of England hierarchy, that is before she had been ordained. Unfortunately once she had begun formal training for the Congregational ministry, and even more after her ordination in 1941, the situation had changed dramatically and critically for his future preferment. Clearly Garrington's intended marriage to a woman minister of any denomination would not receive the approval of his bishop. Therefore, he not only encountered the opposition of the formidable Annie Chamberlain but also that of his superiors in the Church of England. That his fiancée should have acquired such a high public profile, as a result of a heated and prolonged controversy which had involved the Archbishop of Canterbury, did not make the matter any easier, although, in essence, the principles at issue remained the same. An Anglican incumbent's wife was informally required to be active in the parish and, naturally, it was assumed that she would be a confirmed Anglican herself. Elsie's conscience and vocation would not easily allow her to fulfil these expectations, although she wrestled with the problems and later did her best to be supportive.

In these circumstances, John had had to overcome great hurdles before finally obtaining a living of his own within the Church of England. He had already proved a determined suitor, simply refusing at any time to accept that his engagement to Elsie was over. Indeed his letters to her throughout the war became very passionate. She eventually was persuaded to marry him, on condition that he had first obtained his own benefice, and thus acquired a status which would meet at least some of her mother's reservations. Elsie did want to marry, and to have children of her own, but John's endeavours to find a parish had resulted in rebuffs and frustrations at every turn.[1]

---

1. J. Williams, *First Lady of the Pulpit: A Biography of Elsie Chamberlain* (Lewes, Sussex: Book Guild, 1993), pp. 35–38.

Having served his first curacy at St Martin's Church, Kensal Rise in north London 1937–39, he had then moved, as has been noted, to his second curacy at St Mary Abbots, Kensington 1940–46. As his time at Kensington was drawing to a close, and after almost nine years as a curate, he had applied without success to become the incumbent in parishes as far afield as Guernsey, Falmouth, Dunmow, Birmingham, Chester, Shrewsbury, Canterbury and Gloucester. With the mounting number of rejections, he had become increasingly desperate, both in his forlorn search for a parish and in the thwarting of his hopes to marry Elsie.

In a daring effort to ease his path, she herself made a direct approach in writing to the Bishop of London, (John) William Wand (1885–1977), who had replaced Geoffrey Fisher on the latter's elevation to Canterbury in early 1945. She went so far as to assure Wand that she was willing to resign her pastorate after their marriage and that she would even accept confirmation from the bishop. Letters between them were exchanged on a weekly basis, sometimes within a few days. The bishop was unmoved by all Elsie's declarations and supplications because, as he wrote in October 1945, confirmation requires 'a complete readiness to accept whatever is involved in the service with the heart as well as with the mind and there is such a thing as an Anglican ethos', with which she would need to become familiar. He did concede that she would have had 'far greater intellectual grasp than 99%' of the candidates for confirmation at that time but felt that she lacked the appropriate 'disposition'.

Undeterred she pressed her case again, only to be advised by Wand in December 1945, in quite explicit terms, that it would be 'impossible' for John Garrington to find a church while she was still serving a 'Free Church Pastorate'. The bishop betrayed the depth of his feelings, on this affair of the heart, when he was reported as having commented that Garrington could 'go and be a butcher's boy if he wants to marry this welfare worker'! Reduced to utter despondency, Elsie accused Dr Wand of 'Anglican autocracy' and 'holy blackmail', realizing that any hopes she might once have had of bearing children were receding rapidly.[2]

---

2. M. Stansgate, *My Exit Visa: An Autobiography* (London: Hutchinson, 1992), p. 200.

Bishop Wand

(John) William Charles Wand was a scholarly Anglo-Catholic, from a modest background in Grantham in Lincolnshire, and, although his parents had both been confirmed in the Church of England, his father had become the organist for services at a Calvinist chapel near the family home, and played the harmonium there on Sunday mornings. He regularly took his three sons with him. As the bishop later recalled, his father had 'belonged to the most definitely Calvinist section of the evangelicals: the chapel was handy and he enjoyed his job as organist'. The chapel services were not welcome to the future bishop and left a deeply unpleasant impression on him, so that he never forgot these boyhood experiences of 'undiluted Calvinism from the inside', as he called it. Indeed he was sure that, in his early years, he had 'heard a great deal more about freewill and predestination than most' of his 'colleagues in later life'. In reaction he became a confirmed Anglican at school. His mother had not accompanied her husband to the chapel but had remained 'faithful to the parish church'. The result was, in Wand's view, that 'the separation made an uncomfortable breach between them just where two thoroughly religious people would feel it most'.

It seems probable that the personal distaste Wand felt for the religion of his father, and for the austere chapel worship of his childhood, influenced his dealings with John Garrington and Elsie Chamberlain. Perhaps Bishop Wand entertained fears that the strong-minded Elsie would persuade her future husband to share her own Dissenting principles and thus entice him away from Anglican truth, as he saw it. If so, he under-estimated the resolute Garrington, who had a mind of his own. On the other hand, the bishop might have sincerely believed that, through his unbending attitude, he was doing the pair a kindness, by preventing Elsie and John from suffering the awkward separation on Sundays which his own parents had known and which had so grieved him. The genial Wand was noted for his friendly and dignified relations with his clergy yet, in this matter, he was supported by Archbishop Fisher, who had formerly been Garrington's bishop in London, in his opposition to John and Elsie's union, as Fisher himself freely admitted to them both on a later but happier occasion.[3]

3. J.W.C. Wand, *Changeful Page: The Autobiography of William Wand* (London: Hodder & Stoughton, 1965), pp. 16, 25–26. As a boy of 18, Wand often led

However, as we have seen, Elsie had acquired influential friends. These, once alerted to Garrington's pitiful situation, made a crucial intervention. In 1946, Lady Stansgate informed her husband of the impasse in which Elsie and John found themselves. The normally equable Lord Stansgate, so happy in his own marriage, became 'very angry' at the news and acted immediately to bring about the positive change needed by the couple. He broke the deadlock by enlisting the help of his government colleague, the Lord Chancellor, Lord Jowitt, who had within his gift certain Church of England benefices. Jowitt had gained the unenviable reputation in political life of having few real principles yet, in this instance, he seized his chance to share Stansgate's moral outrage. Lord Jowitt, who was born in Stevenage Rectory and was the only son of a Church of England clergyman, offered Garrington the living of All Saints Church, Hampton, Middlesex, within a matter of days. The logjam was burst and, with enormous relief, John promptly accepted. He was formally instituted there in May 1946.[4]

Later that same year, as has been stated, Squadron Officer Elsie Chamberlain was diagnosed as suffering from arthritis yet, in spite of her illness, she and John felt able at last to plan for their wedding which finally occurred in July 1947. The sheer relief, occasioned by John's appointment and the prospect of marriage, hastened her recovery from illness although she was only able to hobble down the aisle. They had been engaged, on and off, for ten years! The wedding was held at St John's, Friern Barnet (the parish church situated a short distance from Christ Church Congregational, also in Friern Barnet Road) and was widely reported in the newspapers, both national and local. It had an obvious attraction for journalists and even appeared, with a photograph, in the South Australian press. How could the marriage of an Anglican priest to a Congregational minister, the first woman chaplain in the British forces, be ignored?

The honeymoon consisted of a week in the vicarage of John's best man, Robert (Wally) Horth, in the village of Shalford, south of Guildford, in Surrey, and a second week at a hotel in Torquay, in Devon, paid for by Jim Chamberlain, Elsie's father. Always loyal to

services at a Church of England mission where he preached extempore, the form approved by his family. Wand, *Changeful Page*, pp. 26–27.

4. Stansgate, *My Exit Visa*, p. 200. Williams, *First Lady of the Pulpit*. For William Allen Jowitt (1885–1957), Earl Jowitt, see, *Oxford Dictionary of National Biography*.

the Church of England, nevertheless John saw that their marriage was a triumph against entrenched Anglican prejudice and, like Elsie, thought that they were 'really pioneers in the matter of church unity'. Yet this marriage had only occurred, as John himself admitted, 'in the teeth of authority' which had been hostile and obstructive throughout.[5]

A New Life Together

The clerical couple set up their first home together in John's vicarage at Hampton. Two months after their wedding, in September 1947, Elsie herself, following her husband's example, was to begin a new ministry. She was to become the minister of the Vineyard Congregational Church, Richmond-upon-Thames, where she had first preached in June that year, shortly after John's move to Hampton, some five miles south west of Richmond, but still astride the river.[6]

In 1947 Elsie was 37 years old. She had faithfully pursued her calling to the ministry and, in doing so, as a woman, she had encountered difficulties, occasional embarrassments, blind prejudice, and downright hostility. After a tough apprenticeship amid the Blitz in Liverpool, she had applied her lessons and proved her worth as a Congregational minister in war-time London, at Friern Barnet. It is true that both Christ Church, Friern Barnet, and Vineyard Congregational Church, Richmond, had initially approached a number of men who had declined to serve as their ministers, at least in part because the stipends offered were low. Indeed, Elsie may only have been acceptable, in the early stages of her ministry, because the churches had been reduced to desperation. On her side, she may have accepted these invitations, in 1941 and 1947, because, as a woman minister, she knew well that the opportunities for her were few and far between and she had to prove herself. In short, like other women ministers, she was not in a position to be choosy.

However, she had confounded and would continue to confound her critics with her industry, style, good spirits, dynamism, and sheer force of character. In contrast to the deprivations of the Second World War and the bleakness of the late 1940s, throughout which

5. Williams, *First Lady of the Pulpit*, pp. 44–48.
6. Williams, *First Lady of the Pulpit*, pp. 44–48.

the churches suffered numerical decline and loss of confidence, Elsie brought excitement and fun. As a minister she would consistently be perceived as a great blessing to her churches – as preacher, pastor, musician, youth worker and inspirer. Hers was always an uplifting presence.

By 1947, of course, she had made a name for herself. She had confronted the obstacles to her becoming a forces' chaplain and she had overcome them, albeit at some cost to her health. The principle of a woman chaplain in the armed forces had been laid down, even if the opposition had been and remained 'implacable'.[7] She had shown similar resolution and fortitude in her dealings with the Church of England authorities who had opposed her marriage to John for so long. In this too she had at last gained the victory and, in the process, she had surrendered none of her scruples. Significantly she had also asserted herself against her dominating mother who had not wanted her to marry John Garrington. She was still actively employed as a Congregational minister and she had gained a measure of recognition in and beyond church circles.

However, her route to that recognition had entailed such defiance of established order that it must have been difficult for her to accept that sometimes the conventional way, the well-trodden path, was the right course to take. Her experience had only reinforced her individualism. Would such waywardness always be a virtue? Having been forced to take her own singular path, would she be able to offer well balanced advice to others? How would she ever know when it was right to conform? Such questions remained still to be answered but in 1947 for this bright star, as Sidney Berry had prophesied, another big job and a bright future beckoned.

Years of Fulfilment: A New Home and Future

After her marriage to John Garrington, a victory over Anglican bullying and stuffiness, as they both understood it, and through her service in the RAF, Elsie Chamberlain had acquired a national celebrity, rare in a Congregational minister, if not unique in the late 1940s. Such fame made her settling down as the minister of Vineyard Congregational Church, Richmond-upon-Thames, awkward both for her and for her church members. She was not only in a new

7. Stansgate, *My Exit Visa*, p. 200.

pastorate and newly married but, in addition, she had to cope with the demands, imposed upon her, as the wife of the vicar of All Saints' Church, Hampton, who in 1947 had 8,000 parishioners in his care.

She had encountered considerable difficulties in her life and ministry so far, at least partially because she was such a tough, uncompromising woman, yet those very qualities of toughness and endurance had enabled her to survive and triumph. These experiences were necessarily to influence her later decisions but her strong will and self-confidence gave her a resilience and the power to overcome vicissitudes and to take her own line against the voices of friend and foe alike. She would not be cowed into submission, no matter what the cause.

Life at Hampton

Hampton village, as it is called by its residents, is a much admired beauty spot in the crowded south-east of England, an expensive and desirable place to live. It is, of course, dominated by the Tudor palace, alongside the river Thames, with its art treasures, its parks, gardens and maze, which is Hampton Court, originally built for the ambitious Cardinal Wolsey, but then acquired by his royal master, King Henry VIII. The village, physically separated from the palace by the large green, has been a fashionable retreat, since the late seventeenth century onwards. In the late 1940s, when Elsie moved to the district, many elegant houses survived and do so still today. However, residents and visitors to Hampton alike must cope with the seemingly incessant traffic, although in the late 1940s and 1950s the volume of traffic, though heavy by contemporary standards, would have been less of a nuisance than it would later become.

All Saint's Church, to which John had been appointed, is not the old Hampton parish church, St Mary's, which stands high up in the centre of the village. Rather it is a more modern building, only begun in 1908.[8] Yet this was to provide Elsie and John with their first home together, of which they had dreamed and for which they had waited patiently. With a constant flow of visitors to the village, especially in summer, and booksellers and antique shops aplenty, Elsie and John settled happily into the vicarage, a detached, double-fronted house,

8. B. Cherry and N. Pevsner, *The Buildings of England: London 2: South* (London: Penguin, 1983), p. 477.

with a large garden. John, of course, was familiar with the area, having lived there for almost a year before their marriage.

Elsie was not a natural housewife and did not easily take to housework. She had never needed to do it and, at Hampton, John overcame this problem by arranging for a parishioner to come in to clean the house. As a result John's study and the lounge, or music room, were always kept in immaculate condition for the reception of visitors. John and Elsie did their best to support each other's ministry and, on occasions, they even preached in each other's churches. At least on one occasion the Vineyard Congregational Church deacons held a formal meeting at All Saints' vicarage.

As she had assured Bishop Wand that she would, Elsie took seriously her role as the vicar's wife, caring for John's church as well as for her own. Her 'terrific enthusiasm and vitality' made her a force in the parish, especially on Sundays. Although Elsie and John were so different – she was teetotal, he liked alcohol, she was tall, he was shorter, she was a Congregationalist, he a High Anglican – theirs proved to be 'a strong and mutually supportive relationship' which was to bring them both lasting happiness. One close friend described their 'improbable marriage' as illustrating 'by their mutual understanding the true ecumenical spirit'. Certainly John and Elsie would have liked that description. At All Saints and in the parish as a whole, Elsie did not resist being known as the vicar's wife. Indeed she was happy to be Mrs Garrington.[9]

Outside the parish, however, she was universally known as Elsie Chamberlain and she continued to use her maiden name for most purposes for the rest of her life. This was in marked contrast to at least one other ordained Congregational woman who, based in Lancashire, was expected, after marriage, to forgo her maiden name and thereafter to use her husband's. Although willing to comply, she later wondered why the rules had been different for Elsie. Was Elsie seen as a special case? Were those in or near London treated differently from those in the north? Elsie was, after all, a friend of Sidney Berry the secretary of the Congregational Union of England and Wales. If he used her maiden name then few Congregationalists

---

9. Stansgate, *My Exit Visa*, p. 200. Williams, *First Lady of the Pulpit*, p. 49. Vineyard Congregational Church, deacons' meeting minutes 1 November 1948. *The Times*, 12 April 1991; *The Guardian*, 15 April 1991; *The Independent*, 20 April 1991.

would question it. Perhaps after the war it was deemed that social conventions had eased somewhat and Elsie, using the surname Chamberlain, had already acquired some distinction.[10]

A Family

Soon after marriage Elsie, at 37 years, and John, at 35, decided to adopt a child rather than try to have children of their own. Elsie's still delicate health and her dedication to her calling were considerations. They chose to adopt a child of an age approximate to any child who might have been born to them, had they married when they had originally hoped to. Janette was in the British Legion children's home at Richmond-upon-Thames, close to Elsie's church, in the Vineyard. The children of the home, ex-servicemen's children, were sent to the Congregational church where Janette was in the Brownies. On a visit to Vineyard one day John took an immediate shine to her and she was fostered with them. Elsie was a little reluctant, judging Janette to be 'a mouse' but John was keen and the fostering in time led to her full adoption.

Like many of her generation, Elsie was thrifty, finding it difficult ever to throw things away. Consequently she kept papers galore and her letters seemed to be everywhere in her study. The vicarage was also full of furniture and crockery, bought at low prices at salerooms, and Elsie and John would also regularly buy second-hand books. Elsie made many of her own clothes and, in the early years, those for Janette also. Elsie was simply too energetic to sleep all night and, well into old age, she would go to bed late and rise very early. Her husband, by contrast, would arise later and have little for breakfast whereas Elsie enjoyed a hearty but healthy meal of lemon juice, cereal, fruit, yoghurt and weak, often herbal, tea. She loved bananas, in particular. Family meals in the vicarage always involved the saying of grace but a daily Bible reading was not included.[11]

Elsie's love of music led her to direct and conduct oratorios at All Saints, Hampton, to which, among others, she would invite members and friends of Vineyard. In similar fashion, but on a smaller scale,

10. When Kathleen Hall married in 1938 she was told by the Lancashire moderator, T.T. James, that she would henceforth be known in the year book by her married name. K. Hendry, *Don't Ask Me Why 60 Years a Woman Minister* (London: United Reformed Church, 1991), p. 45.

11. Williams, *First Lady of the Pulpit*, pp. 50–53.

she would hold musical events at Vineyard. She also ran a children's orchestra in the parish and made the vicarage and its garden available for the summer fete every year. On one occasion the Bishop of London stayed for dinner after presiding at a confirmation service at All Saints. Elsie joined the Mothers' Union in the parish and in November 1947 she founded the Young Wives' Club which she conscientiously attended, even when she was working at the BBC in the 1950s. She realized that young wives especially needed a night out and, at the club, members would listen to music, hear talks, have socials and enjoy each other's company in a relaxed setting. Elsie would take friends from the parish with her on visits to the City churches. In the mid-1990s, the Wives' Club still continued although, after 50 years, it no longer bore the epithet young. Elsie herself continued to run the club up to 1963 when John left Hampton to move to a living in Essex.

Living in Hampton, Janette attended John's church and joined the choir. As a teenager she found John's relaxed view towards social gatherings more congenial than Elsie's strict sabbatarianism. In accordance with her own upbringing, Elsie refused to allow her daughter to do homework or wash her hair on Sundays and, in addition, she expected her teetotal principles to be respected. John's membership of the Working Man's Club and of the freemasons underlined how much he differed from his wife. The uncompromising Elsie also disapproved of make-up, to her a form of female vanity and unnecessary. As a result Janette had some awkward experiences whilst growing into adulthood.[12]

While living at Hampton, John and Elsie bought a cottage in Hampshire, at Chute, near Andover, where they spent holidays and occasional days off. Later they bought other houses, often in a dilapidated state. One cottage, near Plymouth, was used by John as the consulting rooms, for his work as a counsellor and psychotherapist. He would hypnotize people, referred to him, in an effort to help their recovery from emotional and mental problems. He saw this healing as complementary to his Christian work as a priest. Elsie always drove John to Plymouth as he did not drive. She would often take with them the family cat which was free to roam at will in the moving vehicle, a habit she repeated with other cats later when she was a widow. Elsie's ardent teetotalism could cause particular

---

12. Williams, *First Lady of the Pulpit*, pp. 52–55. Information supplied by Mrs B. Smith.

awkwardness, as at Janette's wedding, after which the groom's family wished to serve sherry and wine. Elsie exercised a veto over this suggestion![13]

In 1963, the Garrington family moved from Hampton to the rectory at Greensted near Ongar, in Essex. In this early nineteenth century house, with its whitewashed exterior and large garden, Elsie felt at home while John was proud of the ancient church which he served. He would personally conduct visitors around the church building which is Saxon in origin, having been built to mark the place where St Edmund's body rested, on its way from London to Bury St Edmund's in 1013. Nevertheless Greensted parish church, with its distinctive oak timber walls, curiously is dedicated to St Andrew, and not to St Edmund.[14]

13. *The Independent*, 20 April 1991. Williams, *First Lady of the Pulpit*, pp. 53, 55, 58, 59.

14. Williams, *First Lady of the Pulpit*, p. 57. W.R. Powell (ed.), *Victoria History of the Counties of England: Essex, Vol IV* (London: published for the Institute of Historical Research by Oxford University Press, 1956), pp. 60, 61.

Chapter 7

VINEYARD CONGREGATIONAL CHURCH, RICHMOND-UPON-THAMES

Vineyard Congregational Church at Richmond-upon-Thames had been founded in 1830 and the handsome, grey brick building, designed by John Davies, opened a year later. It is sited adjacent to a Roman Catholic church, dedicated to St Elizabeth, in a side road off Hill Rise, called The Vineyard. The Catholic church had itself been opened for worship, only a few years before its neighbour, in 1824.[1] Both churches, therefore, bear witness to the expansion of the local population at the beginning of the nineteenth century in this part of what was then rural Surrey, but which was close to the heart of the capital city. Only a few years later, with the coming of the railways, Richmond would find itself even more accessible to London.

The Vineyard Congregational Church had been unsuccessful in its attempts to find a minister early in 1947. Elsie's immediate predecessor as minister had been Edward Tait Kirby (1871–1972) who had left New College, London in 1900 and had pastorates in Southport, Whetstone, Havant, and Egham Hill from which he had formally retired in 1940. However, after this retirement, he fulfilled a part-time ministry, first at West Kensington 1940–1941 and then at the Vineyard, Richmond 1942–1946, following the resignation of the young Welsh theologian, Daniel T. Jenkins (1914–2002), whose brief but scholarly ministry at Richmond had lasted from 1940–1942, when he had accepted a post with the Student Christian Movement. Although elderly, Kirby remained a live wire, playing golf until he was 97 and living to be 100 years old. Prior to Jenkins' arrival, the church had spent several years without a minister.[2]

---

1. B. Cherry and N. Pevsner, *The Buildings of England London 2: South* (London: Penguin, 1983), p. 519. H.E. Malden (ed.), *Victoria History of the Counties of England: Surrey, Vol III* (Westminster: Archibald Constable, 1911), p. 541.

2. *Congregational Year Book 1972* (London: Congregational Church in England and Wales, 1972), p. 361. A.W. Austin, *The Surrey Congregational Union 1862–1965* (Banbury, Oxon: the author, nd), pp. 52, 59. G.H. P[reston]

He had come as a young man, to the Vineyard, his first pastoral charge from Mansfield College, Oxford, during the upheaval of the Second World War while, in obvious contrast, Kirby had already retired when he began his Vineyard ministry. In 1947, with the uncertainties of the war ended, the church clearly needed stability and committed leadership.

In June that year Alan Green, who had followed R.J. Evans as the moderator of the London province of the CUEW in 1942, recommended Elsie Chamberlain to the church. Her first visit to Vineyard was 'much appreciated' and the church members were unanimous in their invitation to her to preach again. John fully agreed with Elsie that, after marriage, she should continue with her ministerial work and seek a pastorate. Indeed the church had thoughtfully sent a telegram to Elsie and John congratulating them on their wedding. A special church meeting on 18 September 1947 unanimously confirmed an earlier decision to invite Elsie to be the minister of Vineyard, with a stipend of £300 per annum. Elsie had written to suggest that, in view of the possible effects of the coming winter on her still delicate health, perhaps she should only agree to serve for the next six months, after which the position could be reviewed by both parties.

At Elsie's first church meeting, in October 1947, she announced her plans to hold church membership meetings. Her induction service as minister there was to be held on 14 November when John Huxtable (1912-1990), the minister of Palmer's Green Congregational Church, in north London, 1943-1954, and also then, like Elsie, a rising star in the Congregational Union of England and Wales, was to be the preacher.[3] The deacons' meetings in October and November 1947 outlined a winter programme which included a toy service, a nativity play, and carol services. They also recorded that one couple were transferring their membership from the Vineyard to Richmond Presbyterian Church. Was this move in reaction to the appointment of

Vineyard Congregational Church Richmond 1830–1980 (nd, np), pp. 4–5. For Jenkins, see, *Oxford Dictionary of National Biography; United Reformed Church Year Book 2003* (London: United Reformed Church, 2003), p. 326; and J. Taylor and J.C.G. Binfield (eds), *Who They Were in the Reformed Churches of England and Wales 1901–2000* (Donington: Shaun Tyas for the United Reformed Church History Society, 2007), pp. 114–15.

3. *United Reformed Church Year Book 1991–92* (London: United Reformed Church, 1991), p. 229.

a woman minister? If so, they were out-numbered by those joining the church for in contrast, at this same time, four new women members were added to the roll.[4]

Elsie's interest in music surfaced in the choir's plans to sing Stainer's *Crucifixion* on Palm Sunday 1948 and Handel's *Messiah* on April 3. In January 1948, the church meeting discussed Elsie's infrequent attendances at Sunday evening services. The members hoped that she would be able to preach on Sunday evenings more regularly if the morning rota was adjusted. Elsie was then reliant on public transport and she admitted that she was hoping to buy a motor car soon. In March 1948 the six months which Elsie had initially agreed to serve were completed. The deacons reported that her health had been 'satisfactory' throughout, while the church members were unanimous in renewing their call to Elsie to be their minister. In response, she stated her own belief that there was much left for her to do at Vineyard. An encouraging development was that four more new members were joining the church and two dozen additional communion cups had been ordered.

The Vineyard Ministry Develops

In April three more members were added to the church roll. In June 1948, the deacons recommended that a communion service should be held quarterly, as part of the church meeting at which new members should be formally received. One distinct feature of the church's witness that year was its concern for world Christianity and for ecumenism. That summer the Vineyard members 'adopted' a church in Germany which they could help, Pastor Heuner's church in Dortmund, and gifts of clothing were sent. Fritz Heuner (1891–1962) was a distinguished Lutheran and was the superintendent of the Dortmund church district 1934–1961. He was strongly anti-Nazi, being involved in the Confessing Church, and was instrumental after 1945 in assisting the reconstruction of Lutheran churches in the Dortmund district (Dortmund had been badly damaged by allied bombing from the air in 1943–1944). The Dortmund church, assisted by Vineyard, was probably St Marienkirche in the city centre.

4. Vineyard Congregational Church, deacons' minutes 24 June, 25 August, 29 September, 26 November 1947; church meeting minutes 29 June, 27 August, 18 September, 23 October, 27 November 1947.

In September 1948, the West London Orchestra was given permission to use the schoolroom on Monday evenings for rehearsals and Elsie's old friend, Lady Stansgate, who had just returned from the World Council of Churches' inaugural meeting in Amsterdam, having decided to leave the Church of England in favour of Congregationalism, became a church member. Elsie had herself been present at the World Council of Churches' meeting which left an indelible impression upon her. The deacons also gave consideration to the report of the then current negotiations for unity between the Congregational Union of England and Wales and the Presbyterian Church of England. Local discussions with the Presbyterians in Richmond had occurred as early as 1946 and continued in a cordial atmosphere for some years. On a more domestic issue, the church meeting unanimously approved the deacons' proposal that Elsie's stipend should be augmented, by an expense allowance of £25 per annum.[5]

In late November 1948 the deacons, having studied the documents individually, gave their general approval to the Congregational/Presbyterian talks. The report, they felt, provided 'a basis for fuller and official negotiations'. On 1st December Elsie explained in detail to the church meeting the state of the Congregational/Presbyterian negotiations and the church members, like the deacons, also approved the talks but went further, by urging the Free Church Federal Council to inaugurate moves for a union of all the Free Churches. It is interesting to note that, had this church union been approved nationally in the late 1940s, Elsie would have sided with the uniting party whereas in 1972 she had reversed her position.

The church meeting in late December accepted the plan to assemble a 'gathered choir' to sing Handel's *Messiah* in April. Elsie reviewed the work of the previous year, especially referring to the Missionary Week, the publicity campaign, and the Rotary Club's goodwill Christmas tree which yielded £12 for her to help those in need.

5. Vineyard Congregational Church, church meeting minutes 31 December 1947, 28 January, 31 March, 29 April, 3 June, 29 July, 8, 29 September, 17 October 1948; deacons' minutes 1 March, 30 March, 26 April, 21 June, 26 July, 6, 27 September 1848. E.A. Elders, *The Kirk on the Green: The Story of Richmond's Presbyterian Congregation 1876–1976* (Richmond: Richmond Green United Reformed Church, 1976), pp. 21–22. For further information on Heuner see, Konrad Lorenz (ed.), *Die Ev. St Marienkirche zu Dortmund* (2nd edn, Dortmund: Eigenverlag der Mariengemeinde, 1981).

She intended to begin a junior church in January 1949. At this time Elsie's pastoral work included her visiting absent members and other absentees from the regular congregation. She also announced that her annual vacation that year was to be held over six Sundays in June and July when she would attend the International Congregational Council meetings in the United States of America.[6] Had the church members not imagined that their minister was becoming a figure of influence in the denomination then, after the World Council of Churches' conference of 1948 and the International Congregational Council meetings of 1949, they had little excuse for such an underestimation.

In March 1949, the deacons advised that some names should be removed from the membership roll as they had received no replies to their letters of enquiry. More encouragingly that same month one young woman formally joined the church as a member. In April a new piano was bought at their minister's suggestion, for the beginners' department, and in June Elsie, accompanied by a married couple from Vineyard, set off for the International Congregational Council meetings at Wellesley, Massachusetts.

Rachel Storr

During Elsie's absence in the United States of America, she had arranged for the Revd Rachel Storr to supply the pulpit at her Richmond church. Frances Rachel Storr (1909–2002), when a laywoman, had preached her first sermon in Elsie's former church, Christ Church, Friern Barnet. The two women had met at the inter-denominational group for the ordination of women and had become friends. Rachel had been born in 1909, just one year earlier than Elsie, and had been brought up in a devout Church of England family. She was a graduate in English of Lady Margaret Hall, Oxford, and had been a teacher for 13 years. Her father, Vernon Faithfull Storr (1869–1940), was a canon of Westminster, the rector of St Margaret, Westminster, and the author of *The Development of English Theology in the Nineteenth Century 1800–1860*[7] and of several other theological studies. As their friendship had deepened, Elsie had encouraged

---

6. Vineyard Congregational Church, church meeting minutes 1 December, 30 December 1948, deacons' minutes 22 November 1948.

7. Vernon Faithfull Storr, *The Development of English Theology in the Nineteenth Century* (London: Longmans, Green and Co., 1913).

Rachel, who believed that she had a vocation to ministry, to consider training to become a Congregational minister. In 1944, Rachel became a member of Hammersmith Congregational Church and soon discovered that she felt happy as a Free Churchwoman. From 1945 to 1947 she worked as assistant minister at the Claremont Central Mission, while studying for a diploma in theology. She was ordained in 1948.

Elsie's persuasion, allied to the call of the Holy Spirit, had resulted in Rachel Storr transferring her allegiance to Congregationalism where her sex proved no barrier to her ordination. Elsie and Rachel Storr were to remain lifelong friends. In the summer of 1949, when Rachel preached at the Vineyard, she had only been ordained for one year, although she had gained valuable experience at Claremont Central Mission and had been the temporary minister in 1948 of Putney Congregational Church (geographically close to Richmond-upon-Thames). She was to move as minister to Brentford Congregational Church in August 1949, on which occasion the Vineyard deacons sent their fellowship's good wishes. She was at Brentford for ten years as minister, before moving in 1959 to Thetford in Norfolk where she remained for 15 years. Rachel Storr retired in 1974 and continued preaching until she was nearly 90 years old. A woman of quiet, confident faith, she died in October 2002.[8]

Church Life at Vineyard

Recent repairs to the church organ in the summer of 1949 were marked by invitations to Dr Eric Thiman (1900–1975), the composer, later to be musical editor of the hymn book *Congregational Praise* and much respected organist of The City Temple, and to Sandy Macpherson, the well-known musician and BBC radio broadcaster, to give recitals at Vineyard. Both Thiman and Macpherson enjoyed

8. Vineyard Congregational Church, church meeting minutes 30 March, 28 April, 1 June, 22 August, 28 September 1949; deacons' meeting minutes 17 January, 21 March, 26 April, 26 May 1949. R.T. Jones, *Congregationalism in England, 1662–1962* (London: Independent Press, 1962), p. 429. F.L. Fagley (ed.), *Proceedings of the Sixth International Congregational Council* (London: Independent Press, 1949), pp. 122–27, 180–81. *United Reformed Church Year Book 1999* (London: United Reformed Church,1999), p. 258; *United Reformed Church Year Book 2004* (London: United Reformed Church, 2004), p. 331. *Reform* (July 1975), p. 6. Private conversation with Miss Storr.

some measure of celebrity but a greater contrast in terms of their musical styles could hardly have been found, that is the difference between the academic and the populist. Thiman was regarded as 'the most widely distinguished musician in the history of Congregationalism' and had been professor of harmony at the Royal Academy of Music since 1930.[9] Yet by inviting these two, Elsie was aiming high – one a noted Congregationalist, the other a popular radio communicator.

Perhaps using the educational emphases which she had learned in Liverpool, she often began church meetings at Vineyard with short talks on church history. In September 1949, she introduced a series on the early history of Independency, with reference to the Westminster Assembly of Divines of the 1640s and to the Westminster Confession. The Assembly and the Confession were principally of importance to Presbyterianism, rather than Congregationalism, and Elsie's choice of these subjects probably reflected the Congregational/Presbyterian talks about union of that time. Elsie also announced, to the church meeting, that she would devote one Sunday evening service per month to answering questions, previously submitted by members of the church and congregation, and a box was to be provided in the church in which questions could be placed.

On 28 September 1949 Elsie continued her talks on subjects related to the history of Congregationalism, addressing the members on the Savoy Declaration of 1658. The minutes also record that a Vineyard church magazine had recently been started. In November, Elsie spoke on Christian heritage to the church meeting and later reported on her recent visit to the USA. In December a plan to start a men's club in January 1950 at the church was announced and, in addition, it was noted that a small prayer group had begun meeting. Throughout 1949 several new members joined the church – a man in June, three women in September, a married couple by transfer from Blackheath Congregational Church in October, and two women in January 1950. Most significantly on 1st February 1950 Revd Edward Charles Dudley

9. *The Hymn Society of Great Britain and Ireland. Bulletin* 8(7), (June 1975), pp. 117–20. For Thiman see, J. Taylor and C. Binfield (eds), *Who They Were in the Reformed Churches of England and Wales 1901–2000* (Donington: Shaun Tyas for the United Reformed Church History Society, 2007), p. 224.

Stanford, and his wife and daughter, transferred their memberships to the Vineyard.[10]

Open Air Witness

In March 1950, Elsie proposed to the deacons that on Sundays, before the evening services, 'half an hour of community hymn-singing' should be held outside the church. The idea would not stand up well to detailed analysis. The Vineyard was then, and remains, a narrow street, largely unaltered, of early nineteenth century houses, with a small pavement, outside the Congregational church, which is located a few yards from the very narrow street corner. As has been stated, on one side the Congregational church has a Roman Catholic church as its immediate neighbour. On the other side, the Congregational church is only yards from a junction with a busy and more important road, Hill Rise, leading from Richmond Bridge up Richmond Hill, from which spectacular views of the meandering river Thames in a lush parkland setting may be seen.

Elsie's suggestion of outdoor community hymn singing, on Sunday evenings, in the Vineyard, however superficially attractive, was and is simply impractical. Even ten people there would be a crowd and more would be a dangerous obstruction. One is led to ask, 'Where might they have stood?' Certainly not on the pavement. Surely it would have been dangerous, even for a relatively small congregation in the 1950s, to have sung outside the church? It would have caused an awkwardness and might have proved counter-productive, by annoying the neighbours. The proposal spoke volumes about Elsie's enthusiasm and her wish to take the church to the people. But it was not well thought out.

At the church meeting, Ted Stanford (as he was commonly known) made the sensible suggestion that Vineyard should hold open-air services by the Thames riverside, a short distance from the building, but a lot safer, with more open space and greater potential to gather a crowd than the Vineyard, on Sunday evenings. In May this proposal

10. Vineyard Congregational Church, church meeting minutes 1 September, 28 September, 3 November, 30 November, 22 December 1949. Sandy Macpherson, a former cinema organist and BBC radio broadcaster, presented *Silver Chords* and *Chapel in the Valley* on the Light Programme, playing music and hymns with 'deliberate sentimentality'. K.M. Wolfe, *The Churches and the British Broadcasting Corporation 1922–1956* (London: SCM Press, 1984), pp. 375–76.

was qualified by inviting the Presbyterian and parish churches to co-operate in the venture but, in the absence of any response from either of them, the Congregational church seemed willing to go it alone. Also in May the church meeting unanimously voted Elsie an increase in stipend, to £350 per annum (including expenses), and she was congratulated on being appointed president elect of the Women's Federation of the Congregational Union of England and Wales. In June 1950 the local Presbyterians indicated that they were unwilling to support the proposed open-air meetings, with the result that the scheme was postponed.[11]

11. Vineyard Congregational Church, deacons' minutes 20 March, 24 April, 22 May; church meeting minutes 30 March, 4 May, 31 May.

Chapter 8

LATER YEARS AT VINEYARD

In July 1950 Elsie told the deacons at Vineyard that she had been offered a part-time post in the 'organising of religious broadcasts' for the British Broadcasting Corporation, which she would like to accept. She explained that she hoped to depute to others some of the ministerial tasks at Vineyard although she accepted the need to develop further the church's work in Richmond. In particular she expressed her concern about the need for a 'Free Church on the new housing estate at Ham, where over 300 families were already housed, with the probability of an additional 238 in the near future'. Ham is almost physically a part of Richmond being situated close to it, outside the impressive Richmond Park, along the river to the south. The meeting heard the suggestion that Ted Stanford might be willing to help, if Elsie did take the BBC job, by serving as joint minister of the Vineyard church with Elsie. The church members, although probably shocked and bemused, found this proposal acceptable, in September 1950, when 34 voted in favour with none against. At the same meeting it was announced that one of the church members, Elisabeth Neale, was to begin her studies at King's College, London, where Elsie had herself studied. The young woman hoped to be admitted to train for the Congregational ministry. The church agreed to recommend her formally to the Surrey Congregational Union, as a candidate for the ministry.

Stanford began as co-pastor in December 1950 and from January 1951 onwards he and Elsie alternately chaired the deacons and church meetings. In April 1951, Ted Stanford was appointed to an administrative post in the education department of the British Council of Churches. In June the deacons decided to increase the combined stipend to £400 per annum. One month earlier Stanford had addressed the church members on the recent joint session of the Congregational Union of England and Wales with the Presbyterian Church of England's general assembly, held during the annual May meetings of the Congregational Union in London. He read aloud the

Figure 8.1 Elsie and Ted Stanford – the ministerial partnership at Vineyard, Richmond-upon-Thames, late 1950. Reproduced with permission of Janette Williams.

joint declaration, 'pledging mutual co-operation' between the two bodies. Taking this pledge seriously, the church attempted to find ways of working with the local Presbyterians and, on 22 October 1951, the deacons discussed the possibility of joint social activities with Richmond Presbyterian Church.[1]

E.C.D. Stanford

Ted Stanford (1903–1994) was born in Peckham, south London, and trained for the ministry at Hackney and New College, before serving in pastorates at Bury St Edmund's 1928–1934 and at Olton,

1. Elisabeth Neale studied at Western College, Bristol, qualifying in 1955, having already completed her course at King's College, London. She died in 2009. *The London Gazette*, 16 February 2010, issue no. 59336. Vineyard Congregational Church, church meeting minutes 26 July, 28 September, 2 November 1950; deacons' minutes 17 July, 26 July, 27 October 1950, 22 January, 22 October 1951. R.T. Jones, *Congregationalism in England, 1662–1962* (London: Independent Press, 1962), pp. 432–33.

Birmingham 1934–1945. From 1946 to 1949 he worked in administrative posts for the Congregational Union of England and Wales while, from 1949 to 1951, during which time he joined Vineyard, he was the general secretary of the Christian Auxiliary Movement. From 1950 to 1954, Stanford shared the pastorate of Vineyard with Elsie while continuing to work with the British Council of Churches 1951–1962. Later he served the British and Foreign Bible Society 1962–1963 and then became the Education Secretary of the Congregational Union of England and Wales 1963–1967. In 1967 he had officially retired but was asked that year to collate and report on the replies from local Congregational and Presbyterian churches to the draft basis of union between these two bodies, which basis proved to be part of the preparation for the emergence of the United Reformed Church. In 1968, he produced a 'massive document', setting out the various responses, and in 1972 he opted to join the new United Reformed Church. He retired to Rustington in Sussex where he died in 1994, aged 90.

Stanford's joint ministry with Elsie was deemed to have worked well at Vineyard. He was seven years older than her and had more pastoral experience. She was indeed fortunate to have his willing help at a time, when attractive opportunities were available to her. Like Elsie, he had bookish tastes but, unlike her, he paid great attention to detail and would not allow himself to be carried away with wishful thinking. She always had an outline of the points she wished to make but laid much weight upon sensing the needs of the occasion and immediately responding to them. In contrast, he was always prepared well in advance and had his feet firmly on the ground. Yet Ted Stanford had 'an impish sense of humour' and, again like Elsie, he had 'a love for and interest in people'. Although he was to serve the churches as an administrator for many years, he had no desire to be other than a pastor to a local church and was an undoubted asset to the Vineyard. He was a capable preacher and a tactful and good listener. They worked well together, complementing each other's gifts. His calmness proved a foil to Elsie's fireworks and, most importantly, they liked and respected each other.[2]

2. *United Reformed Church Year Book 1995* (London: United Reformed Church, 1995), p. 268. Surman Index of Congregational Ministers, held at Dr Williams's Library, London. A. Macarthur, 'The Background to the Formation of the United Reformed Church' in *Journal of the United Reformed Church History Society* 4(1) (October 1987), pp. 10–11.

A New Hymn Book

In February 1952 the church, like many others at the time, considered buying the new hymn book, *Congregational Praise*, produced by a committee of the Congregational Union of England and Wales over several years, and first published in 1951. The church meeting decided that the book would enhance the regular worship of the church. Twenty-five music copies were needed, plus two hundred ordinary copies, that is approximately twice as many books as the church had members. Was the regular congregation much larger than those who had formally accepted the privileges and responsibilities of membership? Elsie arranged for the Revd Erik Routley (1917–1982) to conduct an evening of hymn singing, in May 1952 at Vineyard, concentrating on the content of the new book. Routley was the hymn book committee's minutes secretary and also its general secretary. He was, therefore, one of the book's chief compilers and certainly its most energetic advocate. This must have been a thrilling occasion for her, combining her love of music and her Christian devotion to God.

In 1951, 'in readiness for the launching of *Congregational Praise*', Routley had conducted 'a virtually single-handed publicity campaign', arranging and leading musical evenings up and down the country. In the course of his travels, he was to hone his talent for 'popular presentation' and, in the process, came to know a great many ministers and organists. By the early 1950s Routley was well-known as an accomplished organist, a composer and an enthusiastic writer on hymns and their background. He had an engaging manner and could be expected to amuse, inform and even captivate his audience.[3] Elsie had obtained Routley's services at an opportune time. The warmth of his personality, even when confronting a large congregation, was easily communicated. Routley believed that 'only the best was good enough for public worship' and *Congregational Praise* remains a fine hymn book. He had learned from his visits to churches what congregations, like that at Richmond, might profit most from and which hymns were likely to be appreciated. Therefore he offered a judicious mix of old favourites and good new tunes and hymns. Of course, he

---

3. *Who Was Who, 1981–1990* (London: A. & C. Black, 1991). *The Hymn Society of Great Britain and Ireland. Bulletin* 8(6) (February 1975), p. 94. C. Micklem, 'Erik Routley, 1917–1982' in R.A. Leaver and J.H. Litton, *Duty and Delight: Routley Remembered* (Norwich: Canterbury Press, 1985), p. 8.

was really introducing this 'outstanding' hymn book to the church at Richmond and to friends, from other churches, who joined them.[4]

Later Work at the Vineyard

In July 1952, the church returned to the need to evangelize the growing riverside housing estate at Ham, in conjunction with Kingston Congregational Church, situated to the south of Ham, and also with Richmond Presbyterian Church. Services were arranged in the Working Men's Institute at Ham on Sunday evenings for a trial period of six months, although these later were to move to the hall of the new school on the estate. A 'lot of work and prayer' was expended to promote this venture but eventually it seemed that 'the time was not ripe'. The people at Ham had failed to support the services in sufficient numbers, although 'a strong group of keen supporters' had loyally attended 'in all weathers and despite all difficulties'. It was decided to end the experiment in 1954, with the various parties promising to try again in the future. The 'mutual goodwill and ecumenical effort', engendered by the joint mission at Ham, resulted in the Presbyterian Church being invited to join Vineyard for its Christmas Day service in 1952 and a combined service with the Presbyterians was also planned for the following Good Friday.[5]

In March 1953, Elsie asked the deacons for leave of absence for June, July and August, during which time she would expect to forego her stipend. She explained that she felt the need of 'a long vacation owing to pressure of work' and she referred particularly to the 'strenuous task' of pastoral visiting, a task for which, one might assume, her gifts of friendliness and openness were especially suited. The church meeting later endorsed the deacons' prior agreement to this. We must conclude that she was totally sincere, in her comments

---

4. Jones, *Congregationalism in England*, pp. 456-57. J. Taylor and C. Binfield (eds), *Who They Were in the Reformed Churches of England and Wales 1901–2000* (Donington: Shaun Tyas for the United Reformed Church History Society, 2007), pp. 196-97.

5. E.A. Elders, *The Kirk on the Green: The Story of Richmond's Presbyterian Congregation 1876–1976* (Richmond, Surrey: Richmond Green United Reformed Church), p. 22. E.D. Chamberlain, *White to Harvest* (London: Independent Press, 1956), p. 14. Vineyard Congregational Church, church meeting minutes 29 February, 4 July, 31 October; deacons' minutes 20 February, 21 July, 20 October, 24 November 1952, 16 February 1953.

about the emotional strains of visiting, because she returned to this theme three years later, speaking out against 'this exhausting and never ending demand to be visited', in her chairman's address to the Congregational Union of England and Wales in May 1956.

In October 1953, with Elsie in the chair, Ted Stanford addressed the deacons on the shared pastorate. He explained that both ministers felt that they had 'insufficient time to give to the Church', especially in pastoral matters. They believed that they could maintain the church at the present level but sadly 'saw no prospect of the work advancing under the present arrangements'. Therefore they had both decided to terminate their ministry at Vineyard at the end of the year. In the light of this unforeseen and critical development, the deacons decided to approach St Paul's Congregational Church, their neighbour also in Richmond, located to the east of Richmond Bridge and the town centre, with a view to the two churches sharing the services of one minister or even uniting.[6] At that time St Paul's pastorate was vacant and the church building, which had been destroyed by enemy bombing in 1940, had not been replaced. Although discussions between representative deacons of the two Congregational churches were held in early 1954, the churches did not unite. In the summer of 1954 both Elsie and Ted Stanford, who had himself planned to leave six months earlier, were still chairing church meetings at Vineyard and both continued to preach at the church and chair the meetings when required, until Ernest Cruchley was appointed in September 1955.[7] In 1954, Elsie herself moved from part-time work at the BBC to full-time employment for the corporation. Leaving her ministry at Vineyard simply made this an easier step.

Elsie as Minister

Elsie demanded much of her church members. She would adopt, probably unknowingly, the manner of an earnest schoolmistress addressing naughty pupils. Was that what the Berkley Street young people in Liverpool had meant by the term 'church police',

6. Vineyard Congregational Church, church meeting minutes 1 May, 4 December 1953; deacons' minutes 18 March, 20 April, 19 October 1953.

7. St Paul's voted to become part of the United Reformed Church in 1972 and Vineyard joined the Congregational Federation. Vineyard Congregational Church, church meeting minutes 11 July, 30 July 1954. G.H.P[reston], *Vineyard Congregational Church Richmond 1830–1980* (nd, np), p. 5.

which nickname they had fondly given young Elsie? As minister she would, on occasions, telephone any absentees from the church meeting, on the following morning, and ask for explanations. Elsie was notoriously forthright, like her mother, and could be sharp and reproving. Were traces of her own headmistress at Channing School, Miss Haigh, evident in her pastoral attitudes? Although she could be fierce, she was a warm friend and maintained a steady, thoughtful correspondence over the years in her large, characteristically bold handwriting.

Her prayers in public worship were much appreciated, although opinions differed about the quality of her preaching. Her sermons were prepared with some care but were always imbued with her own strong personality and her desire to relate directly to the people before her. Her wide reading of popular theology reinforced her views which were broadly liberal and at least one church member at Vineyard noticed that she rarely, if ever, spoke of Jesus as her saviour. Was that because even as assured a minister as Elsie could feel a little embarrassed to speak openly of her own Christian experiences, and of her personal weaknesses, which she dutifully confided to Christ? She did not wear her heart on her sleeve.

In 1947 when Elsie became minister at Vineyard the church had 94 members, 52 children and 22 teachers. It had no lay preachers. In 1954, the year in which she and Ted Stanford left its ministry, the church had 105 members, 82 children and 13 teachers. In 1955 it had 95 members, in 1956, then with Ernest Cruchley in his first pastorate, it had 82, and in 1957 it had 86. Elsie had made a positive difference to the church. She also had made enduring friends at Vineyard and, 40 years after leaving it, in the mid-1990s, she was recalled with real affection by older church members. In her time at the Vineyard, she had begun her work in religious broadcasting which she was to find fulfilling and which proved to be, in the words of one BBC colleague, 'the central part' of her 'stormy life'. Vineyard had given her the base, the freedom and the support she needed to embark upon this adventure.[8]

8. *Congregational Year Book 1947* (London: Congregational Union of England and Wales, 1947), p. 216, *Congregational Year Book 1954* (London: Congregational Union of England and Wales, 1954), p. 243, *Congregational Year Book 1955* (London: Congregational Union of England and Wales, 1955), p. 245, *Congregational Year Book 1957* (London: Congregational Union of England and Wales, 1957), p. 245. *The Independent*, 20 April 1991.

Elsie and Women Ministers

Elsie sought out and drew women, in particular, to her churches. Of course, they were also drawn throughout her long ministry to her, as also were many men. Her own conspicuous success as a minister, and her apparent control of her chosen course through life, made her a model for a generation and more of women who felt a vocation to the Christian ministry. She herself showed an especial interest in such women and a number of women, from the churches to which she ministered, were subsequently ordained. Some, but not all, of these came originally from other denominations and Elsie's advice to prospective ministers was often to follow her own singular pattern, rather than to follow the established Congregational Union of England and Wales' guidelines. Was she deliberately ignoring the guidelines or did she simply not bother to acquaint herself with procedures? While others might regard her conduct as slipshod and irresponsible, she might see their demands as fussy and bureaucratic. Her own route into ministry had been far from the norm and gave her little understanding of what might be expected from those following a more regular pattern.

Elsie's advice to prospective candidates for the ministry could cause unnecessary embarrassment, both to students and moderators alike. At one point (William) Andrew James, the moderator of the Congregational Union of England and Wales Southern Province 1950-1966, was furious with Elsie, for misleading one student from Vineyard who mistakenly believed that she was accredited as training for the Congregational ministry, although her name had not been forwarded to the moderator and, consequently, she had not been through the formal interviewing process, then required by the Congregational Union of England and Wales. In practice, Elsie really saw little need for moderators and claimed quite seriously that a London Bachelor of Divinity rendered a Congregational or any minister the equal of a Church of England bishop.[9]

---

9. For William Andrew James (1904-1975) see, *United Reformed Church Year Book 1976* (London: United Reformed Church, 1976), pp. 299-300.

Chapter 9

INTERNATIONAL MEETINGS AND THE CUEW CHAIR

In the late 1940s and early 1950s, Elsie Chamberlain came to enjoy a high public profile, both without and within the churches, and not merely among her fellow Congregationalists. At this time she became involved with the International Congregational Council and with the World Council of Churches. Simultaneously her work for the BBC Religious Broadcasting department brought her into contact with many of the leading clergy in Britain's denominations. Indeed that work may have reinforced her desire to attend these major events and may also correspondingly have benefited from such attendance. This rapid rise, from the relative obscurity of a lowly suburban minister to an ecclesiastical celebrity, culminated in her election to the chair of the Congregational Union of England and Wales. These few years were undoubtedly those of her greatest influence. She had come far from the streets of Liverpool 8 and the unusual training for the ministry she had received there in wartime!

The International Congregational Council at Wellesley

In June 1949, Elsie Chamberlain was among the delegates from Britain who gathered at Waterloo Railway Station, in London, and who journeyed by train and by sea, on board the liner, 'Queen Elizabeth', to the United States of America for the sixth International Congregational Council meetings at Wellesley College, Wellesley, Massachusetts. The superb hospitality afforded by the Americans to their visitors in New York and elsewhere was at times, in the words of one Briton, 'almost overwhelming' and 'amazing'. However, given the then current post-war 'British austerity', such generosity would have been impossible to match in this country. One British participant, L. Hector Read, remarked upon the high quality of the 'prepared speeches' and summarized the experience by stating that it was 'good to be at Wellesley'. Yet, in his report, he also questioned the contemporary wisdom of trying to alter Congregationalism that it may fit better into 'a planned society, with all its dangers to the freedom of the individual'. Rather Read emphasized the value of freedom, 'as exemplified in Congregationalism, and practised by our forefathers'. If this were done, he maintained, the realization might dawn that 'in striving for complete union more harm than good may ensue to the church'.[1]

The phrase, 'a planned society', echoes the language of politics in the late 1940s when the Labour government was reforming the British economy, nationalizing key industries and setting up large public corporations. Read appears to have suspected that those within the Congregational Union of England and Wales, who argued that it should become more of a single body, that is a national Church, rather than remain a union of separate, local, gathered churches, were devaluing the strengths of Congregationalism and following too closely the dominant social theories of the day. No evidence exists to support the view that Elsie then shared such fears.

However, she did agree about the warm reception given to the visitors who arrived at the International Congregational Council meetings in the United States of America, in her own words, 'as agog as a charabanc of trippers'. She recalled giving an assurance, to a group of American women, that she would tell her friends at home that 'they were so much nicer' than she had expected! She was especially struck by the fact that American Congregationalism, in and around New York, where existed 'wealthy churches with colossal memberships, highly paid staff, and marvellous equipment (those kitchens! – like ideal home exhibitions on a large scale)', was 'very different' from the English understanding of that tradition. The church at Riverside, New York, she commented with incredulous wonder, had as many as '70 names on its payroll' and she stated, realistically, that church meetings are simply not 'practical' when the membership stands at two or three thousand. She wrote of her participation in worship, at some American churches. 'The central altar with Cross and two candles and the liturgical part of the Service would have made many an Anglican feel at home'. Nevertheless she had found it 'the greatest possible encouragement in ecumenicity', taking a different view from her fellow delegate, Hector Read.[2]

1. L.H. Read, 'Impressions of the Conference', *Congregational Quarterly* XXVII (1949), pp. 356–59.
2. E.D. Chamberlain, 'Impressions of the Conference', *Congregational Quarterly* XXVII (1949), 359–61.

Figure 9.1 Elsie at the World Council of Churches, Amsterdam 1948. Reproduced with permission of Janette Williams.

Figure 9.2 Departing Waterloo for the World Council of Churches, Evanston, August 1954 – photograph by John Garrington. Reproduced with permission of Janette Williams.

At these International Congregational Council meetings, Elsie gave an address to the women's divisional meeting on the 'Life and Work of Women in the World Church'. She also initiated a lengthy discussion, on the number of women to be nominated for the International Congregational Council executive committee, which resulted in an official undertaking being given that in future 'consideration should be given to more complete representation of women' from the different national unions in membership of the International Congregational Council. After the meetings at Wellesley, Elsie reported that the Congregational women planned to send out 'twice a year a bulletin of international news'. Among the delegates in Wellesley was her friend and mentor from Liverpool, Muriel Paulden, for whom she retained a lifelong respect and affection.[3]

The World Council of Churches

Elsie's unbridled enthusiasm for ecclesiastical ecumenism led her in August 1948 to attend the inaugural meetings of the World Council of Churches at Amsterdam, not as an official delegate of the Congregational Union of England and Wales, but rather as an 'accredited visitor'.[4] She was simply very keen, as was her friend, Viscountess Stansgate, and both wanted to be present to lend their support to the assembled church representatives and be part of this historic occasion. Her presence did not go unnoticed.

Six years later, Elsie attended from 15 to 31 August 1954, the second assembly of the World Council of Churches at North Western University, Evanston, Illinois, in the USA. On this occasion she was one of five official representatives from the Congregational Union of England and Wales, among the delegates from 160 Christian denominations worldwide. Accompanying her on this occasion were Dr Leslie Cooke, the Congregational Union of England and Wales' general secretary (1948–1955), who had replaced Sidney Berry in that office; Dr J. Trevor Davies, the minister of Richmond

3. F.L. Fagley (ed.), *Proceedings of the Sixth International Congregational Council* (London: Independent Press, 1949), pp. 16, 17, 19, 22. Muriel Paulden also gave an address to the International Congregational Council at Wellesley.

4. W.A. Visser 't. Hooft (ed.), *The First Assembly of the World Council of Churches* (London: SCM Press Ltd, 1949), p. 261. The delegates from the Congregational Union of England and Wales were Sidney Berry, A.M. Chirgwin, Leslie Cooke and John Marsh. Their alternates were Philip Ashton, John Huxtable, Cecil Northcott and S. Maurice Watts, Visser 't. Hooft, *The First Assembly*, pp. 244, 253.

Hill Congregational Church, Bournemouth 1951-1971, who was to become chairman (1960-1961) of the Congregational Union of England and Wales; B.J. Hartwell, a layman who became chairman (1959-1960) of the Congregational Union of England and Wales; and Dr John Marsh, the principal of Mansfield College, Oxford. Sidney Berry was also present, as a representative of the International Congregational Council. Elsie's star continued to rise. However, given that earlier that same year she had resigned from Vineyard's ministry, ostensibly because of the unrelenting pressure of pastoral work, one is led to ask if the demands of the BBC, the Congregational Union of England and Wales and other more elevated tasks were taking precedence over the humble and more mundane duties of the minister's work at Richmond? Was she in danger of having her head turned by worldly status and flattery?

On the fourth day of the World Council of Churches' assembly at Evanston (18 August), Elsie was both the leader and preacher at the morning service, the only woman delegate chosen to lead worship at these World Council of Churches meetings. She must have preached on that occasion to a minimum of 1,500 people – hundreds of them denominational officials and distinguished theologians in their own countries – an intimidating congregation for any preacher but for a woman, speaking to many who disapproved of women preachers, an even more daunting prospect! She needed all her self-belief! On return to London, Elsie confided to a female colleague at the BBC that, on one sweltering hot day at the World Council of Churches' assembly, the chairman had given permission to the delegates to remove their gowns. Clearly this was intended as a helpful concession, and no doubt helped the men especially, but Elsie was not able to comply with this advice, as she had nothing on beneath her gown![5]

A Festival of Congregationalism

Sidney Berry's successor as general secretary of the Congregational Union of England and Wales, Leslie Cooke, saw it as his task to

5. W.A. Visser 't. Hooft (ed) *The Evanston Report: The Second Assembly of the World Council of Churches 1954* (London: SCM Press Ltd, 1955), pp. 35, 272, 283. J. Williams, *First Lady of the Pulpit: A Biography of Elsie Chamberlain* (Lewes, Sussex: Book Guild, 1993), p. 74. H.G.G. Herklots, *Looking at Evanston: A Study of the Second Assembly of the World Council of Churches* (London: SCM Press, 1954), pp. 14-15.

provide and discover a measure of confidence for the Congregational churches after the Second World War. As a result he promoted a so-called Forward Movement in the early 1950s. This concluded in 'A Festival of Congregationalism entitled Cloud of Witnesses' on Thursday, 21st May 1953 at the Royal Albert Hall. Thus the year of the coronation of Queen Elizabeth II, symbolic of a new age, was marked by this festival (echoing the nomenclature of the successful Festival of Britain of May 1951). The Festival of Congregationalism ended 'three years of preparation for the Forward Movement' and dedicated 'the coming years to continuing advance' – a vain hope, as it turned out. Among those involved in the presentation of the festival were the two comperes, as they were called, Elsie Chamberlain and Cecil Northcott (1902–1987). The latter was then the editorial secretary of the United Society for Christian Literature and the editor of Lutterworth Press.[6]

Elsie's involvement in this festival testified to her growing prominence in the denomination. She brought dignity, self-assurance, friendliness, and grace to an occasion. Above all, she had an infectious sense of fun which readily communicated itself to an audience. Of course, being an obviously warm and natural woman, at ease with herself and others, whatever their status, and often being the only woman on the platform, meant that she stood in marked contrast to the comparatively staid men around her. She was fast becoming an essential element to such ceremonies.

Chairman of the Congregational Union of England and Wales

Elsie Dorothea Chamberlain was elected chairman of the Congregational Union of England and Wales 1956–57. She succeeded the eminent William Gordon Robinson, the principal of Lancashire Independent College since 1943, and she was in turn to be followed by Hubert Cunliffe-Jones, since 1947 principal of Yorkshire Independent College, Bradford. She was an unusual and daring choice. She could not claim the scholarly credentials of these colleagues for, unlike Robinson and Cunliffe-Jones, she had not published books of theological or literary merit. Neither had she served the Congregational Union of England and Wales as a moderator of any of its nine provinces nor given years of service to committee work. The

6. A Festival of Congregationalism, programme in The Congregational Library, Gordon Square, London. *United Reformed Church Year Book 1988–1989*, p. 201.

two churches to which she had ministered were of no great size nor historic importance and both were situated among the unassuming outer suburbs of London. Admittedly she had gained some fame as the first woman chaplain in the armed forces, but such fame is fleeting, and she had left that post some ten years previously. Most unusual of all for a Congregational Union of England and Wales' chairman, she was, of course, a woman and, at that time, 'the decision-making processes of the denomination were still in practice in the hands of men' and women's representation on Congregational Union of England and Wales' committees was minimal. Therefore, her election to the chair was a remarkable personal tribute to her and revealed the confidence, felt by ordinary church members, ministers and officials of the Congregational Union of England and Wales alike, in this commanding but still youthful woman of 46 years.

The only conventional element which she brought to the chair was that she was a minister. Had she been a laywoman her election would have been even more astounding. Yet her appointment was not only seen as a personal tribute but as an extraordinary breakthrough for women in general. A major British denomination was giving public recognition with its own highest honour to a woman minister and thus celebrating her unique success. Despite her election to this high status, John Marsh, her companion at Evanston, described Elsie as 'an entirely normal person', although he admitted, in the same breath, that she had 'quite unusual gifts' and was 'a radiant person with a joyful faith'. Normal but unusual – an uncommon combination, yet these particular attributes were seen as sufficient to qualify her to be the chairman.[7]

She was the first woman (and the only woman) to chair the Congregational Union of England and Wales, serving almost 40 years after Constance Coltman, the first woman to be ordained to the Congregational ministry, had begun her pastorate at the King's Weigh House, London in 1917. Elsie stated that she would not have stood for election against her old friend, Muriel Paulden, had the latter been nominated and had she accepted that nomination, revealing not only Elsie's regard for Miss Paulden, but also Elsie's acceptance that her own nomination represented a landmark both for women ministers and for women in general. Elsie was the first woman to preside over

7. *Reform* (May 1991), p. 18. E. Kaye, J. Lees and K. Thorpe, *Daughters of Dissent* (London: United Reformed Church, 2004), p. 41.

the assembly of any of the main Free Churches in England, which probably means that she was the first woman to preside over any major Christian denomination anywhere at all.[8]

As has been stated, Elsie was, in many ways, an unlikely choice for the chair of the Congregational Union of England and Wales. Probably, more than most, if not all, her predecessors and successors in that post, she was a truly popular choice. As Marsh implied, she had no uniquely outstanding qualifications nor long list of fine achievements, apart from simply being herself and instinctively filled with life. The Congregational Union of England and Wales chair for Elsie was not a reward for a life of service as a college principal, or academic, or denominational official, nor was she, in truth, a great preacher. She had proved herself to be a brave, tenacious woman and her struggles had in some ways become those of others in the Congregational churches who identified with the perceived injustices she had overcome. In addition, hers was an attractive personality and she had seized the imagination of ordinary church members who saw her as one of their own.

Undoubtedly by 1955, when Elsie was chosen to be the chairman-elect of the Congregational Union of England and Wales, she had become very well-known. Not only her long battle with the Church of England hierarchy, in order to marry John Garrington, but also her struggle to gain recognition as the first woman chaplain in the RAF, had brought her to public attention. Most importantly, her work as a broadcaster for the BBC took her voice into almost every home in the country, making hers a familiar name to countless numbers who would never enter a Congregational church. As a genuinely popular minister, with the power to reach many beyond the churches, she must have been an outstanding, but unique, candidate for the chairmanship of the Congregational Union of England and Wales.

Elsie's Distinctive Service

While she was recovering from the arthritis which had laid her low in the RAF, Sidney Berry had predicted that 'another big job' awaited her. He presumably had not seen her as a future chairman of the Congregational Union of England and Wales at that stage, or

8. Williams, *First Lady of the Pulpit*, p. 78. *The Times*, 12 April 1991. Vera Findlay (nee Kenmure) 1904–1973 became president of the Congregational Union of Scotland in 1952. *Reform* (June 2011) 21.

might he just have wondered even then? Leslie Cooke wrote to Elsie to inform her of her election to the chair in May 1955. He assured her that it was in 'recognition of the distinctive service' that she had 'given over the years'. What was that distinctive service which made Elsie so different from other hard-working ministers in the Congregational Union of England and Wales? That unique distinction could only have lain in the extraordinary ups and downs of her ministry – her unprecedented RAF chaplaincy, her defiantly clinging to her love of a high Anglican priest, and her BBC post. Above all, her real distinction lay in her making such a success of being a woman minister. The Congregational women ministers before her had tended to play second fiddle to male colleagues, with churches apologetically placing them as assistants and associates. Elsie had not played second fiddle to a man. Indeed where she had combined with a male colleague at Richmond, he had supported her, rather than the other way round (although later at The City Temple she would support Kenneth Slack who was the chief minister). By the mid-1950s, Elsie had brought women ministers to the centre of the stage. After her, they were no longer kept in the shadows. Now they were to receive their due status and were not to be accepted only under sufferance.

She was by temperament an individualist, always going her own way, rather than following any well-ploughed furrows, but in truth she had been forced to blaze her own path by circumstances beyond her control. Her refusal to compromise on matters of principle, both personally and professionally, had brought her trials and pain before it yielded her eventual triumph. This in 1955 comprised her 'distinctive service' to Congregationalism.[9]

Elsie did not use her position as chairman of the Congregational Union of England and Wales to campaign for the ministry of women. Rather she sought to reassure those who feared she might so act. She stated, 'I believe that a minister is a minister regardless of whether that person is a he or a she. And it is as a minister that I shall be serving the Union'.[10] Yet her election to the chair did indicate much more. Certainly it was an immediate vote of confidence in Elsie Chamberlain as an individual, but it also said very clearly that the Congregational churches were not ashamed of their women ministers, no matter the

9. R.T. Jones, *Congregationalism in England, 1662–1962* (London: Independent Press, 1962), p. 393.

10. Williams, *First Lady of the Pulpit*, p. 79.

attitudes of other denominations. In 1917 the principle of women's ordination had been conceded by the Congregational Union of England and Wales but this had not led to overnight acceptance in the churches and disapproval and suspicion had taken a generation and more to break down. Elsie herself, as a young prospective woman minister, had contemplated being snubbed in the future by some Congregationalists and, indeed, had later suffered some prejudicial treatment because of her sex, but in 1955 this election to the chair revealed that the Congregational Union of England and Wales had collectively turned its back on this behaviour. If a woman minister could be elected to the chair of the union, then women ministers were surely reckoned the equal of men, and as acceptable as men, in every respect? By the mid-1950s, the Congregational Union of England and Wales had learned to be proud of the contribution of its women ministers. Certainly it was proud of Elsie Chamberlain and she, in response, was proud to be chosen!

A 'Disastrous' Chairman

John Marsh recognized in Elsie 'a ready openness of mind that seldom, if ever, left her'. He continued, 'She possessed a great good humour which made her conversation – and public speaking – a lively and enjoyable experience.'[11] Against this encouraging comment must be placed the widely held view that her chairmanship of the Congregational Union of England and Wales was not considered to have been a success, neither by Elsie herself, nor by others. She judged her own performance severely, concluding that she had been a 'disastrous' chairman, although she had loved visiting the churches, attending the Cenotaph service on Remembrance Sunday, and being at a garden party at Buckingham Palace.[12] The term 'disastrous' is very strong. Elsie was usually able to relate to people of all types and backgrounds, with her natural warmth, so why should her chairmanship have gone so badly?

Her relative inexperience with the inner workings of the Congregational Union of England and Wales may have placed her at a disadvantage as its chair and she had few diplomatic skills. She was by nature impatient and, having convinced herself that change

---

11. *Reform* (May 1991), p. 18.
12. Williams, *First Lady of the Pulpit*, p. 80.

was necessary, she expected that change to be effected immediately and would brook no delay. In this, her characteristic decisiveness could work against her. Of course, she could not see that others might need persuading that she had diagnosed the problems correctly. She was in essence an activist and not a committee animal. Instinct and intuition, rather than reasoning, were vital to Elsie's decision making. Tempered by Christian faith, they charged her with the innate impulse and energy which converted her opinions and plans into action.

We should record that in April 1956, one month before she began her year as chairman, Elsie's father, Jim Chamberlain, died at the age of 83. He had been a constant support to his daughter and undoubtedly she felt his loss deeply. If not the dominant influence upon her which her headstrong mother, Annie, clearly was, Jim had been a quiet, reassuring presence. He had exercised a steadying leverage over his wife's excesses and Annie was to survive him by some 19 years, eventually dying in 1975. His death came at a difficult juncture in his daughter's life.[13]

Yet if her year as chairman was a relative failure, in mitigation we can say that she came to the chair at a most awkward time in the history of the Congregational Union. Leslie Cooke had resigned unexpectedly in 1955 as general secretary of the Congregational Union of England and Wales, perhaps frustrated at not being able to effect the positive changes he had worked and prayed for, and he had moved to a permanent position with the World Council of Churches in Geneva. In those circumstances, the Congregational Union of England and Wales' council had been expected to nominate the secretary of the Lancashire Congregational Union who was also the moderator of the Lancashire province of the Congregational Union of England and Wales, the irascible Howard Stanley, as Cooke's successor, at Memorial Hall in London. But the council was divided about Stanley and voted 184 for and 61 against. Stanley felt that this was an insufficient majority to constitute a call to such high office and, therefore, he declined to accept the post. As a result the Congregational Union of England and Wales was thrown into some disorder, without its leading official, an eventuality for which it was quite unprepared. Consequently the veteran Sidney Berry, who had

13. Williams, *First Lady of the Pulpit*, pp. 12, 18. *Oxford Dictionary of National Biography*.

skilfully guided the CUEW from 1923–1948, had been recalled from retirement unanimously by the May assembly in 1955 to fill the breach, albeit temporarily.

Sidney Berry 1955–1956

Leslie Cooke had been Berry's preferred successor and he was particularly disappointed at Cooke's unexpected departure, after only seven years as secretary and at a time of reconstruction for the Congregational Union of England and Wales. Berry, the loyal servant in whom everyone had unbounded belief, dutifully filled the breach between 1955–1956 until Howard Stanley was appointed to the post, one year later than expected. Stanley had been a notable success in Lancashire but he had acquired a reputation as 'a ruffler of feathers' and his bluff manner did not win him friends in every quarter. The aged Berry, with his ability 'to win people's confidence and dispel their suspicions', was supremely competent but he was persuaded only reluctantly to return to office for an interim period. The Congregational Union of England and Wales was, therefore, experiencing a singular crisis and was considering its future leadership, just at the time when Elsie was called to be chairman-elect. Fully aware of these tensions between leading members of the denomination, Elsie must have fielded many awkward questions, as she travelled the country, speaking to church gatherings, attending and chairing meetings, and trying to inspire ministers and members alike. All was not well in the higher councils of the Congregational Union of England and Wales and she could not easily convey the opposite impression, nor wave a magic wand and make it better.[14]

In May 1956, at the May assembly of the Congregational Union of England and Wales, Elsie, as chairman, presided at Westminster Chapel at the service of dedication of the newly-elected secretary of the union. At the central part of the service, she put the required questions to both Howard Stanley and to the assembly delegates. Aware of the sensitivities and of the mixture of feelings among the delegates present in the chapel, Elsie needed a steady nerve and great strength of mind.[15]

14. Jones, *Congregationalism in England*, pp. 392–93.
15. Jones, *Congregationalism in England*, p. 428. *Congregational Year Book 1956* (London: Congregational Union of England and Wales, 1956), pp. 91–93;

In addition to these tensions in the Congregational Union of England and Wales, Elsie brought to the chairman's role some awkwardness of her own. Her gift for clarity and for cutting through needlessly long and tedious perorations, an asset at the BBC, could be seen, in different settings, as sheer curtness and intolerance and, during her year as chairman of the Congregational Union of England and Wales, she injured the pride of some experienced but sensitive colleagues who felt that she 'was teaching them their job'.[16] She is recalled as bluntly putting people in what she felt was their place. Even her friends realized that she was confronting long established practice too much, thereby riding roughshod over those who 'had always done it this way'. As chairman, at this critical time, she might have achieved more with tact and charm than with the sword.

Elsie's Chairman's Address

In her chairman's address in May 1956, Elsie spoke modestly of her achievements. 'I have no learned theory to expound' and 'can – and will – only speak of knowledge gained through practical experiences'. She stressed her upbringing in, what she termed, her 'ecumenical home' (that is having a Church of England father and a Congregational mother) as her 'training for future work' and for her own eventual marriage. She recalled Islington Chapel, 'the downtown London church to which we belonged', as 'notable for the consecutive ministries of two brothers – Joseph and Robert Shepherd' and referred tongue in cheek to her time at King's College, London, where all her fellow students 'were out of step' except her, as the sole Congregationalist. She paid tribute to her formative work in wartime Liverpool, where she had 'discovered that theology is practical and knowledge of the Bible relevant to daily life', and spoke of her learning pastoralia from Muriel Paulden, who by then had been the minister at Berkley Street Congregational Church, for 37 years and who was present to hear her former *protégée's* address. She briefly mentioned her own ministry to two churches in the London suburbs and her service in the Royal Air Force, describing these aspects of her life as being 'mostly quite ordinary experiences of the Ministry'.

Congregational Year Book 1957 (London: Congregational Union of England and Wales, 1957), pp. 92, 99–101.

16. *The Guardian*, 15 April 1991.

She explained the title of her address, *White to Harvest*, believing that Christ himself would say to this generation, 'Say not ye, There are yet four months and then cometh harvest? Behold I say unto you lift up your eyes and look on the fields, for they are white already to harvest'. She continued, as we have forgotten our calling to be 'fellow-labourers with Christ', and have done 'nothing to deserve such a harvest, ... we have failed to notice fields inside and outside the Church that are white to harvest'.

Elsie went on to decry the divisions of the Christian denominations, arising from the Reformation, and reached as far back as the split between the Eastern and Western churches of 1054, but she praised the World Council of Churches, which she identified as 'the greatest movement that the Church has known'. Curiously for such a self-reliant woman, she denounced those who took refuge in independence, both economic and spiritual, and she cast doubt upon the accepted interpretation of the term independent. She held that 'the first and last quality of real faith is dependence, utter, self-abandoning dependence on Christ'. She noted that the British Council of Churches was not merely Anglican in character, for it had an English Presbyterian, Kenneth Slack, as its general secretary and her colleague from Vineyard, Ted Stanford, as its education secretary.

Continuing with her ecumenical theme, she stated her belief that 'it is time the Free Church Council started to plan its own demise, that out of its ashes might rise in every place a council of churches, as interdenominational as the World Council of Churches'. She wondered whether anyone was 'working against the unity that Christ planned for his followers, because he would rather be a big fish in a little puddle, than a little fish in a big puddle', which is exactly the accusation which some critics would level at her 20 years later. She recalled that issues of church unity called for remedies, even within Congregationalism, and that 'closer relationships' were needed between the Congregational Union of England and Wales, the London Missionary Society and the Commonwealth Missionary Society.

She criticized those churches which sought to conduct their affairs as if nothing had changed for 50 or more years, saying that 'if all the world mills round your church from 9–5 Monday to Friday, a locked building is not much witness to a living faith. And a minister might more usefully preach on the steps of his church on week days than shout ineffectually to the handful of people who come miles on Sunday to sit at the very back of the church, presumably to avoid hearing what he has to say.' This advice she took seriously both at Richmond and, years later, at Taunton.

Elsie referred to herself, in her chairman's address in 1956, as an 'ecumaniac'. She also spoke of her broadcasting work for the BBC which she termed 'a bigger missionary venture than I ever dreamed of sharing'. She was 'proud' to be part of such a venture, with programmes which regularly numbered their audiences in the millions. To her that again suggested 'a field that is white to harvest'. She believed that ministers certainly needed more encouragement but she admitted that, having lived 'in a church circle' all her life, she felt that she and other ministers had tended 'to lose touch with ordinary people'. Yet she was 'not pessimistic' but saw reasons for 'hope for the Church's future', in young people training for the ministry, and in those taking courses to become lay preachers, and in the interests of many outside the churches in moral and spiritual questions.[17]

17. E.D. Chamberlain, *White to Harvest* (London: Independent Press, 1956), pp. 5–7, 10, 20.

Chapter 10

ELSIE AT THE BBC

Elsie had acquired some small experience of broadcasting before she was employed by the British Broadcasting Corporation. In August 1945, she had been invited to give six brief talks in the popular wireless programme *Lift Up Your Hearts* which had been on the air since 1939. These talks, of four to four and a half minutes each (650–700 words), went out in the week October 22–27 from 7.55 to 8 am. In preparation for the broadcast, Elsie had been advised to put her thoughts into simple words, avoiding traditional phrases of Christian piety (that is churchy language), but encapsulating 'some truth of the Gospel'. She clearly acquitted herself well for she was later congratulated for these 'really excellent broadcasts' by Kenneth Grayston, the assistant head of religious broadcasting (1944–1949) and a Methodist minister. Three years later, in November 1948, Elsie took part in a discussion on 'Women as Ordained Clergy', to be transmitted to Sweden.[1] Therefore this brief taste of broadcasting had given her some valuable knowledge of how things were done at the BBC and had whetted her appetite for more.

On the basis of these forays into radio, Elsie was encouraged by her mother in May 1950 to apply for the post of assistant producer in the Religious Broadcasting department of the BBC. Hundreds of hopeful applications were sent in to the BBC, from recently unseated former Labour MPs, and Christian ministers and laypersons of all denominations. The advertisement had stipulated that two posts were to be filled and, on the day appointed, Elsie was one of the last to be interviewed. The selection board had more or less finalized its choices by the time of her interview but, having been seen, the verdict of one interviewer was that 'she was never in danger' of not being appointed. He recalled that 'Once she entered the room we knew that she was the person we wanted and the interview was

---

1. BBC Written Archive – Contributors' Talks, File I 1945–1962, Revd Elsie Chamberlain.

memorable, as were the next seven years that I worked with her'. In fact, the department accommodated all the interviewing panel's choices and three appointments were subsequently confirmed. Elsie's newly recruited fellows were Richard Tatlock who had been a naval chaplain and was to be employed on a full-time basis and J. Ormerod Greenwood, a radio dramatist, who like her was to work part-time.

Elsie began working part-time for the Religious Broadcasting department in July 1950. Soon her own considerable gifts 'began to define her job in the department' and it became obvious to her colleagues that 'she was the right person' to produce *Lift Up Your Hearts* which was then reaching 'an audience of about three million listeners, most of whom were non-churchgoers'. *Lift Up Your Hearts* had begun in Scotland as a thought and a prayer before the morning news was broadcast and, although it sounded like a simple talk, it had in truth come to be regarded as 'a species of small sermon'. It was designed for those Christians who could not benefit from the daily service, which was broadcast later in the morning, when many would have been at their workplace, and also for listeners who may have been interested in, but were not committed to the Christian faith.

Elsie took responsibility for the yearly schedule for these broadcasts and, most significantly, she vetted the scripts of the broadcasters. Her colleagues had total confidence in her power to communicate, in her own 'plain and simple' way, as well as in her ability to help others to use successfully 'that crucial spot'. Elsie would 'clean up scripts', sweeping away 'complex theological ideas' and highfaluting Christian dogma. Thus she 'decanted the parson's voice and made sure that all could understand what was being said'. Ironically among the contributors to *Lift Up Your Hearts* was Bishop William Wand who had blocked John Garrington's advancement. His talks on 'Aspects of the Cross' and on 'Aspects of Advent' were broadcast in March and December 1956 respectively and were later published, in a series of BBC Talks, by the Congregational publishing house, the Independent Press. Elsie was at pains to vary the themes and the subject matter in *Lift Up Your Hearts*.[2]

---

2. K.M. Wolfe, *The Churches and the British Broadcasting Corporation 1922–1956* (London: SCM Press, 1984), p. 407. J. Williams, *First Lady of the Pulpit: A Biography of Elsie Chamberlain* (Lewes, Sussex: Book Guild, 1993), pp. 61–62. *The Independent*, 20 April 1991. J.W.C. Wand, *Aspects of the Cross* (London: Independent Press, 1956), *Aspects of Advent* (London: Independent Press, 1957).

Another occasional broadcaster on the programme was Elsie's friend, John Huxtable, the minister of Palmer's Green Congregational Church, in north London, who was destined for distinction in the denomination. He probably spoke for most contributors to the programme when he stated how much he valued the privilege of being able to speak to 'those about to catch their office trains, for the good of their eternal souls'. He noted that the programme 'seemed to have much greater success' than many might have expected and, 'whatever good may have been done by what was said' to the listeners, 'it is certain that those who did the speaking profited enormously'. He appreciated trying 'to say something worthwhile in just over 4 minutes' which he found to be 'an excellent discipline' because it improved one's style and 'cut down – even out – many of the frills'.[3]

Elsie wrote that she had agreed to work full-time for the BBC in 1954 because 'I had discovered that whereas a church tended to engulf the whole of a minister's time the BBC gave me a missionary job'. Was that really fair to the Vineyard Congregational Church which had given her the freedom to accept a position with the BBC? As a prolific broadcaster, she had a status beyond the humble church minister and it is difficult to avoid the conclusion that Elsie was in part carried along by the thrill of broadcasting, and the sensation of being at the heart of so much stimulation and excitement.

She valued the privilege and the opportunity, afforded by radio, 'to go into factories and clubs, the circle of local government and education'. She explained that, in contrast to work in a local church, the BBC allowed her 'to work for those outside the Church', and to try to meet their wants and needs. She felt that BBC religious broadcasting over the years had 'been building a bridge across the gulf of irreligion'. She denied, however, that there was such a thing as a 'Radio Church' and argued that the 'finishing of the bridge' must lie 'with the local community of the Church'. The BBC enabled Elsie to 'reach the 'outsider', as she had hoped to do in all her ministry, being a 'true evangelist'.[4]

This seems to denigrate the work of ordinary ministers in the churches, up and down the land, by implying, probably truthfully,

3. J. Huxtable, *As It Seemed To Me* (London: United Reformed Church, 1990), p. 40.

4. E.D. Chamberlain, *White to Harvest* (London: Independent Press, 1956), p. 16. *Reform*, May 1991.

that they were failing to take the Christian gospel to the masses, although Elsie did state that the completion of 'the bridge' remained the work of the local churches. Therefore she had a prestigious job, as a radio evangelist, awakening and stirring up hearts and minds, while the local ministers, with little or no glamour, still had the often thankless task of turning that germ of interest into a sustaining and saving faith. Yet if some criticisms may be levelled at Elsie, it is undeniable that she scaled the heights as a religious broadcaster, and there are no reasons for believing that she was any less than sincere in what she tried to do.

Broadcasting Work

Lift Up Your Hearts, still adhering to its basic format of a story, a hymn and a prayer, went out live on the BBC Home Service and Elsie developed an exceptional skill in helping the invited speakers to broadcast effectively, as if they were having a friendly chat around the fireside with their listeners at home. Elsie received a steady correspondence from listeners, with comments both favourable and unfavourable. *Lift Up Your Hearts* was not only broadcast in Britain but also went out on the overseas service. She had responsibility for *Work and Worship* too, an overseas programme aimed specifically at a target audience of missionaries. The audience for such a programme in the mid-1950s might be expected to be dwindling but the subjects covered by it were up to date. In October 1956, this programme carried a report by Kenneth Slack (1917–1987) about the World Council of Churches' central committee meeting, recently held in Hungary. The Presbyterian Slack was the general secretary of the British Council of Churches during the years 1955–1965. He had earlier spent three years (1943–1946), in India as a chaplain in the RAF (another point in common with Elsie) and had developed a deep and lasting interest in the worldwide missionary task of the Church. He was to attend most major meetings of the World Council of Churches during his lifetime. Two years after that programme was aired, Elsie interviewed Kenneth Slack again for *Work and Worship* on his work for the British Council of Churches.[5] Kenneth and Millicent Slack were to become and remain good friends with Elsie.

5. BBC Archive – Religious scripts on microfilm.

In the summer of 1952, Elsie was asked to take part in an unscripted discussion programme with Bishop George Bell of Chichester (1883–1958), noted especially for his outspoken pronouncements on the allies' reprisals and obliteration bombing of Germany in the last years of the Second World War, and Father Thomas Corbishley (1903–1976), the Jesuit scholar and principal of Campion Hall, Oxford, who was a versatile popular theologian and a pioneer in ecumenical affairs. William Clark (1916–1985), the then diplomatic correspondent of the Sunday newspaper, *The Observer*, who became the Prime Minister's public relations adviser 1955–1956, and who was especially interested in reconstruction and world development, was to be the chairman. Realizing that she probably lacked the required gravitas and might be out of her depth, Elsie confessed that she felt 'inadequate to the role'. The programme was entitled 'How can the churches help to solve world problems?'[6]

Why was she asked to join in such a discussion? Arguably she was an intellectual lightweight for such a highbrow programme, as she herself suspected. Perhaps she was chosen because she could bring to such a forum her own very normal but concerned thinking and conscience. She was popular for many reasons, of course, but probably the main reason for her popularity was her sheer normality, her ability to speak for the average listener and to voice his or her concerns. As a result she was trusted by the audience and took the role of the woman in the street, even though she was simultaneously the skilled professional, used to guiding interviews with guests in the studios. Her superiors in the BBC fully grasped her particular value to the Religious Broadcasting Department, so that inviting her to be a member of this high powered group may have been a deliberate attempt to bring the voice of the average person into the discussion.

Elsie was the first woman to lead *The Daily Service* which she conducted 'with a special kind of naturalness', her own distinctive quality. Of course, some listeners in the 1950s objected to a woman leading worship to the nation, when woman ministers were exceptional, but others commented on her 'very beautiful voice' and 'delightful' tones. Some found that her 'deep and distinctive' voice had an 'allure' which drew them to listen more attentively, while yet others found that Elsie's voice was insistent and authoritative.

---

6. BBC Written Archive – Contributors' Talks. For Bell, Corbishley and Clark, see *Oxford Dictionary of National Biography*.

Probably it could carry all these nuances and meanings, by turns. Her colleague, (Andrew) Stuart Hibberd (1893–1983), who was known for his clear enunciation and cultivated voice, took some pains to help Elsie use her voice most effectively. Just after Elsie's death in 1991, BBC Radio Four broadcast a brief excerpt from one of her recordings, giving at least one old friend a sharp pang of sadness. She would take her turn to conduct *Saturday Night Prayers*, about once a quarter, and she helped on occasions with the production of outside broadcasts of religious services, especially in the London area.

Elsie was also responsible for a kind of 'agony column of the air', entitled *The Silver Lining*. This programme brought 'comfort to people handicapped or housebound' and was devised as a means of replying to and helping the many distressed listeners who wrote in to the Religious Broadcasting Department. It had a clear pastoral aim, responding to the emotional needs and misery, revealed in this unsolicited correspondence, and it quickly gained a 'very considerable' audience, particularly among working-class women. The staple fare of the programme was 'simple prayers and comfortable words'. *The Silver Lining* showed that 'a vast tract of the population' could be regarded as in need of the kind of pastoral care which local clergy were willing to provide but were often not called upon to give.[7]

The Head of Religious Broadcasting was uncertain what reactions Elsie's first broadcasts would produce. She was the first ordained woman producer in the BBC and the first woman presenter of *The Daily Service*. He need not have feared overmuch because the reactions to her were 'wholly favourable'. Although the department then had some very able people on its staff, Elsie is judged to have 'more than held her own' in such company.[8]

She appeared also on non-religious programmes, like *Woman's Hour*, from time to time, talking about topics of a Christian nature, from books to children's upbringing, and, in addition, she made a few television appearances. Elsie did take the required training course for television but was never at her ease with this visual medium. She had grown up with radio and believed that it was designed 'for communication' and that it was particularly 'her medium'. Like many other broadcasters, Elsie saw radio as calling for a more creative and

---

7. Wolfe, *The Churches and the British Broadcasting Corporation*, pp. 372–73. For Hibberd, see *Oxford Dictionary of National Biography*.
8. BBC Written Archive.

imaginative response from its audience than television. She felt able to help make Christianity alive and interesting at a popular level on the radio. To her, television seemed principally for 'demonstration and entertainment'. She felt that television placed too much stress upon the speaker, to the detriment of the message which he or she was trying to impart.[9] In short she did not feel at home on the television.

Publications

During her time at the BBC, Elsie published a small book of broadcast talks in 1959 which derived its title from her principal programme *Lift Up Your Hearts*. In this she had selected and edited 19 talks by various contributors to the programme. The authors included old friends like H.F. Lovell Cocks, Kenneth Slack and John Huxtable but also, among others, Cuthbert Bardsley, the Bishop of Coventry, and the evangelical John Stott, the rector of All Souls Church, Langham Place, which stands in the shadow of Broadcasting House. Of the 19 contributors, 12 were ministers, five were laypeople and only one was a woman, Janet Lacey, who was then the director of the Inter-Church Aid and Refugee Service of the British Council of Churches.

Elsie explained, in the preface, that the talks had been shortened for publication in book form but it was hoped that something of the speaker's 'original inspiration' would survive. The BBC received a steady trickle of correspondence from listeners who wished to comment on some aspect of the daily broadcasts and now, with the book, they had access to the talks in print. She understood that those who listened to *Lift Up Your Hearts* on the wireless were 'as busy as most people' and she also admitted that they were 'affectionately known to the producer' of the programme, that is to Elsie herself, as 'the Bacon-friers and Shavers'.[10]

In 1961 she published a second book, *Calm Delight*, which was intended to start her readers 'thinking – perhaps praying – each day of a month'. The book was based on the hymn 'Eternal Light', written by the nineteenth century Congregational minister, Thomas Binney (1798–1874). Elsie explained that as a child her favourite hymn had been Binney's 'Eternal Light' which had attracted her by the 'mystery

9. J. Williams, *First Lady of the Pulpit: A Biography of Elsie Chamberlain* (Lewes, Sussex: Book Guild, 1993), pp. 62, 64, 65, 66. *The Independent*, 20 April 1991. *The Times*, 12 April 1991.

10. E.D. Chamberlain, *Lift Up Your Hearts* (London: Max Parrish, 1959), p. 7.

and greatness it expressed'. She continued, 'I loved the spaciousness and grandeur, the feeling of being on the outskirts of eternity, and I often sang myself to sleep with it'. Even at that young age, she felt sure, with Binney, that 'there is a way for man to rise to that sublime abode'. As an adult she acknowledged that, if real progress was to be made on the way to the 'sublime abode', then 'we need daily the impetus of forgiveness' which enables men and women 'to perceive goodness without its being a reminder of guilt'.

In this second book she took a passage from the hymn as the source of a thought or reflection for each day of the month, supporting scriptural texts and her own reflections, with literary and theological quotations from such disparate spiritual sources as St Augustine, St Francis, Martin Luther, Richard Hooker, Thomas Traherne, William Law, and Søren Kierkegaard, among others. Her selection of quotations was not only drawn from the established Christian classics but also included such modern writers and theologians as G.K. Chesterton, D.M. Baillie, Emil Brunner, Arnold J. Toynbee, Martin Buber, W.R. Matthews, Evelyn Underhill, Dietrich Bonhoeffer, Charles Gore, Eric L. Mascall, Dom Gregory Dix, Olive Wyon, William Temple, Lesslie Newbigin, Karl Barth and her old sparring partner, Bishop J.W.C. Wand. She also called on the works of contemporary Congregationalists like Nathaniel Micklem, H.F. Lovell Cocks and the New Testament specialist G.B. Caird. This broad range of sources reveals wide reading on her part, at least in preparation for the book, and a degree of intellectual curiosity. The book may have served as an introduction to these writers but it does not demand a profound engagement, with their thinking, and nor does it demonstrate that Elsie herself had engaged deeply nor systematically with her sources.

Personal Revelations

Inevitably, however, Elsie necessarily revealed something of herself in her books. In *Calm Delight* she wrote of purity of heart as being 'essentially innocence', but 'certainly not ignorance', and stated that 'purity of heart depends on being absolutely sure that God is good and that you don't need sordidness to make life exciting'. That statement smacks of Elsie's childhood home and of Elsie herself who never betrayed any attraction for the vices of this world. She described the reward of 'the humble seeker after God' as getting 'a fresh glimpse of purpose and pattern and upholding creative love'. Was that how she saw herself and her own experience? Certainly the listeners to her programmes were, in her eyes, potential seekers after God and she wanted to offer them 'a fresh glimpse of ... creative love'. She continued, 'Any adventure of faith that demands more than the all we can put into it will achieve something of purity of heart and the vision of the living God that goes with it'.[11]

She wrote of 'burning bliss' and of the excitement of falling in love. 'When we are young and our experience is still limited there are times when we are in heaven. It may be the first time we fall in love; we live in an unreal world, part dream, part imagination, part rosy spectacles'. Was that drawn from Elsie's own love for John? She went on to state that, as we grow older, we 'know we might get hurt, so we seldom reach that sort of bliss again ... we see the not-so-good more clearly than the good.' Yet, by following the example of St Paul and determining to know nothing but Jesus Christ and Him crucified, we too may be 'caught up into Paradise' and hear 'unspeakable words'. We may 'achieve that childlike simplification of purpose' and, therefore, 'the sort of perfection we saw in moments of youthful bliss ... will be ours in a new and real way'. In this Elsie was clearly drawing upon her own experience of life and faith.

She also returned to the theme of church unity in writing of the Holy Spirit. 'In our day the Holy Spirit's energies have driven us to create a World Council of Churches. But there is so much yet to be done that one wonders if those who call themselves the Church will move fast enough to demonstrate a peaceful community before the world totters over the brink of war'.[12] She saw ecumenism as one means to break down the mistrust and suspicion that had led in the past and might yet lead to war. Her stated aim with both these short books, at one with her broadcasting, was to bring the reader nearer to God.

Latter Days at the BBC

Those who worked with Elsie at the BBC recalled her as tall and imposing, with a very strong personality. Although formidable, she was always kind and sympathetic to those with problems but knew

11. For Binney, see *Oxford Dictionary of National Biography*. E.D. Chamberlain, *Calm Delight* (London: Hodder & Stoughton, 1960).
12. Chamberlain, *Calm Delight*, pp. 42, 118.

how to be brusque and dismissive, when she felt it necessary, to others. She would show characteristic annoyance if men held doors open for her to pass through first, as a woman, but when Cardinal Heenan, the Roman Catholic Archbishop of Westminster, was in the same corridor she recalled, with some humour, that he did not wait for her but rather smartly nipped through first! Was he making a point?

Elsie was not a tidy worker. If her home in Hampton revealed in part her own singular method of keeping notes and filing letters etc, then her office, in the old Langham Hotel, opposite Broadcasting House, in Langham Place, had papers everywhere, piled high in stacks. It was painted in battleship grey by the BBC who did not keep it scrupulously clean. During a protracted conversation on the telephone one day, Elsie used her rubber to draw, in the dust and dirt, a mural of Jacob's dream of a ladder, reaching up to heaven, with angels ascending and descending, as in Genesis 28:12. Her impromptu artistry was much admired.[13]

The Storms Break: Leaving the BBC

In 1967 *Lift Up Your Hearts* was axed, in line with 'the secularising tendencies' of the BBC's then director-general, Sir Hugh Greene (1910–1987), who from his appointment in 1960 deliberately set out to transform the BBC's 'Auntie' image. It soon became clear that Greene had little sympathy with the 'specifically Christian principles' of his predecessors, like Sir John Reith. No longer would the Corporation present itself as an uncritical pillar of the establishment. Greene's policy was to challenge the robust competition it had received from Independent Television, by giving priority to television over radio. He believed that the BBC should widen the limits of discussion and challenge 'the old taboos' and he was dismissive of those who did not share his views. Popular with the younger members of the staff, Greene, who had 'an air of impish mischief about him', clearly favoured 'the new republic rather then the ancien regime'.

In the Religious Broadcasting Department, it was argued that a new programme to replace the old favourite, *Lift Up Your Hearts*, was urgently needed so that this valuable early morning broadcast would not go stale. However, Elsie strongly disagreed, believing that *Lift Up Your Hearts* still had lots of life left in it and she herself had

13. Williams, *First Lady of the Pulpit*, p. 63.

many more ideas both for it and also for other programmes. She also held to her oft-stated view that the BBC should have a missionary function rather than merely offer an analysis.[14] As a woman with a well-earned reputation for principle, Elsie eventually came to feel that she had no alternative but resignation. She had initially refused to attend her annual interview but, eventually the advice of friends prevailed. The ensuing interview was awkward for all concerned and failed to clear the air. Rather it served to confirm her position that, as the long-serving producer of *Lift Up Your Hearts*, she should leave with her programme. She maintained that, if the programme had faults, then she must take responsibility for them and, therefore, she had to go. A colleague in the Religious Broadcasting department later described her as having been 'driven out of the BBC'. Clearly she was very unhappy at the manner of her leaving, for she had enjoyed radio broadcasting and was undoubtedly good at it.

Yet she was on the air frequently after her resignation in January 1967. She conducted six services on the World Service which were broadcast in February. She filled the *Ten to Seven* slot on the Home Service also that same month. She led *The Daily Service* at All Souls Church, Langham Place in April, and in May she did the readings and comments on four consecutive Sundays for the programme *The First Day of the Week*. In June she broadcast once more on the World Service when she was again leading *The Daily Service*. In September, October, November and December 1967 she appeared on *The Hymns We Love* for the African/Cultural Services at Bush House. She also frequently broadcast on various radio programmes during 1968–1972. In 1973, she appeared on Radio Four's Sunday programme, she was interviewed by Jeanine McMullen for *On Reflection*, and she again led *The Daily Service* on several occasions that year for the BBC World Service. Years later she was to broadcast on BBC Radio Nottingham's *Thought for the Day* and she was still writing scripts up to her death.[15] In 1988, she was the guest of honour at the 60th anniversary of *The Daily Service*, once more from All Souls. On this occasion she

14. *Broadcasting, Society and the Church: Report of the Broadcasting Commission of the General Synod of the Church of England* (London: Church Information Office, 1973), p. 1, in which Greene was described as the most controversial of all the Directors-General since Reith. For Greene, see *Oxford Dictionary of National Biography*, *The Times*, 21 February 1987; R. Dougall, *In and Out of the Box* (London: Collins, Harvill Press, 1975), pp. 235–36, 280.

15. BBC Written Archive – Contributors' Talks.

was again interviewed on *Woman's Hour*, although she confided afterwards that she had not enjoyed that particular interview.[16]

In June 1953, Elsie was among the delegates of the Congregational Union of England and Wales to the Seventh International Congregational Council meetings at St Andrew's, Scotland, as was again her old friend, Muriel Paulden of Liverpool, whilst Margaret Stansgate was present as an associate delegate. At St Andrew's Elsie was elected to serve on the executive committee of the International Congregational Council. On Sunday June 28, the service from the meetings was broadcast live on BBC radio. Sidney Berry led the service and the sermon was preached by the distinguished American Congregationalist, Douglas Horton. Naturally Elsie, with her broadcasting expertise, was involved. Given the importance of accurate timing on live radio, she took personal responsibility for that broadcast service and is remembered as enthusiastically conducting the entire assembly, from the platform, in the singing of the final hymn and then, with total control and aplomb, silencing them all as one – an impressive authority![17]

After Broadcasting

Elsie Chamberlain had found her metier with the BBC. In radio broadcasting she came into her own, accomplished much of worth and enjoyed herself immensely. Part of her achievement was that, as a pioneer, seemingly effortlessly, invading a man's world, she made millions of listeners familiar with a woman's voice, in leading worship and setting out Christian views in a direct and acceptable style, so that other women broadcasters, following her, faced less hostility. However, to Elsie herself, even more important than this breakthrough for women was her accomplishment as a Christian minister who had discovered and exploited the possibilities, afforded to the churches, by the medium with which she worked.

If Elsie was good for the BBC, the BBC was in its turn good for Elsie. Through her broadcasting career she had gained an independent status. She was not reliant on a local church which could never have given her a national appeal and would have paid her only a small

16. Williams, *First Lady of the Pulpit*, pp. 67–71.
17. R.F.G. Calder (ed.), *Proceedings of the Seventh International Congregational Council* (London: Independent Press, 1953), pp. 14, 152, 170, 171, 178.

stipend – even if her being a woman minister had been acceptable. Of course, by acquiring that independence she was removed from the daily experience of other ministers and, particularly, of other women ministers. Notwithstanding, the BBC had given Elsie a prominence which otherwise would have been denied her. John Marsh wrote accurately of her that 'Few ministers have had, and seized so effectively, the opportunity to reach the large and secular world' in which the churches of our day must work.[18]

By 1967 Elsie Chamberlain had realized her supreme gift as a 'communicator of the Gospel' to the widest possible audience. At the BBC her ability and desire to strip away all 'pretence and obscurity' in Christian communication had been given free rein. Henceforth, in her preaching and public speaking, she would strive to make the Christian message effective and heard by all possible means, that is she would never forget the lessons she had learned when working for the Corporation. She left the BBC, in trying and difficult circumstances, at the height of her fame and of her powers. She was by no means a spent force in her own estimation, nor in that of her many friends, nor in the world's opinion. On the contrary she was greatly loved and respected. She was energetic and willing to serve. The coming years would hold a few surprises for Elsie and, ever the Independent, she would produce not a few of her own.[19]

18. *Reform*, May 1991.
19. *The Independent*, 20 April 1991.

Chapter 11

AFTER THE BBC: THE CITY TEMPLE

By leaving the BBC in 1967 Elsie Chamberlain had made a stand for principle. She had proved herself to be a resourceful and capable woman who would resist any attempt to force her compliance, especially with a policy which made her uneasy. Elsie may not have been an intellectual but she trusted her judgment and her instincts and, if her feelings told her that something was wrong, she took them seriously and would rarely override them. Her resignation from the BBC gained her much admiration, then and later, but, although brave, hers proved to be a lone stand. Yet broadcasting, allied to her constant willingness to speak up and down the country, had enabled her 'to symbolise for many the place that women were coming to have in the public ministry of the churches'.[1] Indeed working in the BBC, in an environment where being a woman was far less of an apparent disadvantage than in the churches, had served to give her talents and her vocation even more liberty than she had enjoyed hitherto. But that season of her life, however fruitful it had been, was over.

She was left with her principles intact, a national reputation and an impressive list of achievements but, although not poor, nor was she wealthy and she had no job. She was too dynamic, too vigorous to be idle for long. She could not resign herself to be only the good vicar's wife. That would confine her spirit more than she could bear but what should she do? Several options presented themselves. She might use her fame to continue in public life in some way. She might align herself more closely to the emerging women's movement. She might write more books and seek a future in journalism. Or she might return to her first calling, in the pastoral ministry. To an extent she explored all these options.

---

1. *The Times*, 12 April 1991.

Writing

Her fame as a broadcaster and as an advocate of women's equality led her to become involved in a project to highlight the social injustice and prejudice from which women still suffered. Elsie contributed a chapter, 'The World in Which We Worship', to the book, *In Her Own Right*, produced in 1968 by the Six Point Group. This was a non-party political organization, founded in 1921, and its original membership had consisted of former militant suffragettes keen to promote the cause of women in social, economic and political spheres of activity. In the 1960s the group still aimed to work for 'equality between men and women in status, in opportunities, in rewards, in rights, and in responsibilities' and to encourage practical action. The book emerged from a conference which explored the 'movement towards emancipation'. It correctly praised the successes of the women's movement but also identified those problems remaining for women, 50 years after they had first gained the franchise. Contributors included the writer Marghanita Laski, the Labour MP Lena Jeger, the journalist Jacky Gillott, the Conservative politician Dame Patricia Hornsby-Smith, and the lawyer and academic Olive M. Stone, among others. All were high-achievers, well-known women in their various fields, among whom Elsie was not out of place.

In her chapter Elsie lashed out at the Church in general, describing it as 'one of the last bastions of male entrenchment', and pointing out that women have become successful missionaries overseas, like her older but near-contemporaries Mildred Cable (1878–1952), Francesca Law French (1871–1960), and Gladys Aylward (1902–1970), all having been active in China, and the earlier but outstanding social reformers, like Elizabeth Fry (1780–1845) and Josephine Butler (1828–1906).[2] Of course, all these were among Elsie's heroines. They offered positive models upon which young Christian women could base their lives, as she herself had tried to do. Indeed as a group they seem to resemble the collection of saints which her home church, Islington Chapel, had made familiar to Elsie in her girlhood. She maintained that the chief reasons for the entrenched opposition to the ordination of women were 'tradition, expediency and prejudice'. Elsie recalled the response of a 'High Church priest' to her preaching – 'he told me he was so surprised that the sermon was like a man's!' She was taken aback at

2. For all these see, *Oxford Dictionary of National Biography*.

this because she had 'never considered sermons to be masculine or feminine'. The chapter is mainly directed against those denominations which did not then ordain women, that is the Church of England, the Church of Scotland, and the Roman Catholic Church.

On a personal and practical note, Elsie stated that, in her 28 years of ministry, all those problems envisaged by the churches which had refused to ordain women had 'either not materialized' or had not 'been of noticeable size'. She had found that after a short while, she was readily accepted by those who had earlier entertained misgivings. Women have said that they 'could talk to another woman' and men, especially in the Forces, were glad to 'talk over their home problems with a woman'. In addition she had found that her conducting the daily service on the BBC each week, for over 16 years, had accustomed many correspondents to the fact that a woman can lead them perfectly satisfactorily in the worship of God.[3]

In that book, regarded as a 'significant' contribution to the furtherance of women's rights, Elsie described herself in 1968 as 'at present involved in religious education'. The editor, Hazel Hunkins Hallinan (1890–1982), was a determined and doughty American campaigner for women's rights who had been long resident in the United Kingdom and had been the chairman of the Six Point Group since the 1950s. She introduced Elsie as an 'exceptional' woman who lived 'a more emancipated role than most' and who had 'fought her battles to give the Church the benefits of women's talents and in so doing has reaped her own'.[4] Elsie's reputation at this time, as a champion of women's rights, as a communicator with scruples, and as a woman of devotion, was deservedly high.

Mini-Commentaries

Between 1968 and 1970 the publishing house, Mowbrays, issued a series of *Mini-Commentaries*, based on the text of the recently published Jerusalem Bible. Elsie Chamberlain was the general editor of this series of 12 short commentaries. These inexpensive books were intended to be brief 'guideposts' for Bible study and discussion and

3. H. Hunkins Hallinan (ed.), *In Her Own Right* (London: Harrap, 1968), pp. 7, 121, 124, 125, 128, 131.
4. Hallinan, *In Her Own Right*, pp. 17, 160. For Hazel Hunkins Hallinan, see *Oxford Dictionary of National Biography*.

did not offer detailed, academic expositions. Elsie's skill at pruning and simplifying over-wordy texts, acquired and honed in her years editing scripts every day for the BBC, served her well in this work. Number one in this series, a composite volume on the Gospels of Matthew, Mark and Luke and the Acts of the Apostles, was written by her friend, Kenneth Slack.[5]

Other volumes in the series were contributed, among others, by Ulrich Simon and Peter Ackroyd, distinguished academics from the theology department of King's College, London, by Harold Moulton, of the British and Foreign Bible Society, by the Baptist Edwin Robertson, another close friend and former colleague at the BBC, by the Methodist William Simpson, general secretary of the Council of Christians and Jews, and by Ian Thomson, director of the Bible Reading Fellowship. This variety of authors shows the breadth of contacts which Elsie Chamberlain had built up during her time as a broadcaster and suggests that her understanding of Christ's Church reflected that breadth.

A Possible Life Peerage

Viscountess Stansgate's son, Tony Benn, the Labour politician, recalled in his diaries the possibility of Elsie Chamberlain receiving a peerage in 1968. At that time Benn was Minister of Technology, with a seat in the Cabinet, while Harold Wilson, the leader of the Labour Party, was the Prime Minister. One afternoon in late April 1968 Benn visited Wilson to discuss his proposals for the forthcoming honours list. Wilson told him that John Stonehouse was to become a privy councillor, and that Trevor Huddleston was to be the Bishop of Birmingham but that 'he couldn't give the Reverend Elsie Chamberlain a peerage because he wanted it for the Lord Mayor of Liverpool, who was a woman'.[6]

---

5. K. Slack, *Matthew, Mark, Luke and Acts* (London: A. & R. Mowbray, 1968).

6. Tony Benn, *Office Without Power: Diaries 1968–72* (London: Hutchinson, 1988), pp. 63, 138. John Stonehouse (1925–1988) was Minister of State for Technology in 1968 and rose to higher political office. He was made a Privy Councillor in 1968 but suffered disgrace after committing fraud and faking his own death in 1974, *Oxford Dictionary of National Biography*. Trevor Huddleston (1913–1998), a well-known anti-apartheid campaigner, did not become Bishop of Birmingham. He was Bishop Suffragan of Stepney 1968–1978, and Archbishop of the Indian Ocean 1978–1983, *Oxford Dictionary of National Biography*.

Benn's approach to Harold Wilson on behalf of Elsie Chamberlain at this time suggests a friend, probably prompted by his mother, Lady Stansgate, recognizing Elsie's talent, and the lack of women in Parliament, who wanted to help her at a time in her life when, after her resignation from the BBC, she was seen as being at a loose end. Wilson's reply to Benn's enquiry indicates that this was no frivolous proposal to be easily dismissed. Rather Wilson had given serious thought to the suggestion but felt compelled, through political necessity, to strengthen the Labour presence in the upper chamber. He seems to have seen no objection in principle to Elsie's elevation to the peerage.

Wilson's own Congregational allegiance may have reinforced his willingness to consider Elsie's becoming a peer. He had himself been brought up as a Congregationalist and, with his family, had attended Highfield Congregational Church, Rock Ferry, in the Wirral. At Oxford he attended the Congregational Society meetings at Mansfield College and the Sunday morning services at Mansfield College Chapel, where he and Mary had been married in January 1940 by the college principal, Nathaniel Micklem, and by the Revd Daniel Baldwin, the bride's father, who was himself a Congregational minister. In London during the early 1940s the Wilsons had regularly attended The Vineyard Congregational Church, Richmond-upon-Thames, when Daniel T. Jenkins was the minister there and where Elsie herself was to be the minister a few years later. After moving home in 1948, Wilson transferred his membership in 1950 to Hampstead Garden Suburb Free Church where he was to preach on a number of occasions. As Prime Minister from 1964 onwards, he regarded himself as remaining a Congregationalist.[7]

The episode raises the intriguing thought that Elsie Chamberlain might have become the first ordained woman to sit in the House of Lords (indeed in either of the Houses of Parliament). It would have been a popular appointment because she enjoyed a large following. Indeed Wilson was to reveal, in successive appointments lists, his

7. E. Kay, *Pragmatic Premier An Intimate Portrait of Harold Wilson* (London: Leslie Frewin, 1967), pp. 18, 19. L. Smith, *Harold Wilson The Authentic Portrait* (London: Hodder & Stoughton, 1964), p. 128. E. Kaye, *Mansfield College, Oxford: Its Origin, History and Significance* (Oxford: Oxford University Press, 1996), p. 211; J. Taylor and C. Binfield (eds), *Who They Were in the Reformed Churches of England and Wales 1901–2000* (Donington: Shaun Tyas for the United Reformed Church History Society, 2007), pp. 246–48.

inclination to use the honours system to challenge the established order and to broaden his own appeal, by bestowing awards on sporting champions, entertainers and musicians. Elsie would not have been overawed in the House of Lords but rather would have been a colourful contributor to debates. Tony Benn believed that she would have made 'a fine peer'. One wonders what influence as a peer she might have had in the churches (especially in the coming debates about the United Reformed Church) and beyond them, but it was not to be and an opportunity was missed. Some 30 years later Revd Kathleen Richardson, a Methodist minister, was created Baroness Richardson of Calow in 1998, thus becoming the first woman minister to sit in the upper chamber.[8]

The City Temple

After some months of teaching and lecturing, Elsie returned to the pastoral ministry which was her original vocation and, in 1968, she accepted the call to be the associate minister of The City Temple, on Holborn Viaduct, in the City of London, where her heroine, Maude Royden, had once championed women's ministry. The City Temple, which claimed its foundation year to be as early as 1640, had long enjoyed international fame as the most prominent free church in England. It had only recently appointed a minister to replace the Canadian Leonard Griffith (Leslie Weatherhead's successor) who had left in June 1966 after six years. On 31 May 1967, The City Temple church meeting had called Kenneth Slack, then minister of St Andrew's Presbyterian Church, Cheam, to become its minister. Slack had privately confided in Weatherhead, some two months earlier, that after two years, he was unhappy at Cheam and would 'eagerly welcome a call to The City Temple'.[9] Slack was well-known to The City Temple faithful and to Weatherhead who retained the status of minister emeritus there. After 24 years as minister at The City Temple Weatherhead, who had drawn large congregations and enjoyed something of a personality cult, remained a powerful influence in the church.[10]

8. Private correspondence. *Who's Who 2001*.

9. J. Williams, *First Lady of the Pulpit: A Biography of Elsie Chamberlain* (Lewes, Sussex: Book Guild, 1993), p. 80. J. Travell, *Doctor of Souls* (London: Lutterworth Press, 1999), pp. 274–75.

10. For Weatherhead (1893–1976) see Travell, *Doctor of Souls*; also *Oxford Dictionary of National Biography* and H. Davies, *Worship and Theology in England*

When Slack took up his ministry at The City Temple the church already had a pastoral assistant, Colin Campbell, who had been there since 1961, and an assistant minister Anthony Coates, who had been appointed in 1964. The two brought contrasting gifts to the ministerial team. Whereas Campbell was an experienced minister who had been ordained in 1921, Coates was in his first pastorate after leaving Mansfield College, Oxford. Unlike Slack, both had trained to be Congregational ministers. They had both arrived during Leonard Griffith's ministry at The City Temple and both left soon after Slack's arrival. Campbell retired and Coates was to marry and then become free church chaplain at Keele University in 1968.[11]

Campbell had officially retired in 1960 but, after only five months, had received 'the irresistible call' to serve pro-tem at The City Temple. His services to this church were deemed 'a remarkable personal ministry' in which he brought 'comfort, cheer and guidance to countless people'. He was described as an able preacher and a fine pastor who simply 'loved people'. Curiously he was the same Colin Campbell who had succeeded Elsie in 1947 as minister of her former charge, Christ Church, Friern Barnet, where he had remained until his first retirement in 1960, when he had moved south of the Thames to Cheam (from which district Slack was to move to The City Temple, a second coincidence). Cheam is some 14 miles by rail from Holborn Viaduct and Campbell, therefore, would have had the journey of a commuter each time he came to The City Temple. Elsie and Campbell would have known of each other from many sources. Certainly he enhanced his reputation while at The City Temple, doing much to ease the transition for the congregation from the long and celebrated ministry of Leslie Weatherhead to the less newsworthy pastorate of Leonard Griffith.

Even as late as 1965, Weatherhead was described as 'Britain's most popular preacher'. The City Temple congregation, which he had gathered and held, consisted of 'a cabinet minister, and others of rank, position and authority, and also the lowliest and poorest – people who

– *The Ecumenical Century 1900–65* (Princeton, NJ: Princeton University Press, 1965), pp. 219–25.

11. *Congregational Year Book 1967–1968* (London: Congregational Church in England and Wales, 1967), pp. 219, 339, 342. In fact Slack was admitted to the Congregational Church in England and Wales roll of ministers in May 1967 by transfer from the Presbyterian Church of England. *Congregational Year Book 1967–1968*, p. 420.

have been unemployed, people who have been in prison'. A few years later, in Kenneth Slack's, and Elsie Chamberlain's, time at the church, the members similarly ranged from the occupants of Regency-style flats in Mayfair, and a High Court judge and his family from Gray's Inn, to the more humble residents of the Golden Lane estate. The congregation assembled from all over London and, like Campbell, from the inner home counties. It had an international character with, at times, 14 different nationalities represented at any one service.[12]

By 1968 Coates and Campbell had left and Slack had two different ministers working with him at The City Temple. Of course, he had come to know Elsie well at the BBC when was himself a frequent broadcaster. She had helped to put Slack at his ease behind the microphone and had assisted in his preparing and presenting an effective script. The two were firm friends and Elsie had even mentioned Slack in her chairman's address to the Congregational Union of England and Wales' May assembly in 1956 – referring to the wonder that the British Council of Churches, with so many Episcopalians involved in its work, had appointed an English Presbyterian, Kenneth Slack, as its general secretary.[13] Some months after Elsie's arrival at The City Temple as the associate minister, a young man fresh from college, Timothy Cornford, was ordained there and he served as the assistant minister 1968–73. The associate minister was an experienced colleague to the senior minister and had something approaching equal status, although serving only part-time, while the assistant minister lacked both experience and equal status but worked full-time.

Any suggestion that Slack had cleared out his predecessor's team of ministers, in order to start afresh with his own people, does not accord with the facts. Colin Campbell, although well-respected, had already retired once, was 72 years old in 1967, and had more than earned an easier life. Anthony Coates had spent four years at The City Temple and, it was felt, as a young minister would benefit from experience of a different kind than that which this central London church could offer. It was always understood that he would leave

12. *Congregational Year Book 1972* (London: Congregational Church in England and Wales 1972), pp. 352–53. Davies, *Worship and Theology in England*, pp. 222, 225. L. Weatherhead, *The Significance of Silence* (London: Epworth Press, 1945), see Preface.

13. E.D. Chamberlain, *White to Harvest* (London: Independent Press, 1956), p. 7.

after Kenneth Slack had settled there. Elsie's involvement arose, at least in part, from Slack's pastoral concern for her which led to his raising her case at a City Temple ministers' meeting. He felt that she had been badly treated by the BBC and wanted to help. He believed that she needed a community and a role and that a minister of Elsie's eminence would benefit The City Temple which, in return, would benefit Elsie. He was motivated by sympathy and compassion and the church members recall that these ministers worked well and happily together.[14] Therefore in 1968 it was announced that, following the retirement of Colin Campbell at The City Temple, Elsie Chamberlain had been appointed the associate minister. Doubtless she accepted for a variety of reasons but preaching where Maude Royden had stood and working with her friend, Slack, would have helped to persuade her. She began work in April. She went to The City Temple for a fixed term only but, after the formal appointment had ended, she continued to be frequently heard there.[15]

Tim Cornford recalled his first meeting with Elsie. She arrived late one evening at the flat which he rented in West Hampstead, 'bounding up the stairs to the second floor'. She impressed him from the outset as an 'energetic woman, mentally and physically'. Like him, she was to travel 'miles on the pastoral side of the job'. They divided Greater London into two. Elsie took London north of the Thames while Cornford took south of the river. The young man found his older colleague 'an unworldly woman' who 'wore her reputation very lightly and never flaunted her connections'. She was unassuming and kind and could easily engage in conversation with anyone and everyone.

Slack himself was a lively, good-humoured conversationalist with a ready laugh. He had a confident and commanding air, like Elsie herself, and his sermons were direct, forceful and, like his

14. *Congregational Year Book 1968–69* (London: Congregational Church in England and Wales, 1968), p. 221; *Congregational Year Book 1969–1970* (London: Congregational Church in England and Wales, 1969), p. 342. Cornford resigned his ministry in the United Reformed Church in 1975. The City Temple was an attractive church at which a young minister might serve his first pastorate but it was untypical and peculiarly demanding.

15. *Congregational Monthly* (March 1968), p. 22, private correspondence. The manuscript records of The City Temple, including church meeting minutes, appear to have been lost. Repeated attempts to locate them have yielded no positive results.

broadcasting, often flavoured with contemporary allusions. A superficial judgement might conclude that Kenneth Slack, with his striking, powerful personality, and Elsie Chamberlain, with her own strong will, were ill matched. Indeed Slack has been likened to 'a benevolent dictator', a description which might have easily fitted Elsie. Perhaps the post at The City Temple should in theory have proved 'a death job' for Elsie but she and Slack made their collaboration in the ministerial team a success. Tim Cornford remembered Elsie as 'a lovely colleague: warm, friendly, outgoing, generous and kind'.

Women's Ministry at The City Temple

At The City Temple Elsie took her place in a succession of women who had served 'that historic pulpit' and its church, although always doing so in supporting roles. Not only had Maude Royden been assistant preacher at The City Temple 1917-1920, during Joseph Fort Newton's ministry, but Dorothy Wilson, a Congregational minister and Elsie's friend, had served there as Weatherhead's 'pulpit associate' from late 1937 to 1939. Other women also had played and were to play key parts in The City Temple ministry.

Undoubtedly Maude Royden (1876–1956) had set the standard for women in the churches in the first half of the twentieth century. She had campaigned for women's suffrage before World War One but had discovered her true vocation in preaching on Sunday evenings at The City Temple. Having preached there early in 1917, she had created such a good impression that the invitation to her to become the assistant to Fort Newton was unanimous. Although she later moved to an interdenominational pulpit, with the 'Fellowship Services' at the Guildhouse in Eccleston Square, London, Maude Royden remained a regular visitor to The City Temple pulpit for many years. An outspoken pacifist throughout the First World War and later, Maude influenced many Congregationalists on this score too.[16] Even after she had left The City Temple her following, within the Congregational churches, remained strong. In the centenary year of the Congregational Union of England and Wales, in 1931, she was among the speakers at the Congregational Union of England and

16. *Oxford Dictionary of National Biography*. K. Slack, *The City Temple – A Hundred Years* (London: the Elders' Meeting, The City Temple, 1974), p. 27.

Wales' October assembly in Manchester taking as her subject 'The Challenge of Christianity to Women'.[17]

The City Temple was not the first church to call a woman to preach regularly from its pulpit but it was, at that date, the most important church to have done so. The members of The City Temple were proud of this series of accomplished women preachers who had added lustre to its reputation. Dorothy Wilson (1893–1956) who had preached for Elsie at Christ Church, Friern Barnet, was the daughter of Sir William Courthope Wilson (1865–1944), Vice-Chancellor of the Duchy of Lancaster 1925–1936. She had been brought up as a Presbyterian but, after her application to train for the Presbyterian ministry had been rejected, in 1924 she had accepted the invitation of W.B. Selbie, to study at Mansfield College, Oxford, to prepare for ministry within the Congregational churches. Sadly, her career was cut short by ill-health.[18]

More recently Marjorie Inkster had been assistant minister to Leslie Weatherhead at The City Temple for nearly two years 1959–1961. She was herself a 'former City Templar' and, after studying at Cheshunt College, Cambridge, had been a chaplain's assistant in the RAF 1952–1957 (not a full chaplain as Elsie had been before her – though Marjorie had not then been ordained) and was later a psychiatric social worker in West Middlesex Hospital. She was ordained to the Congregational ministry at The City Temple in April 1959. In 1961, illness prompted her resignation both from The City Temple and from the ministry. Marjorie Inkster herself had replaced Winifred Barton who had been 'Minister's Assistant' at the City Temple for 23 years. Winifred Barton was not ordained and did not preach but she visited the sick and needy and interviewed those who hoped to marry, or have children baptised at The City Temple.[19] After Elsie Chamberlain's time, Barbara Meachin was to be assistant minister 1971–1977, and Mia Hilborn was part-time minister there 1997–2000, so continuing the tradition of ordained women's ministry in the

For M. Royden, see, S. Fletcher, *Maude Royden: A Life* (Oxford: Basil Blackwell, 1989), and *Oxford Dictionary of National Biography*.

17. *Congregational Year Book 1932*, p. 74.

18. *Congregational Year Book 1944*, p. 367. Kaye, *Mansfield College*, p. 182, *Who Was Who 1941–1950*. Travell, *Doctor of Souls*, p. 133. E. Kaye, J. Lees and K. Thorpe, *Daughters of Dissent* (London: United Reformed Church, 2004), pp. 46, 57, 73–74, 169.

19. *Congregational Year Book 1960*, p. 341. Travell, *Doctor of Souls*, p. 234.

church, although by 2010 no woman had been chosen as the leading minister of The City Temple.[20]

Kenneth Slack

Kenneth Slack (1917–1987) was from Wallasey, in Cheshire. After education at Liverpool University and training for the ministry at Westminster College, Cambridge, he became a Presbyterian minister in 1941, having a pastorate in Shrewsbury for one year, before becoming a chaplain in the Royal Air Force Volunteer Reserve in 1942. He served in the Far East 1943–1946, with distinction, and was awarded the MBE. From 1946 to 1955 he was minister of St James's Presbyterian Church, Edgware, and then was appointed general secretary of the British Council of Churches. This latter position gave Slack, when a relatively young man, unique access to the leaders of all the Protestant denominations in Britain. As the British Council of Churches gained in importance and influence, with ecumenical relations becoming an indispensable element of British church life, so his own star rose. In 1965 he accepted the call to St Andrew's Presbyterian Church, Cheam, moving some two years later to The City Temple where he remained until 1975.[21]

Not only was Slack well-known to Elsie Chamberlain but, as has been stated, he was also well-known to Leslie Weatherhead and The City Temple congregation which had worshipped for 11 years, from 1947, at the Presbyterian Church, George Street, Marylebone, until its new building emerged from the bomb-damaged shell on Holborn Viaduct. Slack had preached one Sunday a month at Marylebone during 1957 and 1958 and had often sat in the pew to hear Weatherhead. The new City Temple, rebuilt after the ravages of fire bombs in the war years, was officially opened on 30 October 1958, in the presence of Queen Elizabeth, the Queen Mother. Throughout his ministry, Slack proved a prolific and popular author who wrote on a wide variety of subjects of Christian interest, including successive assemblies of the World Council of Churches.[22]

20. *Congregational Year Book 1972*, pp. 298, 341, 343. *United Reformed Church Year Book 1978*, p. 214; *United Reformed Church Year Book 2001*, p. 212. Mia Hilborn transferred to the Church of England in 2002. Kaye, Lees and Thorpe, *Daughters of Dissent*, p. 241.

21. *Oxford Dictionary of National Biography*. Taylor and Binfield, *Who They Were*, pp. 206–207.

22. Slack, *The City Temple*, pp. 38, 41, 43. *Oxford Dictionary of National Biography*.

The appointment of a Presbyterian to The City Temple ministry is not in itself a matter to wonder at. R.J. Campbell, who had resigned from the church in 1915, prior to his joining the Church of England, was at that time the last Congregationalist (albeit an unrepresentative Congregationalist) appointed to the senior ministerial position. Leonard Griffith came from the United Church of Canada, Leslie Weatherhead was a Methodist and remained so throughout his ministry at The City Temple, and his two predecessors were an Australian Baptist and an American Liberal Christian.[23] The City Temple had long gone its own way, often appointing as minister an outstanding Protestant preacher without regard to his denominational allegiance. Slack was to become 1975–1982 the director of Christian Aid, the relief agency through which the British churches channelled their international charitable giving.[24]

Associate Minister

The City Temple already held a regular mid-week lunchtime service of half an hour when Elsie Chamberlain arrived at the church. Its basic format was a cut-down version of the normal Sunday service. The ministers wanted to develop events which would make an impact on the working population of the area and so Elsie imported an idea from her BBC experience. She began an early weekday morning event, consisting of a reading and a prayer, with a brief introduction. In all this lasted only five minutes, a mere turning aside for the City worker on the way from Holborn Viaduct railway station to the office. The main church building was opened and the 'presenter' just stood in the middle of the assembled group and read. Elsie persuaded some well-known personalities to help. Obviously she was an attraction in her own right but she brought in friends from her BBC years, including Joyce Grenfell (1910–1979), the actress, broadcaster and comedienne, and Alvar Lidell (1908–1981), the radio newsreader and chief announcer, who retired in 1969 and was notable for his distinctive reading of the news bulletins, especially at the outbreak of, and throughout the Second World War. This brief worship event

23. Dr Fort Newton was minister at The City Temple during 1917–1919. He had formerly served Cedar Rapids Liberal Christian Church, Iowa, from 1908. F.W. Norwood was City Temple minister during 1919–1936. A. Clare, *The City Temple 1640–1940* (London: Independent Press, 1940), pp. 176, 182, 201, 222.
24. *Oxford Dictionary of National Biography.*

(almost a variant on the *Lift Up Your Hearts* broadcasts) was held on Tuesday, Wednesday and Thursday each week for some time but it did not last beyond Elsie's leaving.

Joyce Grenfell, a lifelong Christian Scientist, had a deep interest in metaphysics. She had often contributed to the BBC's early morning religious programmes on the radio, like 'Thought for the Day', and spoke frequently in St Mary-le-Bow Church in Cheapside, London, as well as in Westminster Abbey and Truro Cathedral. She enjoyed life thoroughly and had 'a genuine love of goodness' which she sought and found 'in all things, in music, literature, nature, and above all people'. She had gained a 'huge following' and was loved for 'her artistry, kind-heartedness, and sense of humour'. Elsie would have naturally been drawn to Joyce, by her strength of character, her religious seriousness and her zest for life – in many ways not unlike Elsie herself.[25]

Elsie would tell of her first meeting, some years before, with Alvar Lidell who was universally regarded as 'an exemplary stylist of the spoken word'. Her host had placed her at dinner next to Alvar and said that he would not introduce him because Elsie would be sure to recognize his distinctive voice. Before he had a chance to speak a word, she turned to him and said, 'And why should I recognise your voice?' She told the story against herself and it typifies her modesty and other-worldliness.

Both Joyce Grenfell and Alvar Lidell were noted for their compassion and generosity to good causes. That Elsie could attract such luminaries to these short reflections speaks well of her reputation and influence at this time, as it speaks well of them too. Slack was wise to involve her in The City Temple's ministry. These early morning services brought nothing but benefit to The City Temple, although the short reflection was judged only a qualified success. Huge crowds did not come but it did draw a very respectable 40 to 50 people on good days, while on others only 10 or 15 attended. However, the regulars appreciated the pause for thought and the peace, before they were overtaken by the busyness of the working day.

Elsie played little part in the governance of The City Temple which had never been run like a typical Congregational church. The minister there exercised more authority than might be expected

25. For Joyce Grenfell and Alvar Lidell see, *Oxford Dictionary of National Biography*.

elsewhere. Her part-time capacity as associate minister meant that she did not always attend its business meetings, so she was not in a position where she felt it necessary to declare her views on issues confronting the church.

Other Activities

After leaving the BBC, Elsie had not been idle. Her position at The City Temple left her time enough to accept engagements all over the country and she did so with gusto. Slack was amazed at the distances his colleague travelled but she dismissed his friendly criticism as 'daft'. Such travelling was neither a problem nor a trial to her for she enjoyed driving. Notoriously she had little sense of geography or direction. On one occasion during her time at The City Temple she had accepted an engagement in West Bromwich. On looking in her motorist's atlas, on the day before the engagement, she was shocked to learn that it was in the English Midlands. She explained that she knew a place called Bromley and had supposed that it couldn't be too far from there! Elsie was quite happy to tell this story against herself.

The Congregational Monthly announced in January 1968 that she was to open the annual garden party in June at Fen Place, Turner's Hill, near Crawley, in Sussex. Fen Place had grown from an early seventeenth century foundation into a handsome, great house which was completed in 1904 and had been acquired in 1951 by the Congregational Union of England and Wales for retirement flats for ministers and their dependants. The mansion had a dignified front entrance hall and was topped by a series of tall, ornate Jacobean style chimneys. During the Second World War it had been requisitioned by the government to house, first Canadian troops, and then Italian prisoners. They left it in a derelict state which was how the Revd S. Maurice Watts had found it when he was looking for a suitable place for a retirement home for retired Congregational ministers and their spouses. It had opened in May 1952 and was able to offer accommodation for up to 36 residents, with places for eight more in four bungalows in the drive. With fine views over the Sussex downs, Fen Place was set in grounds of 11 acres which were used for an annual garden party which came to rival the steps of Westminster Chapel, at the time of the Congregational Union of England and Wales's May assembly, as a meeting place and reunion for Congregationalists.

There, in Jessie Forsyth Andrews' words, 'distant friends' would 'meet each other under our great trees in rhododendron time'.

An even larger gathering than the 600 who had attended the garden party in 1967 was expected the following year and the organizers were not disappointed when 900 attended in June 1968! Elsie was undeniably an added attraction. These visitors in June 1968 journeyed through the rain to be present and the marquee was full to overflowing. Elsie herself addressed the crowd at the garden party, by stating her surprise at being asked to open the proceedings because, she said, 'whenever I do this sort of thing it always rains'. At that point Elsie's unique magic worked and, somewhat dramatically, the sun appeared and from then on 'it was practically all sunshine'. The Fen Place garden party that year was judged to have been 'an outstanding success'.[26]

In June 1968 the Bedfordshire Union of Churches ceased to exist. The rather unhelpful explanation given was that 'Changes in denominational life have made this inevitable'. The Bedfordshire Union, in the tradition of Bunyan Meeting, Bedford, had always consisted of both Baptist and Congregational churches in the county but, with the probability of a united national church of Presbyterians and Congregationalists coming into being, it was deemed necessary to sever these formal and long-standing links. The churches in Bedfordshire joined with those in neighbouring counties – Hertfordshire, Northamptonshire, Cambridgeshire and Huntingdonshire – while, in addition, the passing of the Bedfordshire Women's Committee was marked. At the Bedfordshire Union's final rally in Bury Park Church, Luton, Elsie Chamberlain was the speaker. Her text, 'The Grain of Wheat Dies', was considered 'most appropriate'. Honestly recognizing that this was a 'funeral', she properly laid stress on all their hopes for the future.[27]

---

26. For S. Maurice Watts (1898–1979) see, *United Reformed Church Year Book 1980* (London: United Reformed Church, 1980), p. 259. For Fen Place see, R.T. Jones, *Congregationalism in England 1662–1962* (London: Independent Press, 1962), p. 400. By 1968 this should refer to the Congregational Church in England and Wales, not the Congregational Union, but the reference in *Congregational Monthly* (January 1968), p. 18 is to the Congregational Union of England and Wales. *Congregational Monthly* (December 1968), p. 18. Fen Place News-Letter (August 1964, April, October 1968) held at The Congregational Library, Gordon Square, London, WC 1.

27. *Congregational Monthly* (July 1968), p. 20.

In December 1968, Elsie was the guest speaker at the district rally of Congregational Women at Leiston, Suffolk. The minister there from 1954 was Blanche Reita Searle (1900–93) who herself was to retire in 1970 to Fen Place. She was also an old friend of Elsie's.[28] In December 1970, Elsie preached at the anniversary of Woodbridge Congregational Church, also in Suffolk.[29] In July 1972 she led a festival of praise at Ridgewell Congregational Church, Essex as part of the celebrations occasioned by the flower festival there.[30]

Theological Questions

Elsie's training for the ministry, 'on the job' in Liverpool with Muriel Paulden and not at a ministerial college, might have been understood as making her less comfortable with academic theology. However she was proud to hold a degree from King's, London, and, even when advanced in years, she still bought works of theology although, at times, her own views raised questions. Whilst at The City Temple, one of the major Christian festivals was being marked by a series of Bible studies, in which a set reading was Genesis 1:1-25, where the reading closed on day five, with God saying that it was good. When the question was asked why the reading had stopped there, Elsie pointed out that it was all good, up to the point where man came on the scene and messed things up. This seemed satisfactory until it was noted that, at the end of day six, God surveys everything and still calls it all very good – including man. What was Elsie trying to get at? The only aspect of the creation story that goes wrong is man – everything else stays good. Was it a quasi-serious anti-male comment or merely a throwaway line?

On another occasion the group meeting was discussing guilt and forgiveness and Elsie ventured that she thought people could only really understand and feel divine forgiveness, if they had experienced and understood forgiveness from another person. Was Elsie's religion anthropomorphic or not? Probably what she was doing, in her inimitable, matter of fact way, was insisting that the divine is not a rarefied 'something other' but someone who connects directly with us, in ways we can and should see.

28. *United Reformed Church Year Book 1994* (London: United Reformed Church 1994), p. 277. *Congregational Monthly* (December 1968), p. 18.
   29. *Congregational Monthly* (December 1970), p. 20.
   30. *Congregational Monthly* (July 1972), p. 19.

The City Temple had been good for Elsie but by 1970 she was faced with yet another crisis, with personal and denominational elements to it. The decisions she reached at this time would affect her for the rest of her life.

Chapter 12

THE SKY TURNS BLACK: ANOTHER CRISIS

During the 1960s Kenneth Slack made 'a unique contribution' to the negotiations between the Presbyterian Church of England and the Congregational Church in England and Wales which led to the formation of the United Reformed Church in 1972. Recognition of this came in his nomination by the joint committee to be the first full term Moderator of the United Reformed Church, for 1973–1974. In those years he was among those who encouraged the infant United Reformed Church to engage in consultations about further ecclesiastical unions.[1]

Although personal relations between Slack and Elsie always remained friendly, the two were to differ on the union of the Presbyterians and Congregationalists. Elsie had openly proclaimed herself in 1956, when chairman of the Congregational Union of England and Wales, an 'ecumaniac'. She had praised the World Council of Churches and had exhorted the Free Church Federal Council to work towards its becoming a more inter-denominational forum. Above all, she had berated the different church bodies for their divisions. 'The divided church is not whole or holy but weakened and spiritually impoverished, and Christ's purpose is delayed', she had stressed. As she had reminded her listeners and readers on that occasion, she was the child of an Anglican father and a Congregational mother, and she was married to an Anglican parson of high church views. Her personal circumstances seemed to her, then and later, to demand her commitment to the ecumenical cause. Certainly she admitted to a passionate and personal commitment to ecumenism.

Contemporaries, therefore, saw her correctly as at one with those Congregationalists who favoured union with the Presbyterians. Yet she came to change her views, as she said, 'very late in the day'. Although this change cannot precisely be dated it is probable

---

1. *Oxford Dictionary of National Biography. United Reformed Church Year Book 1988–89* (London: United Reformed Church, 1988), pp. 202-203.

that while at the BBC, her energy and thoughts were largely taken up with broadcasting and latterly with the struggles which led to her resignation. Although broadly favouring church unity in these years, she had not had the opportunity to familiarize herself with the questions at issue between the Congregationalists and the Presbyterians, and certainly not in any detail. Therefore we must conclude that, during her two years' ministry at The City Temple, in which she was brought closer to the immediate implications of the proposed union of churches, and had the opportunity to discuss these with her ministerial colleagues, especially with Slack, one of the architects of the United Reformed Church, she rethought her position. Allowing for this, one must reiterate that tensions about the United Reformed Church never intruded into Elsie's relationship with Slack when the two worked together at The City Temple, and none of the church members recalled this issue as causing any problem for her or others.

Yet, in January 1972 Elsie admitted that she had been 'sitting' on 'the fence' for two years and that, when she was associate minister at The City Temple, she had come near to a decision against the United Reformed Church. She claimed that while there she had been given the choice of 'four formulae allowed in the proposed URC constitution as invitation to our Lord's table'. She did not like such formulae, preferring rather to invite 'all who love our Lord and desire to serve and follow Him' to share in communion. In response to this, both Kenneth Slack and John Huxtable, the minister secretary of the Congregational Church in England and Wales, contended in print that these formulae were not intended to be part of the United Reformed Church constitution. Slack wrote that he had asked Elsie to use any of four formulae of invitation which had been suggested by the Congregational committee set up to consider such issues. Nevertheless, if in truth she had laboured under a misconception, it was a misconception which she had gained at The City Temple and which had not been dispelled during her time there. Elsie suspected that the 'lengthy constitutions' of the proposed United Reformed Church were 'purposely expressed in phrases that can be turned two ways'.[2]

Elsie Chamberlain had spent 16 years, simplifying scripts, cutting through needlessly long and tedious perorations. She had met and

2. *British Weekly*, 21 January, 4 February 1972. *The Guardian*, 22 January 1972.

befriended cardinals, bishops and professors and had tidied up their thoughts and writings, striving not to offend but rather to help them. She knew her audience and understood that ordinary people, like her, needed complex ideas put simply and directly. After all, as John Marsh wrote, she was 'an entirely normal person' and simplicity was her own need.[3] Being straightforward herself, she distrusted ideas and structures which rendered complex and opaque that which she believed should be simple and transparent. In time then she came to distrust the proposed United Reformed Church and to question the motives of its chief promoters. Why did it seem to take that which was natural and unqualified, that is to Elsie the Congregational gathered church, the body of believers, and hedge it round with limitations and regulations? Was this the price of church unity required by Christ himself? Or was it only required by human beings, by church bureaucrats (i.e. men) with vested interests? To her, the proponents of the United Reformed Church were not being open with the people in the pews. What was their hidden agenda which necessitated a centralized structure and a hierarchy of officials? Elsie found herself unable to proceed from the unassuming form she understood to the impenetrable legalism she profoundly suspected.

In like fashion she became uncertain about much ecumenical jargon, just as she had distrusted the experts' complicated and indigestible pre-breakfast scripts at the BBC. Was this jargon a characteristically 'masculine stumbling block to a simple spiritual unity ... based on love for the Church's Lord?', she asked.[4] Given her public declaration that she was an 'ecumaniac', reinforced by her father's devotion to the Church of England and her marriage to an Anglican parson, which had resulted in her commitment to church unity, nationally and internationally, it caused her considerable heartache to surrender her hopes for the immediate future, and to change sides. In doing so this proud woman ate huge portions of humble pie.

We should consider the possibility that Elsie may have found it difficult to be number two to Slack at The City Temple. There the minister's word carried great authority. He could act unilaterally without consultation and, although her preaching, her prayers and her pastoral care were appreciated, she would only ever remain the associate minister. We have no reason for suggesting that she

---

3. *Reform* (May 1991), p. 18.
4. *The Times*, 12 April 1991.

entertained any hope of succeeding Slack there. On leaving The City Temple in 1970, she was freed to seek a church where she might be the sole minister. Her growing scepticism over the United Reformed Church probably contributed to her desire to leave The City Temple, although other factors were at play. She began by thinking what the United Reformed Church would be like, if too much power was concentrated in the hands of a few. Any discomfort she may have felt at The City Temple may then have caused her to fear the growth of clericalism in the united church.

Another factor giving Elsie serious concern in the 1970s was her husband John's deteriorating health and she wanted to spend more time with him. During the 1950s and 1960s she had frequently been away from home but now she realized that she was increasingly needed there. Driving from Greensted, near Ongar in Essex, where her husband's church was situated, to The City Temple and back again, took more time than she wanted to give so, for all these reasons, Elsie decided to look for a pastorate nearer home.[5]

Nevertheless leaving The City Temple in 1970 meant that she was again in the wilderness. Having defied convention and officialdom over her desire to marry John Garrington, having overcome Anglican prejudice, as she saw it, by becoming the first female chaplain in the RAF, and having left the BBC on a matter of principle, Elsie was strong enough not to be intimidated by any opprobrium she might meet in questioning the basis of the United Reformed Church. What might she do? Where would she go? She could hardly expect her old friend, John Huxtable, in his role as the minister secretary of the Congregational Church in England and Wales, who was the chief deviser of and advocate for the United Reformed Church, within Congregationalism at least, to commend her to a prominent Congregational church which her experience might otherwise have merited. He would fear that her newly found doubts about his understanding of ecumenism might sway that church's members and, therefore, lead to that church's defiance of the officially approved union with the Presbyterians. Even worse, given Elsie's national reputation and charm, he might have feared that her influence would sway other ministers and churches to doubt this scheme. She could expect no encouragement from that quarter and she knew it. To Huxtable she must have seemed almost a

5. J. Williams, *First Lady of the Pulpit: A Biography of Elsie Chamberlain* (Lewes, Sussex: Book Guild, 1993), pp. 77, 80.

traitor to the cause which he had served so faithfully all his ministry, so that he would have suffered annoyance and disappointment at her defection. Her tender conscience had again left her exposed. However, by accepting a preaching engagement, she was to find a pastorate for herself nearer home.

Off The Fence

On 12 May 1971 Elsie told the deacons of her church in Hutton, Essex, to which she had recently been inducted, that she had voted against the proposed United Reformed Church at the assembly of the Congregational Church in England and Wales, which was meeting in London that week. In fact the debate on the United Reformed Church had occurred only the previous day and among the speakers for the motion were Kenneth Slack, while Reginald W. Cleaves, a Congregational minister from Leicester, and others had opposed it. As a former chairman of the Congregational Union of England and Wales, Elsie sat with the other dignitaries on the assembly platform, so that she had a privileged position from which to watch the proceedings. Later she stated that she had been moved to pity, by witnessing the unfair and partisan treatment, meted out to Cleaves, as he had tried to deliver a brief speech in opposition to many vociferous delegates who favoured the United Reformed Church. She explained her vote, against the United Reformed Church at this Congregational Church in England and Wales May assembly in 1971, to the Hutton deacons, stating that, in her view, 'the cause of general church union was not ... helped by this move'.[6]

Elsie Chamberlain first publicly aligned herself with those Congregationalists who objected to the expected United Reformed Church in January 1972. Her anxieties about the scheme of union led her then to side with 'the dissenters' proposed Congregational Federation'. She stated that 'she could not accept any restrictions on those permitted to receive Holy Communion' – a reference to the 'limited invitation' to communion, deemed a 'constitutional necessity' by the proponents of the United Reformed Church. Her decision was reported firstly in the Christian newspaper, *The British Weekly*, where

6. Hutton Free Church (HFC) Deacons' Meeting Minutes Book 1970–1974 – 12 May 1971. *Congregational Year Book 1971–1972* (London: Congregational Church in England and Wales, 1971), p. 88. Among others who spoke in the debate were G.M. Adams, Revd E.S. Guest, Revd Ivor Morris, and David Watson.

she commented on her attendance at a recent meeting of continuing Congregationalists which she had found 'exhilarating'. She was pleasantly surprised to discover that several of her old friends were at this meeting and that she was not so isolated in having reservations about the future. She indicated that what finally proved 'the last straw on the camel's back' was her being asked to give an assurance that, if she preached from 'a certain pulpit', there would be no obligation on her conscience to bear testimony against the United Reformed Church. She expressed grave misgivings 'about any organisation that tries to tidy up consciences'. If they were so certain that what they proposed was God's will, as was often repeated by United Reformed Church advocates in the early 1970s, why did they fear those who took a different view?

The comment, that she was asked to give such an assurance, does suggest that at this time some advocates of the United Reformed Church were worried about Elsie's ability to sway any waverers about the proposed new ecclesiastical body. Of course, the attempt to silence Elsie on this score (or any other) was ill-conceived because it was bound to backfire, and have exactly the opposite effect from that intended. It only served to confirm her suspicions that all her doubts about the coming ecclesiastical union were justified.

Having decided to remain a Congregationalist, rather than join the United Reformed Church, Elsie felt free, as she put it, from 'the institutionalism that is killing the Spirit and making ordinary people weary of the Church that binds on them burdens grievous to be borne'. At that stage she believed that about 700 Congregational churches would stand aside from 'the merger' and would resist those 'pressures toward uniformity and conformity that are entirely contrary to the spirit of unity'. She believed that if people could be 'bull-dozed into the Kingdom, it would certainly be visible on earth now' – clearly implying that, in her opinion, undue pressure was applied by the proponents of the United Reformed Church to gain support for their cause. Having made this decision Elsie felt a sense of relief. 'For myself', she confessed, 'I'm glad to be free of the pressures of power politics which seem to be the order of the day in bringing a new denomination to birth.' She added the judgement, 'It does not savour of the Kingdom of God'. Only the next day the daily newspaper, *The Guardian*, publicized her decision not to join the United Reformed Church and, one week later, it published a letter from her on this subject. Thus Elsie came to commit herself to those pledged to continue what they understood to be historic Congregationalism and who had organized themselves under the title the Congregational Association (which, in time, was to prove the nucleus of those who formed the Congregational Federation).

The Congregational Association had begun life in 1964 and by the following year Reginald Cleaves, the Welsh minister of Clarendon Park Congregational Church, Leicester, had become its chairman and John Wilcox of Loughborough its secretary. The Congregational Association stated that its members hoped to persuade Congregationalists to 'be faithful to historic Independency'. By 1965, Viscountess Stansgate had become involved with this 'Congregational Association for the Continuance and Extension of Congregationalism'. It is probable that Lady Stansgate first persuaded Elsie to examine afresh the concessions Congregationalists would be required to make, in order to proceed with the United Reformed Church, concessions which Margaret Stansgate had decided were too costly as early as May 1965. From at least 1966 the committee of the Congregational Association regularly met in Lady Stansgate's flat in Westminster. Clearly Lady Stansgate's involvement with those planning for a continuing Congregational presence in England and Wales was known to Elsie. She would have had many opportunities to present her case to her friend, when the implications of the proposed Congregational-Presbyterian union came up in conversation.[7]

If the Congregational Association's declared aim was to be 'faithful to historic Independency', we may ask how faithful Elsie was to this undefined concept. She was after all no great respecter of traditions or conventions and never, even later in the Congregational Federation, displayed any particular affection for, or sensitivity to, Congregational traditions. Ever the pragmatist, she demanded that tradition should take a back seat and allow the practical needs of the day to occupy the foreground. The Congregational Federation might well be underpinned by a concern for the traditions which had helped to make Congregationalism (a corrective, as some saw

---

7. R.W. Cleaves, *Congregationalism 1960–1976: The Story of the Federation* (Swansea: John Penry Press, 1977), pp. 20, 29, 42, 67, 68. *Congregational Year Book 1992–1993* (Nottingham: Congregational Federation, 1992), pp. 38–39. *The Guardian*, 22 January, 29 January 1972. *British Weekly*, 21 January 1972. For Cleaves see, J. Taylor and C. Binfield (eds), *Who They Were in the Reformed Churches of England and Wales 1901–2000* (Donington: Shaun Tyas for the United Reformed Church History Society, 2007), pp. 36–37.

it, to the insufficient place they held in the United Reformed Church)
but this concern was more likely to be found in others, like Reginald
Cleaves, than in Elsie. Her forte had always been the puncturing of
pretentiousness, and the blowing of draughts of fresh air so as to
scatter the dust of tired traditions. Surely she felt safer with innovation
than with tradition. One might wonder if she felt that the relative
openness of Congregationalism, which she hoped to find in the
Congregational Federation, would allow more space for her own
peerless individuality than would the threatening efficiency of the
nascent United Reformed Church. Nevertheless her involvement with
the makers of the Congregational Federation was extraordinary. Her
distrust for the coming United Reformed Church must have been
deeply disturbing.

An Open Letter

Two weeks after Elsie had announced, in her terms, that she had
come 'off the fence', and her decision had been given publicity in a
national newspaper, her friend, Kenneth Slack, replied in an 'open
letter', published on the front page of *The British Weekly*. He corrected
what he described as her mistake that the United Reformed Church's
'scheme of union' placed restrictions upon who might be admitted
to communion, and also dissociated himself from the suggestion
that pressure had been placed upon her in this regard, when she
was at The City Temple. He stated that he had been brought up, as
a Presbyterian, in a church which followed the same custom as that
practiced by Elsie, that is extending an open invitation to communion,
and that this was also practiced at his last Presbyterian Church, in
Cheam 1965–1967. However, he allowed that John Huxtable, the
minister secretary of the Congregational Church in England and
Wales ('surely a not unrepresentative figure', as Slack put it), had
always invited 'members of any church', a more exclusive form of
words.

Slack did not understand precisely what Elsie meant by the phrase,
'the pressures of power politics', but saw it as having 'a rather
more emotive flavour' than he would 'readily welcome in a serious
debate between Christians'. He felt sure that she would not impute
'unworthy motives' to many who have long been friends to them
both and, therefore, suggested her phrase might mean 'order' in the
Church. Slack conceded that the balance between order and freedom

is difficult to strike but he understood that Christian freedom must not be debased into 'a dangerous individualism' nor an 'individualistic licence'. He claimed that those 'drawing up the scheme of union', between Presbyterians and Congregationalists, had not engaged in 'the pressures of power politics' but rather had been 'ordering ... the church's life to help us to serve Christ'. What allowance did Slack and the advocates of the new church make for the movement of the Holy Spirit and the believer's need to make an immediate response to it, a freedom in which Congregationalism had traditionally gloried and had never been able to muzzle? In addition, we may ask if Slack and his fellow advocates of the United Reformed Church saw Elsie then as 'a dangerous individualist'?

He argued that the scheme of union which had been approved by 'assemblies, county unions, presbyteries, churches and congregations' was only 'a starting point'. He continued, 'It may be that we have not got the balance between freedom and order right, or (as I would prefer to put it) have not found quite the right way of ordering the church's life to make it free from both a deadening rigidity and from a lawless individualism that destroys fellowship'. Then he appealed directly to her, and others like her, 'who always refreshingly challenge what "the establishment" proposes', to be of the uniting 'company'.

He asked rhetorically, 'Surely you never believed that unity could come about by all of us becoming Independents?' for 'that is what your statement reads like to me. Is there in your mind no place at all in the church of the future for any of the insights that have been given to other forms of churchmanship?' He saw that 'coming together' in a united church would enable Christians to 'learn from one another' rather than 'caricature one another'.[8]

Of course, Slack's letter was only ostensibly intended for Elsie Chamberlain. In reality, it was aimed at all those who may have been swayed by her decision not to join the United Reformed Church. Nor did he mean that she had herself caricatured Christians of other denominations but that such caricature had happened in the past through ignorance. Knowing her well, he could have entertained few illusions that he would be able to change her mind but he hoped to minimize the damage which her defection might cause. The impact of her declaration to remain Congregational is witnessed to by the fact that *The British Weekly*, traditionally a Nonconformist Christian

8. *British Weekly*, 4 February 1972.

newspaper, devoted not only its front page on that day to Slack's letter but almost one page to a selection of letters, drawn from 'the flood', received in response to Elsie's 'Off the Fence' article.

A Reply

A fortnight later Elsie Chamberlain chose to reply to Kenneth Slack with her own 'open letter'. She stated that she had deliberately delayed making public her decision about the United Reformed Church until 'everyone had had a chance to vote', so as not to exercise undue influence. Then, having found that 'pressure was ... brought to bear on the "noes"', she had felt compelled to stand with the continuing Congregationalists. She challenged the authority of those who claimed that any particular decision was at one with 'God's will' but did not doubt Christ's prayer for the church's unity. However she believed that he was not praying for 'organic or constitutional unity' but for 'a unity of spirit that would be of the same essential unity that he shared with the Father'. Christ, she claimed, did not 'aim at or expect' uniformity.

She denied that she had ever believed that church 'unity would come about by us all becoming Independents', pointing towards her Anglican father and husband, but stated that 'there must be room for all the given insights of all forms of churchmanship'. In contrast to this, the United Reformed Church seemed to her a 'steamrollering together of two forms of churchmanship, each with very different insights', rather than 'a step towards unity'. She feared that 'some things of value' would inevitably 'go down the drain' in this union. That the form of union the United Reformed Church represented could not readily contain Independents like her was to prove a problem for it.

Realizing that she could probably do little to inhibit the coming into being of the United Reformed Church, Elsie took comfort, from The Acts of the Apostles chapter 5, verses 34–39, in 'the judgement of Gamaliel' that, 'if this thing is of God, it will stand – whether it is United Reformed Church or Congregational Federation or both or neither'. She pledged herself to go on 'working and praying for the unity of Christ's Church' and concluded that 'The Spirit, like the wind, still blows where it pleases. Ordinary people must be free to breathe it – freer, I think than the tight lacing of the constitutional corset of the United Reformed Church allows'.[9]

9. *British Weekly*, 25 February 1972.

This surprising analogy surely reveals much of Elsie's feeling, as she likened the United Reformed Church to a woman, forced to wear tight undergarments so that she might appear conventionally attractive, but also disguise her true shape and possibly even who she really is. Elsie's becoming a minister had entailed a conscious rejection of corsets and the image and perception of womanhood which they represented. This rejection almost defined Elsie's life and work. Having been a successful dress designer, as a young woman, she knew well female vanity and the lengths to which it could go. The United Reformed Church's 'tight lacing' threatened Elsie as a woman, and as an 'ordinary' person, disabling her freedom to be who she was born to be and who she felt that the spirit had called her to become. This 'lacing' would be too tight for her, she had concluded. Did she also feel that the United Reformed Church had dressed itself up so as to make a positive, attractive impression but, in reality, it was not all it seemed? Good reasons existed, she felt, to distrust the smiles of the United Reformed Church's advocates. If one raised questions or hesitated to accept the approved line, one was seen as awkward, as siding against God's will, and as fair game to be shot at by the big guns. Was this a positive Christian development which one would be pleased to belong to?

Slack, as a Presbyterian, used to a measure of control from the centre, simply had not understood how uneasy Elsie and other free spirits would feel at this restriction of their natural, God-given freedom. He could not conceive the price which he and his United Reformed Church colleagues were asking Elsie to pay – a price she simply could not pay and remain true to herself and to the God she had strived to serve, often in defiance of social conventions, all her life. Her mother had taught her to be an independent woman. Muriel Paulden had taught her how to be a woman minister in a male dominated society. She had long been a member of the Society for the Ministry of Women in the Church, as had her friend, Viscountess Stansgate, and her exemplar Maude Royden – both of whom were founder members. Her many heroines from history reinforced the possibility of suffering and sacrifice for principle. Many of these had been traduced and rejected. Her own association with the Six Point Group gave her further encouragement for the fight for women's rights and for her own principles, no matter the obstacles.[10] The

10. M. Stansgate, *My Exit Visa: An Autobiography* (London: Hutchinson, 1992), p. 75.

experience of successive struggles against entrenched authority in the past, and male dominated authority at that, had merely added strength to Elsie Chamberlain's already powerful resolve. No amount of pressure would make her buckle now. Rather it would simply stiffen that resolve and confirm her worst fears of an intolerant new order which Slack and Huxtable were about to usher in and which they were inviting her to endorse. How could she conscientiously do so?

Chapter 13

SOMETIMES A LIGHT SURPRISES: THE
CONGREGATIONAL FEDERATION

It has been suggested that the formation of the United Reformed
Church in 1972 caused Elsie Chamberlain 'more distress than
anything else' in her ministry – a bold claim in a stormy life! Some
of her friends found Elsie's decision not to join the United Reformed
Church bewildering. One woman minister knew that Elsie objected
to the Basis of Union between the Congregationalists and the
Presbyterians but did not really know why. Another felt that Elsie
simply had not studied that basis properly. Yet another friend
believed that Elsie had stayed out of the United Reformed Church
because she felt that in it there would be people, trying 'to order
her about', although he readily conceded that she would have been
a 'presence' at assemblies and that the United Reformed Church
would have been 'richer and more effective', had she joined it.[1]
Kenneth Slack, as late as February 1972, still hoped that Elsie would
change her mind and join the United Reformed Church. He stated
that otherwise she would be missed for herself but 'more seriously'
she would be missed for 'the challenge' she would bring, as United
Reformed Church ministers and members adjusted the scheme
in the light of experience. Another minister wanted Elsie to think
again simply because 'we don't want to lose her from the family'.
The difficulty with that was that the existing family was rightly or
wrongly dividing anyway and the United Reformed Church was
not a family of which she wished to be a part. Her intention was
simply to stay in the family into which she had almost been born.[2]
Her decision not to join the United Reformed Church was a blow to
its upholders, while her support for the Congregational Federation
was a major coup for its promoters.

1. J. Williams, *First Lady of the Pulpit: A Biography of Elsie Chamberlain*
(Lewes, Sussex: Book Guild, 1993), p. 87. *The Guardian*, 15 April 1991.
    2. *British Weekly*, 4 February 1972.

None, among her critics and her friends, accepted the view that Elsie Chamberlain opted to join the Congregational Federation, rather than the United Reformed Church, because she preferred to be a big fish in a small pond. The truth is that Elsie Chamberlain would have graced any fellowship she had chosen to join and that she would have made a significant contribution to its life. That this contribution, after 1972, was to be in the Congregational Federation was to its advantage, although her decision, not to join the United Reformed Church, arguably removed her from a position of wider influence in British church life as a whole. Admittedly she would probably have disagreed with that verdict. After all, the Congregational Federation, at her request, was to choose her to represent it in ecumenical affairs and she continued to have an active and fulfilling ministry until her death in 1991. As a member of the United Reformed Church, she almost certainly would not have been able to remain a delegate for so long at ecumenical councils, even if she had been chosen to represent it, and her pastoral ministry may well have been curtailed earlier.

Yet Elsie was a big fish in the Congregational Federation's small pond. Indeed it could be argued that Elsie was too big a fish for the Congregational Federation. Her hope had been that, after October 1972, as many as 700 churches would together continue to represent Congregationalism, perhaps with some degree of unity and fellowship between them. However, an Evangelical Fellowship of Congregational Churches chose to separate itself from Christians of a broader doctrinal interpretation and remained apart from the Congregational Federation, and some Congregational churches deliberately opted not to affiliate to any larger body, staying aloof from the United Reformed Church, Congregational Federation and an Evangelical Fellowship of Congregational Churches. Therefore the Congregational Federation, although it contained the majority of continuing Congregational churches with over 300 affiliated to it, never came close in its total number of churches to Elsie's most optimistic hopes. This fragmentation of continuing Congregationalism was obviously a blow to the advocates of the Congregational Federation.

Elsie Chamberlain brought to the Congregational Federation a recognizable face. Broadcasting had made her a well-known figure and, although such celebrity is relatively short-lived, it rendered the Congregational Federation a higher public profile than it otherwise would have had. Conversely this had its negative aspect too. On more than one occasion, when explaining what the Congregational Federation was, the commonly accepted explanation was that it consisted of 'Elsie Chamberlain and her crowd'! In the late 1970s at a Congregational Federation ministers' conference in Cheltenham, the Baptist minister and writer, Edwin Robertson, Elsie's friend and one of the speakers, apologized to his hearers, in Elsie's presence, for his mistaken belief that the Congregational Federation was only Elsie and a few others. This misconception was, however, to be repeated by Robertson in his obituary of Elsie in April 1991, where he stated that in 1972, 'she led her cohorts out in defence of the congregational nature of the local church and continued in the leadership of the Congregational Federation'. More accurately but still not entirely satisfactorily, later in 1991, Robertson wrote of Lady Stansgate that she and Elsie 'had led the "rump" of churches which formed the Congregational Federation'. In truth the Congregational Federation was never merely a vehicle for Elsie Chamberlain. Reg Cleaves, John Wilcox, Lady Stansgate and others had brought the Congregational Federation into being, with much of the planning being done before Elsie had joined the fight. As she herself admitted on several occasions, she had come only late to the continuing Congregational cause while others had rallied to its banner since the mid-1960s. Of course, she did not claim to lead the Congregational Federation but to Robertson and many others, perhaps understandably, these Congregationalists after 1972 would remain her people, if not in reality 'her cohorts'.[3]

Viscountess Stansgate as Congregational Federation President

On 13 May 1972 a conference of Congregationalists, called together by some of the leading figures opposed to the United Reformed Church, was held at Lyndhurst Road Congregational Church, Hampstead, in north London. At this meeting the Congregational Federation properly came into being. Elsie Chamberlain conducted the devotions and Lady Stansgate was invited to be the first president of the planned Congregational Federation. After this meeting the Congregational Association would no longer make contingency plans for the possibility of an unknown number of churches and individuals who might seek fellowship together, should they decide not to join

3. *The Independent*, 20 April 1991; *The Guardian*, 23 October 1991.

the United Reformed Church, as the association's own members intended. Now these concerned but continuing Congregationalists had a certain future in the immediate and longer term for which to prepare. For them the prospect of some light, at the end of a darkened tunnel perhaps, was realistic. We shall return to consider this assembly at more length in a later chapter.

Some five months later, on 14 October 1972 the inaugural assembly of the Congregational Federation was held at Westminster Chapel where again Elsie Chamberlain led the worship. There the Congregational Federation was founded on a 'distinctive principle', that is 'the scriptural right of every separate church to maintain perfect independence in the government and administration of its own affairs'. Churches and their delegates were assured that the Congregational Federation would not in any case 'assume legislative authority or become a court of appeal'.

Lady Stansgate, in her presidential address to the assembly, emphasized her alternative approach to ecumenism. 'Federation excludes uniformity. Instead it brings ... the delight and refreshment of variety, of the many ways in which truth can be experienced and expressed. For us there will always be the ... validity of the Gathered Church'. But wisely she stated that we do not ask 'others to forsake their ways. There are many royal roads to the Throne of Grace'. She commended to the delegates present the watchword 'unity in diversity'. The uniformity which she denounced, in her view, clearly was asked for by others, implying that among these were the advocates of the United Reformed Church, with whom she and the majority of those present disagreed.

In May 1973, in Leicester, at the Congregational Federation's second assembly, Elsie Chamberlain was inducted to be Lady Stansgate's successor as president for the coming year. Evidently the infant Congregational Federation showed no fear of promoting women to positions of influence! With characteristic informality, Elsie kicked off her shoes as she began to speak, shocking and delighting the delegates in about equal measure. The shackles were off and she was at home with friends and was going to behave as she would with friends. Would this behaviour have been tolerated by the United Reformed Church, keen to impress other denominations, with its seriousness, and with its leadership in ecumenical matters in England? One suspects her disarming informality would have been frowned upon and checked in the United Reformed Church. At this Congregational Federation gathering, she made an immediate impression upon the churches' representatives, who had become used to more sober meetings in the former Congregational Church in England and Wales, where their views, if opposed to the officially preferred interpretation of ecumenism, had had to be suppressed, unless they had been prepared to risk derision.

Elsie's playfulness, her sense of humour and her unaffected openness and unforced friendliness dispelled the delegates' fears that this new body would repeat the stiffness of the Congregational Church in England and Wales. Her warmth and modesty were fine advertisements for this new grouping of Congregationalists. Remarkably she made the delegates, in a large public meeting, where those present may have been among relative strangers, feel at ease. Indeed, with such a relaxed way of conducting its affairs, the Congregational Federation already stood in marked contrast to those earlier Congregational Church in England and Wales meetings where all had appeared formal and impersonal. From these refreshing beginnings, it was clear that the Congregational Federation would not model itself upon the former Congregational Church in England and Wales. This was in large part Elsie's achievement and it arose out of her own character. She could not abide stuffiness and pretence and she would use her influence to ensure that the Congregational Federation would reflect her breezy naturalness. In consequence, the churches and their members paid her the highest compliment they could, for she was not only respected but she was loved.

In May 1973, in her address as president of the Congregational Federation, Elsie set out her own no frills approach to ecumenism, still the subject turning over in her head, as also in many of her listeners' heads. She stated that 'In the simplicity of our basic faith as Congregationalists lies the basis for the unity of all Christendom … Let us stay a Church without power except the power of the Holy Spirit.'[4] We may note in passing that the Congregational Federation was in truth not a Church (as Elsie had stated) but rather a group of independent churches: Elsie's gift was not for the preciseness of details, however vital. Did she feel that her friends and former colleagues, in the United Reformed Church, had sought power and place, through the pursuit of this form of church union? It would

---

4. R.W. Cleaves, *Congregationalism 1960–1976: The Story of the Federation* (Swansea: John Penry Press, 1977), pp. 75–76, 81, 82, 85–86, 103.

appear that she did and she saw such power as corrupting and corrosive of Christian humility. In contrast, the Congregational Federation was far too small and insignificant to seek such power, although it did offer a lively, if irritating to some, criticism of the aims and activities of its friends in the United Reformed Church, and of those who favoured similar organic unions in other denominations. These early meetings of the Congregational Federation demand a fuller description and we shall consider them in more detail later.

Elsie in the Early 1970s

Elsie had come to a parting of the ways. Although she maintained good personal relations with United Reformed Church friends – on one occasion Kenneth and Millicent Slack gave her a lift from the English Midlands to Taunton when Elsie's car was misbehaving – her choice to join the Congregational Federation led her to follow a different path from the English ecumenical mainstream. Her views on ecumenism might in the long run be vindicated but, in the early and mid-1970s, her decision flew in the face of the prevailing theological winds and again she suffered for not overriding the tenderness of her conscience. Yet she was never to doubt the wisdom of her choice in 1972. Certainly she regretted not being in the same denomination as many friends and former colleagues but she never doubted her decision to stay out of the United Reformed Church. Indeed she pledged herself and repeatedly exhorted others 'to disagree without being disagreeable'.[5]

Her commitment to the Congregational Federation was complete and binding. She expended her energies in better acquainting herself with its churches and with their ministers, members and friends. As ever, she was a great encourager of young people and especially of women (of all ages) to enter the ministry. In the Congregational Federation she had found a people to serve and invigorate and, in the revived Congregationalism it professed, she had rediscovered a cause to live for and, in large part, as Edwin Robertson realized, to embody. The Congregational Federation released Elsie, as it did

5. Ebenezer Griffith-Jones (1860–1942), principal of Yorkshire United College 1907–1932, taught students his motto, 'We must learn to disagree without being disagreeable'. *Congregational Year Book 1943* (London: Congregational Union of England and Wales, 1943), pp. 428–29.

others, from compliance to a policy then dominant, and superficially appealing, but, in its details, as Elsie saw it, too controlling, exclusive and restrictive. Henceforth her candour and freshness would be employed, with its 'tornado-like force', in attacking the 'male-dominated ecclesiasticism' which she detected mainly in the ecumenical proposals from which she dissented.[6]

Male Dominated Denominations

Was she correct in this latter judgment, at least in part, that is that the ecumenical proposals then being put forward vigorously were redolent of male domination? Would women have behaved differently? The chief advocates of the United Reformed Church were all men, with the notable exception of Gwen Hall who had been the chairman of the council of the Congregational Church in England and Wales 1969–1972, and who was married to the moderator of the London Congregational Union, Richard J. Hall, who himself became, after October 1972, the first moderator of the Thames North province of the United Reformed Church. Certainly the United Reformed Church's leading officers at the outset were all men. Perhaps this is not surprising for the Christian denominations as a whole were all effectively run by men at that time. Yet Congregationalism, prior to 1972, had been the exception in which women had gained remarkable inroads. Comparable recognition and progress had not been made in other leading British denominations.

However, those who steered the United Reformed Church into being were careful to ensure that positions of authority remained in the hands of tried and trusted officers, again all men. More significantly, of the twelve provincial moderators, appointed by the assembly of the United Reformed Church in England and Wales in October 1972, a judicious selection of experienced former Congregationalists and Presbyterians, over whose nomination great thought was probably expended, not one was a woman. Was any woman even considered for a moderator's role? In 1972 few women sat on United Reformed Church committees – Gwen Hall was the sole woman chairing one of the four departments and she again was the only woman to chair one of the 24 standing committees of the United Reformed Church. None of the secretaries of the departments, nor of these committees,

6. *The Times*, 12 April 1991.

was a woman. The full-time officers of the United Reformed Church at the headquarters in London were also almost entirely male.[7] Perhaps the framers of the United Reformed Church were at pains to ensure that possible partners for further unions, that is principally the Methodists and the Church of England, were not frightened away from the United Reformed Church by its having women, especially women ministers, in leading posts. Certainly they would have been aware of such sensitivities.

A key figure in the 'comparatively low key' Society for the Ministry of Women, which had been founded in 1929, was Margaret Stansgate. She had used her 'wide contacts', charm, determination, and 'enthusiasm for theology' to provide support for scores of Christian women. Having left the Church of England in 1948 and become a Congregationalist, Lady Stansgate was appointed the free church president of the Society. Elaine Kaye has concluded that for many women 'denominational loyalties were less important than equality in ministry', so that several felt they had made no fundamental compromise of their principles in changing denominations and then, for example, seeking ordination as Congregational ministers, after suitable training.[8] Elsie's encouragement of many women, who had a genuine call to the ministry, to leave their former denominations and become Congregationalists should be seen in this context.

Elsie shared the passionate concern of Lady Stansgate and her fellows in the Society for the Ministry of Women. Both felt unable to commend the United Reformed Church which, they feared, would lead the churches backwards on this vitally important matter of the equal status of women ministers. They feared that the United Reformed Church might make concessions to appease other 'male

7. *Congregational Year Book 1972* (London: Congregational Church in England and Wales, 1972), p. 25. *United Reformed Church Year Book 1973–1974* (London: United Reformed Church, 1973), pp. 10–13. Gwen Hall was the second wife of Richard John Hall (1911–1990). See *United Reformed Church Year Book 1991–92* (London: United Reformed Church, 1991), p. 228. For Gwen Hall see, J. Taylor and C. Binfield (eds), *Who They Were in the Reformed Churches of England and Wales 1901–2000* (Donington: Shaun Tyas for the United Reformed Church History Society, 2007), pp. 93–94. Although the Congregationalists had had women ministers since 1917, and moderators since 1919, no women had served the Congregational churches as a provincial moderator.

8. E. Kaye, 'From "Woman Minister" to "Minister"?' in *Journal of the United Reformed Church History Society* 6, no. 10 (July 2002): pp. 770–71.

dominated ecclesiasticisms' with which the United Reformed Church sought further acts of union.

On the face of it, Elsie certainly had reason to criticize what she saw as a masculine re-ordering of denominational divisions to secure and perpetuate men's advantages. To her mind the new ecumenical order seemed to reinforce the injustices which had existed in the former denominations before the union of October 1972. Despite the protestations of progress and modernity, it gave little visible recognition to women and held out little promise for them. Although she had been the chairman of the Congregational Union of England and Wales 1956–1957, no other woman had succeeded her in that post and the Presbyterian Church of England had never had a woman moderator of the general assembly. The English Presbyterians had accepted the ordination of women in principle as early as 1921, but the first ordination of a woman, after regular training in the Presbyterian Church of England, had occurred only in 1965, in contrast to the Congregational Union of England and Wales's acceptance of women ministers on its roll since 1917. For its part, the Church of Scotland to which the Presbyterian Church of England had traditionally looked for fellowship and fraternal guidance had ordained women as ministers, only as recently as 1968.

Did the former Presbyterian churches still harbour suspicions of women ministers? Elsie may have discovered this prejudice lurking beneath the basis of union. Why should she believe that the Presbyterian ministers, overwhelmingly male, had seen the light and regarded women as anything better than second class Christians? Her instincts led her to conclusions, which she felt unable to keep to herself. She probably felt the creation of the United Reformed Church was a step backwards for Congregational women, while it did nothing for their Presbyterian counterparts.

She also understood that the United Reformed Church was intended, by its devisers and promoters, to be the first step to further ecclesiastical unions, as has been stated, and such further unions would most likely be sought with the Methodist Church and with the Church of England, both centralized denominations and both then with little formal recognition of the place of women in the Church and of women's ministry, in particular. The Methodist Church in England was to accept women as fully ordained ministers in 1974, while suitably qualified women, with a ministerial vocation in the Church of England, waited another 20 years, that is until 1994 (three years after Elsie's death), before they might be considered for ordination to the priesthood.[9] Elsie tended to dismiss those Anglican arguments which reflected a sensitivity to that church tradition, that the priesthood (and the episcopate) belong to the mysteries of God's gifts and are not merely the products of human reason. Those mysteries, thus interpreted, had excluded women for centuries.

As the wife of a high Anglican priest, Elsie knew well the weight of opposition to women's ministry within the Church of England. She had suffered because of it. Repeatedly she asked, of the United Reformed Church's championing the cause of organic union, 'Was this the only way to practise church unity?' She reasoned that she had been the victim of male prejudice against women ministers, both in the long wait before she was to marry, in her encountering the enmity of the establishment to her appointment as an RAF chaplain, and in other matters. Elsie could be forgiven for detecting no significant advances for women in the United Reformed Church, and for failing to see any immediate prospects for such advances, if the United Reformed Church's priorities were to look for further unity with Christians who gave women a lower status than they had long enjoyed within Congregationalism. Although these factors reinforced her suspicions of the United Reformed Church and of its chief supporters, they were not alone in persuading her to dissent from it.

Elsie's Unique Position

One doubts if Elsie herself ever sat down to consider it – she was not given to self-regard, being too busy and practical – but in 1972, when she remained outside the United Reformed Church, the new body which received all the public plaudits while those who stayed Congregational were often roundly condemned and reviled at local and national levels for prayerfully exercising their conscientious rights, she was the most prominent Christian woman in this country. She was the only woman to have held the highest office in any Christian denomination in Britain but she was not a careerist who placed personal ambition at the top of her priorities. Rather she cared deeply about the status and respect paid to women, especially by the

9. See article on 'Women, ordination of' in *The Oxford Dictionary of the Christian Church* (Oxford: Oxford University Press, 1997).

churches. She was not a political campaigner, nor did she wear her principles on her sleeve, but it would be a mistake to assume that she was indifferent to the cause of women.

Her decision to continue as a Congregationalist was important, not only to her, nor merely to those she chose to join at that time, but crucially to those whose overtures she spurned, whom she refused to accompany down, what she saw as, an ecumenical cul de sac. That decision deprived the infant United Reformed Church of a prominent woman apologist but gave one (not counting Lady Stansgate, herself an articulate campaigner, and the younger women she would influence) to its critics in the Congregational Federation. Try as she did, Elsie could not persuade herself to join the United Reformed Church because it seemed to her, and to others, retrogressive, essentially moving away from the God-given freedom and independence of the local church, from the growth into maturity, responsibility and holiness of ordinary church members, and also from the justice and trust due to Christian women.

Is this what Slack had meant when he had asked her whether, in her vision of the coming united Church, she had expected other Christians to become Independents? She had then denied the charge but surely he had a point. After all, she was content with the freedom which Congregationalism had given her all her life, so much so that she advocated its advantages to those Christian women who were dissatisfied with their lot in other denominations. More than this, she was 'the outstanding example', indeed the only example, of a woman whose abilities had been given national recognition by the churches.[10] She wanted other women to be equally recognized and honoured. Perhaps she did hope and expect the other Christian denominations to do this, especially if they were to merge with the Congregationalists. If they would not do so, then church unity, of the United Reformed Church type, was not worth having.

Free to serve in the Congregational Federation

Having agonized about what choice she should make, with regards to the United Reformed Church in the early 1970s, and having decided to throw in her lot with the Congregational Federation, Elsie did not sit on her hands pining, nor did she let the grass grow under her feet.

10. Kaye, 'From "Woman Minister" to "Minister"?' p. 769.

That was never her way. She had an energetic spirit which drove her to activity. In the Congregational Federation in the 1970s much remained to be done. Consequently she would be busy and attempt to do all that she could. This proved a time of great satisfaction for her because she was to achieve much of lasting worth.

In 1972, at an age, 62 years, when most women would consider slowing down and enjoying a well-earned retirement, Elsie increased her activities. Her vim and vigour were simply redeployed. For the remaining 19 years of her life Elsie felt free, of the threatening corsets of a stifling form of ecumenism, to witness to the Lord she had served, and would yet serve, in different ways. The churches to which she was to minister, at Hutton, in Essex, at Chulmleigh, in Devon, and Taunton, and Nottingham, would not be uncritical of her – she always had about her an air of naturally superior authority – but they would all, without exception, become proud of her. In time their pride would turn to affection and the warmth of a family's love. She was their mother, grandmother, aunt and big sister, as well as their minister and trusted confidante. Of course, she knew they loved her, probably she expected it, and some adored her, but she did not seek to exploit her position. She loved them in return.

Chapter 14

HUTTON FREE CHURCH, 1971

In 1970, having resigned from The City Temple, after rejecting the proposed United Reformed Church, and living in the rectory at Greensted, near Ongar, in Essex, where her husband was the incumbent, Elsie was seeking a pastorate. In 1971, she found one at Hutton, near Brentwood, in London's outer suburban green belt, nearer her home than her previous post. In wartime Liverpool she had learned to be a minister, at Friern Barnet she had stamped her own character, authority and interests on her church, in a time of rebuilding the community, and at middle class Richmond-upon-Thames she had successfully combined the role of pastor, Anglican parson's wife and BBC broadcaster, while working in partnership with a colleague in the ministry. In addition, in the years after the Second World War, she had overcome the objections to her serving as a woman chaplain in the RAF. At The City Temple she had experienced the distinctive demands of a unique City centre church and congregation, while working with a number of part-time and full-time junior and senior colleagues.

Therefore by the early 1970s, Elsie Chamberlain had served in a variety of settings and locations – inner city Liverpool, north London, the armed forces, south west London, religious broadcasting and, most unusual of all, the City of London.[1] She had gained a national reputation, well beyond the confines of Congregationalism by working for the BBC. Indeed she was that most unusual of beings, a mid-twentieth century celebrity whose fame rested entirely on her presentation of the Christian faith.

1. It may not be evident to those unfamiliar with London that its suburbs have separate and distinctive characters. Friern Barnet, although only 14 miles from Richmond-upon-Thames and 23 miles from Hutton, is very different in feel, atmosphere and mood from either of these, as they are also different from each other. It goes without saying that The City Temple, the only Free Church in the City of London, on Holborn Viaduct, is unique.

Elsie Chamberlain in Demand

In 1971 Elsie remained much in demand as a speaker. In the spring she addressed nearly 200 women, from the churches of the Leicestershire and Rutland Congregational Union, at their rally in Westcotes Congregational Church, Leicester. There she gave answers and commented on questions which had been submitted earlier to the churches.

'Women are sometimes content to do very practical things in the Church but do not use their brains enough to help people who want to know about the faith', she stated with characteristic trenchancy. She felt that women had not always made the most of the options open to them. 'We have had the vote for fifty years but we have not been growing up as fast in knowledge or as fast as the opportunities of our times ought to allow us', she asserted.[2] Elsie remained keen to prompt women to take the initiative in the churches. Never one to sit submissively on the back pew herself, she urged other women to take on leadership roles.

She conducted a festival of praise in the summer of 1972 during a flower festival at Ridgewell Congregational Church, Essex, where the pastor was Miss Frances Cleeves. Both the church and Frances Cleeves were to join the Congregational Federation later that year. In late 1972 Elsie was the visiting preacher at the anniversary of Southam Congregational Church in Warwickshire. This church also joined the Congregational Federation.[3] That Elsie would willingly take on a demanding schedule of activities was not surprising. No invitation was too insignificant. She did not see herself as a dignitary, above the humdrum level of ordinary church life, and regularly accepted invitations to preach, to speak to mid-week meetings, to share her faith and her spirit. This did not tire her. Rather it invigorated her. She always enjoyed meeting people, making new friends, and becoming familiar with hitherto unknown churches. She was good at these functions, bringing not only her beaming smile and grace but also a sense of dignity and authority to the most unprepossessing of gatherings.

However, it is appropriate to consider the beginnings of the Congregational Federation in greater detail than has been possible

2. *Congregational Monthly* (June 1971), p. 17.
3. *Congregational Monthly* (July 1972), p. 19. *Congregational News* (January 1973), p. 8.

hitherto, and to examine Elsie's role in shaping the Federation. Her contribution to its beginnings, though belated, proved an enormous boon to its advocates and to prospective member churches alike.

The Congregational Federation's Beginnings

In 1972 plans had been revealed to continue in some fashion the former Congregational Union of England and Wales and a provisional committee to that end was set up at a meeting at Church House, Westminster, in January, on which committee Elsie Chamberlain sat. In order to discover what interest and support might exist in the country for their plans and hopes, the committee decided to convene a national assembly of continuing Congregationalists on 13 May in London. Before that assembly, in April 1972, 50 people, from Congregational churches in the south-east of England, attended a meeting at East Ham Congregational/Methodist Church where they unanimously agreed to form an area association of the Congregational Federation. Lady Stansgate chaired this meeting and Elsie was among the speakers.[4]

As already noted, the planned national conference was held at Lyndhurst Road Congregational Church, Hampstead, London, on 13 May 1972, for those considering whether they should remain Congregationalists. It was arranged with the express purpose of finding 'a simple way of uniting' those Congregational churches which had chosen not to join the coming United Reformed Church. Elsie not only led the opening devotions but she also gave a brief summary of the day's decisions before the meeting closed in prayer.[5] On the day of the meeting, industrial action had caused a 'go-slow' on the railways which occasioned the organizers some anxiety about how many might be able to attend. However the church, which claimed a seating capacity of over 700, was described as being full on the ground floor, while a number of people were seated in the galleries. Certainly the fellowship was animated and a spirit of expectancy permeated the gathering.[6]

4. *Congregational News* (February 1972), pp. 2, 3; *Congregational News* (April 1972), p. 10. Both in typescript held by Revd Christopher Damp.

5. *Congregational News* (June 1972), pp. 1–5. *Congregational Monthly* (May 1972), p. 19.

6. *Congregational Monthly* (May 1972), p. 19. *Congregational Year Book 1972* (London: Congregational Church in England and Wales, 1972), p. 145.

Although not involved in the original planning of the meeting, Edward Stanley Guest, not sympathetic to the proponents of the Congregational Federation but just as opposed as they were to the United Reformed Church, was invited to address the assembly. As he had done often before at Congregational Union of England and Wales' gatherings, Guest put forward a plea for continuing Congregationalists to uphold a conservative evangelical position. He and his colleagues, unlike Cleaves, were not so much interested in defending Congregational polity but rather in maintaining their own theological viewpoint against the encroachments of liberalism. Those attending listened carefully and respectfully which had not always occurred at former Congregational assemblies.

Later in the day Reginald Cleaves, from the platform, argued for a broad based union of those seeking a deeper understanding of the potential of Congregationalism. He engendered such optimism among his hearers that they returned home, believing that, although the cause of Congregationalism had suffered setbacks in recent years, as Cleaves had put it, these losses need not be fatal. It seemed possible to him, and then at least to some of his listeners, even at the eleventh hour, that these continuing Congregationalists might salvage something of value from the wreckage. The meeting revealed an appetite and enthusiasm for Congregationalism which had been missing, perhaps suppressed, for some time. Yet not all present at the conference were to join either the Congregational Federation or an Evangelical Fellowship of Congregational Churches (favoured by Stan Guest). Some present were from churches which, at the first ballot, had not opted to join the United Reformed Church (like A.T. Illingworth Jagger [1911–1992], the minister of Lyndhurst Road Congregational Church from 1953), but which would later reverse their decisions, once it was clear that the proposed union would come into being.[7]

The significance of this conference for continuing Congregationalism can hardly be overstated. From it, as has been noted, the Congregational Federation proper had its beginning. The former name, the Congregational Union of England and Wales, which many would have preferred to retain, had to be abandoned, chiefly for legal and charitable reasons. Lady Stansgate proposed the alternative title,

7. *United Reformed Church Year Book 1994* (London: United Reformed Church, 1994), p. 272.

Congregational Federation, to the meeting, claiming for the term federation a significance for all 'those joined together in the bonds of a common faith'. The conference endorsed the appointments of Lady Stansgate as president of the Congregational Federation, Reginald Cleaves as chairman and John Wilcox as secretary. Cleaves explained that the conference had been called 'to secure and perpetuate the Congregational way of worship and concept of the Church... We are met to strengthen our faith and our belief in the co-operation of autonomous churches working to maintain the Christian way of life. Many differences existed, theological, political, social, but there was room for all in Congregationalism'.[8]

Cleaves had argued, therefore, for a more inclusive position for the Congregational Federation than that put forward by an Evangelical Fellowship of Congregational Churches with its more sharply defined boundaries. Yet the organizers of the assembly generously had given Stan Guest the opportunity to plead his cause. Many, but not all, of the churches which chose to stand out from the United Reformed Church were evangelical in stance and some of these, but not all, would join an Evangelical Fellowship of Congregational Churches. That Guest, and his fellows in an Evangelical Fellowship of Congregational Churches, felt unable to co-operate in one Christian body with Cleaves, Elsie Chamberlain and others meant that the coming of the United Reformed Church had reinforced suspicions and revealed deep fissures within Congregationalism, perhaps making them even deeper. Henceforth continuing Congregationalism would be regrettably fragmented into the Congregational Federation, an Evangelical Fellowship of Congregational Churches, and the unaffiliated Congregational churches, with little contact between them (although a minority have chosen to join both Congregational Federation and Evangelical Fellowship of Congregational Churches).[9]

8. R.W. Cleaves, *Congregationalism 1960–1976: The Story of the Federation* (Swansea: John Penry Press, 1977), pp. 75–76.

9. Arguably the Countess of Huntingdon's Connexion also should be included. It had churches which had been listed in the *Congregational Year Book* as members of both the Congregational Union of England and Wales and the Connexion, such as Goring, Southstoke, Mortimer West (all near Reading, Berkshire), Ely (Cambridgeshire), Bodmin and Zion, St Ives^ (Cornwall), Ashbourne (Derbyshire), Fordham*^ (Essex), Ebley (Gloucestershire), Immanuel* (Basingstoke), High St, Cheshunt, Hertford Heath, Stanstead Abbotts and Wormley (Hertfordshire), Broad Oak* (Canterbury), Emmanuel* and Bell's

That Elsie was not given any formal post at this stage should not be interpreted as her not being fully trusted by the movers of the Congregational Federation, nor did it indicate any lack of commitment on her part. Those attending the Lyndhurst Road meeting were enormously heartened by her presence on the platform. 'Doesn't she look young?' … 'She looks no different than she did years ago', were among comments overheard. Elsie herself was charged with zeal for her cause and, as always, her liveliness communicated itself to her listeners. This was her calling. She brought confidence and spirit to the Congregational Federation from these early days. As Edwin Robertson sensed, she was the star in the continuing Congregational firmament, invariably giving effortless bravura performances.

Conversely this very advantage, which Elsie's involvement brought, could cause the Congregational Federation difficulties. Elsie was to occupy several posts within the Federation in the years to come – chairman of council, officer for ecumenical relationships, president – but no formal post could provide an entirely satisfactory channel for her unique gifts and zest. Valuable though Elsie was to the Congregational Federation, her talents sat awkwardly within the conventional job description. In truth, in the jargon of a later age, she was not really a team player. Unless she was given the freedom to follow her own inclinations, she would feel constrained and penned in. Where might such qualities be best employed, in the councils of the Church? Some observers believe that those in the Congregational Federation who sought to find a place for her, on its committees and boards, never quite came to terms with who she really was. Did Elsie herself really understand this aspect of her character and free spirit?

Elsie Chamberlain gave the Congregational Federation her own healthy contempt for the staid. Her vigour could not be constrained by cold formality. Her spirit rebelled against it. This rebelliousness stood

---

Yew Green* (both in Tunbridge Wells), Zion* (East Grinstead), Shoreham, Turner's Hill*, Copthorne*, West Hoathly* (Sussex), Bearfield~ (Wiltshire), Malvern Link, Leigh Sinton*, Suckley* (Worcestershire). *Congregational Year Book 1962* (London: Congregational Union of England and Wales, 1962). Churches marked with an asterisk do not appear in *Congregational Year Book 1970–1971*. Churches marked ^ joined an EFCC *Evangelical Fellowship of Congregational, Churches Year Book 1992–1993* (Beverley, E. Yorks: an Evangelical Fellowship of Congregational Churches, 1993). The church marked ~ joined the Congregational Federation, *Congregational Year Book 1979–1980* (Nottingham: Congregational Federation, 1980).

in contrast to the formalism of the moderators of the Congregational Church in England and Wales who appeared to perform their duties with an air of pomposity and self importance. Elsie's girlish audacity seemed especially suited to the new beginning being made by the Congregationalists in the Congregational Federation. Despite her age and experience, she brought youthful freedom and hope which reinforced the release from those shackles, seemingly imposed by the proponents of church union schemes in the former Congregational Church in England and Wales. The control of the ecumenists had been broken for these continuing Congregationalists and many in the Congregational Federation came to find that participle 'continuing' unnecessary and inadequate. Rather than continuing, as if they were conservative diehards, they felt released to defend Congregationalism, which they saw as more progressive than the United Reformed Church. They felt reborn, a rebirth exemplified by Elsie and her exuberance. Whereas the term continuing suggested the same as ever, and an unwillingness to adapt, the word reborn spoke of freshness and energy. Elsie guided the Congregational Federation churches out of the winter of an uncertain future into the spring of new growth.

An Induction for the Congregational Federation

The first ministerial settlement to be arranged by the Congregational Federation took place in early 1972 when Ivor Morris was inducted to the pastorate of Bocking End Congregational Church, Braintree, Essex. The presiding minister was the moderator of the Congregational Church in England and Wales's Eastern province, Clifford John Buckingham (1907-1995) who, from May to October 1972, was the last president of the CCEW. Reginald Cleaves gave the charge to the minister and Percy Wiseman (1900-1985), then in retirement in Braintree, gave the charge to the church. Others taking part in the service included Donald Pattinson (1910-1976), minister-secretary of the Essex Congregational Union, Stan Guest of an Evangelical Fellowship of Congregational Churches, Elsie Chamberlain and Viscountess Stansgate – a remarkably inclusive fellowship. A party of 50 attended the service from Ivor Morris's former church at Knebworth in Hertfordshire where he had ministered since 1968.[10]

---

10. *Congregational Monthly* (May 1972), p. 19.

This induction service displayed a rare spirit of happy co-operation between Congregationalists who were within months of separating in three different ways. The various participants in the service would have known fairly clearly the positions of each other on the subject of the United Reformed Church. Buckingham, Wiseman and Pattinson were to join the United Reformed Church, Guest was a leading spirit in an Evangelical Fellowship of Congregational Churches, while Lady Stansgate, Elsie, Cleaves and Morris himself were all committed to the Congregational Federation.

Buckingham was a modest, independent man whose willingness to preside at this induction was greatly to his credit during a time of division. Percy Wiseman and his wife 'always felt at home in small causes'. He had been brought up in Essex by his grandparents and had served several small churches, many in his home county. Pattinson had been minister of Baddow Road, Chelmsford, 1947–1960, before becoming full time minister-secretary of Essex Congregational Union. Never merely an administrator, he saw his work in pastoral terms and was regarded as serving selflessly the churches and ministers of Essex.[11]

Guest had served at Southchurch Park, Southend-on-Sea, Essex, during the years 1950–1956 and from 1956 Sawbridgeworth, Hertfordshire. From 1964 he also had the oversight of Hadham Cross and Little Hadham. He had been a consistent advocate of the conservative evangelical position within English Congregationalism for years and, like Cleaves, had been barracked at national assemblies for his defiance of the programme put forward by the platform. Guest suspected that the Congregational Federation would stand for liberal Christianity and feared that he and those sharing his views would compromise their position, were they to join it.

Congregational Assemblies

At the 140th Congregational spring assembly, chaired by Buckingham, Ivor Morris returned the new president's favour to him, at his Bocking End induction, by bringing 'a gracious greeting' from the continuing Congregationalists, though it was understood by one

11. *United Reformed Church Year Book 1977* (London: United Reformed Church, 1977), pp. 270; *United Reformed Church Year Book 1984* (London: United Reformed Church, 1984), p. 269; *United Reformed Church Year Book 1996* (London: United Reformed Church, 1996), p. 260. *Congregational Monthly* (June 1972), p. 2.

commentator, somewhat harshly but revealing the ill feeling of those days, as bearing the 'courteous flick of a backlash'.[12] Feelings among Congregationalists of all persuasions in 1972 were acutely sensitive. Observers were quick to attribute mischievous motives to remarks which on other occasions might seem entirely innocent.

As stated, on 14 October 1972, the Congregational Federation held its first annual assembly at Westminster Chapel. At this Elsie acknowledged the validity of the contemporary demand for church unity and of the call to each denomination to develop closer relations with other Christians and, alongside this, the need for each local church to proclaim the gospel and bear witness to their unity in Christ. However, she made no bones about her regarding the freedom Congregationalists enjoy as the 'agency' which could bring about the desired unity of the churches.[13]

Invitation to Hutton

By early 1971, when Elsie was living with her husband in Greensted rectory, near Ongar, in Essex, she had preached on a number of occasions at Hutton Free Church and had discovered that the members there were looking for a minister. Their previous pastor, Allen Robert Kemp, had been in the Methodist ministry 1963–1969, but had then become a Baptist, and from 1969 was officially described as the assistant minister of the neighbouring Hutton and Shenfield Union Church. In fact, Kemp had served as minister of Hutton Free Church which, like Union Church, was affiliated to both the Baptist Union and the Congregational Church in England and Wales. Kemp remained the minister there only briefly 1969–1970.[14]

On one of her visits during the pastoral vacancy, in conversation with the church secretary, Elsie let it be known that she was herself looking for a pastorate. She was invited to meet the deacons formally who reported these conversations to the church. At a special church meeting, in February 1971, 27 members were in favour of continuing to explore the possibility of her becoming their minister while four abstained and one church member voted against her.

12. *Congregational Monthly* (June 1972), p. 20.

13. *Congregational News* (November 1972), p. 7. This was the first printed copy of this bi-monthly magazine.

14. *Congregational Year Book 1970–1971*, p. 158. *The Baptist Handbook 1970* (London: Baptist Union of Great Britain and Ireland, 1970), pp. 130, 291.

In early March she outlined to the deacons her vision for her possible ministry at Hutton. She foresaw a half-time pastorate of three to four Sundays preaching, with one Sunday off each month. She would also work for them on two full days each week, and one evening. She explained that she and her husband were committed to being in Plymouth for the first week in every month. John's desire to help, and his talent for helping, people with various psychological problems made necessary his continuing to use their cottage, near Plymouth, as a consulting room. These trips also allowed the pair to have short rests away from the stresses of their normal lives. Elsie stated to the deacons at Hutton that she understood the pastor's role to be that of a trainer, instructor and missionary, while she insisted that the deacons themselves should be prepared to undertake some pastoral visiting, alongside the church administration which they already tackled. She suggested a trial period of six to 12 months.[15]

On 16 March Elsie met the church members at her own request. Two days later the church meeting unanimously asked her to preach with a view. On 15 April 65 votes were cast in her favour with five against. At this stage, Elsie decided that she must meet the officers of both the Baptist Union and the Congregational Church in England and Wales, before she could make a final decision. The suggested stipend was £600 pa, which included a travel allowance of £100 tax free, while the church was also prepared to meet the minister's telephone bills.

In May 1971, with all preliminaries satisfactorily concluded, Elsie accepted the call to the pastorate at Hutton Free Church and attended her first church meeting there as the minister. She was elderly, her denomination's future was in the balance and she was taking a leading role in the formation of a new but probably small body of churches. Yet she was undaunted. She thrived in a crisis and was irrepressible. Her new church at Hutton was to play a significant part in her engaging with these challenges.

One month earlier the question of the United Reformed Church had arisen at the Hutton Free church meeting. The Baptist Union had recommended that all union churches (like Hutton Free, in being

15. Hutton Free Church, Church Meeting Minutes Book 1968–1975, 18 February 1971; Deacons' Meeting Minutes Book 1970–1974, 10 February 1971, 10 March 1971. J. Williams, *First Lady of the Pulpit: A Biography of Elsie Chamberlain* (Lewes, Sussex: Book Guild, 1993), p. 55.

jointly affiliated to both the Baptist Union and the Congregational Church in England and Wales) should abstain at the coming vote on the United Reformed Church. One deacon went further and proposed that Hutton Free Church should vote against the United Reformed Church but his proposal found no seconder and, consequently, it was dropped.[16]

Hutton

Hutton Free Church is set within London's commuter belt with some City workers in membership, so evening meetings there took the times of the London trains into consideration. At this church Elsie was to bring all her varied experience, her maturity and wisdom, as well as her inexhaustible enthusiasm and energy, to bear on the church's life. The impression she made on the church and on many in the area was unforgettable.

In May 1971, Elsie told the church that she would only accept £465 per annum as a stipend, in order to underline the fact that her pastorate was part-time. It was noted that she would conduct an average of six services a month and would normally be in Plymouth on the first Sunday of each month. In June Elsie was criticized, in her absence, by one man who was disturbed by the 'question and answer method' she had introduced during Sunday evening services. His preference was for 'expository preaching' but he was emphatically told that the minister was free to employ various methods in the conduct of worship.[17]

In July 1971, Elsie mentioned at the church meeting that she intended to hold 'enquirers classes' for those seeking church membership. She was pleased at the response to the call for Sunday School teachers but was displeased to learn that church business had been discussed carelessly outside the church. It was also noted that the neighbouring Hutton and Shenfield Union Church, following advice from the Baptist Union, had recommended that no vote should be taken on the United Reformed Church.

Concern was expressed, at the church meeting in October 1971, about whether the church might remain Baptist, if it were to join the

16. Hutton Free Church, Church Meeting Minutes Book 1968–1975, 8 March 1971, 15 April 1971.
17. Hutton Free Church, Church Meeting Minutes Book 1968–1975, 20 May 1971, 17 June 1971.

United Reformed Church. The following month Elsie reminded the church members of the rehearsals for *The Messiah* which was to be sung at Christmas. In the minister's absence, a special church meeting, held on 14 December 1971, had voted on the issue of whether or not the church should join the United Reformed Church. No votes were recorded in favour of the motion, although 23 voted against it. In November 1971 a children's play-group was set up at Hutton.[18]

In February 1972 the church secretary reported on the past year. He recorded that Elsie had first come merely to lead worship at Hutton and had been asked by a deacon if she was interested in becoming their minister. At that time, he revealed, Baptist ministers had been frightened away by the prospect of the United Reformed Church while he had found that Congregational ministers were just not available. Although Elsie was the first Congregational minister this union church had ever called, he stated, 'our growth spiritually and numerically is entirely through her efforts'.[19] Without doubt, Elsie was beginning to make her presence felt in this Essex commuter town.

Hutton Free Church's Development

In 1970-71 Hutton Free Church had 91 members, 145 children, 11 teachers and 1 lay preacher. A year later the members had increased to 102, children to 175, and teachers to 13. A further year later there were 110 church members, 180 children, 15 teachers and 3 lay preachers.[20] In a relatively short time Elsie had made a positive difference to Hutton Free Church and to its impact in the neighbourhood. This was revealed not merely in statistical returns but also in a more positive attitude among the church members.

In 1980-1981, the year after Elsie resigned from Hutton's ministry, the figures returned suggest a falling back to the situation before she arrived there. The church members stood at 94, the children at 195 although there were still 3 lay preachers. However, the church listed 53 adherents, a considerable number. Elsie clearly had a

18. Hutton Free Church, Church Meeting Minutes Book 1968-1975, 20 July 1971, 19 October 1971, 14 December 1971; Deacons' Meeting Minutes Book 1970-1974, 10 November 1971.

19. Hutton Free Church, Church Meeting Minutes Book 1968-1975, 22 February 1972.

20. *Congregational Year Book 1970-1971*, pp. 158; *Congregational Year Book 1971-1972*, p. 158; *Congregational Year Book 1972*, p. 83.

powerful impact on Hutton, its church and its community and she is remembered with respect and affection.[21]

By the mid-1970s the church had developed in many ways since Elsie's arrival. Members recall that the building was packed every Sunday morning when she was preaching, so much so that an extension had to be built from the entrance to the building into the car park. Early in her ministry at Hutton, while the church halls were being erected, services for worship were held in Brookfield School. Yet even this did not deter newcomers from joining the congregation. Although some at Hutton had been biased against women ministers, many church members came to feel that she was the 'best minister we ever had'. Undoubtedly new people were attracted to the church by Elsie's warm personality and charisma. She would speak at women's meetings in the area and on Sundays the congregation would be swollen by her mid-week hearers keen to hear more.

In March 1972 the church held half hour services on Monday, Tuesday and Wednesday of Holy Week. On Maundy Thursday a united service with Brentwood Congregational Church was held and on Good Friday that old favourite of Elsie, Stainer's *Crucifixion*, was sung by the choir and congregation at Hutton. In May 1972 the church's ministry was reviewed and thanks were expressed to Elsie. The church members hoped not to overtax her physical resources but praised her good work, especially with young people. The words are reminiscent of the first report on her ministry, given 30 years before, at Christ Church, Friern Barnet. In October 1972, Elsie reported that she had been given a 'huge Christmas tree' for the church. The church members were properly apprehensive because it was as tall as a two storey house. The gift was received 'with some hilarity' and is remembered as only just fitting into the building.[22]

In May 1973 the deacons recommended to the church meeting that Elsie be asked to stay for another year and the church members unanimously agreed. By this time Elsie had been appointed the president of the Congregational Federation, although it was noted in November 1973, doubtless with some red faces in the room, that Hutton Free Church had not formally affiliated to the Congregational Federation. The church meeting readily agreed, with some

21. *Congregational Year Book 1980–1981*, p. 93.
22. Hutton Free Church, Church Meeting Minutes Book *1968–1975*, 21 March 1972, 16 May 1972, 17 October 1972.

embarrassment, that the affiliation fees should be paid promptly. Elsie began regularly to include, on church meeting agendas, an item headed the 'Minister's Concerns'. She would report on her pastoral visits and comment on matters of spiritual importance at this time.

In 1976, Elsie proposed that the church should hold a 'thinking weekend' to aid the fellowship's spiritual growth and to consider the needs of the world. She hoped to involve her ministerial colleague from Hutton and Shenfield Union Church (which had joined the United Reformed Church) the former Congregationalist, Edmund Banyard, for whom she had a high regard. His church had been a consistent support to Hutton Free in the past and would be again in the future.[23]

Good Neighbours

To the relief of many, therefore, the coming of the United Reformed Church made no difference to the close relations between the Union Church and Hutton Free Church. Their ministers in the mid-1970s, respecting each other, enjoyed a close friendship. Edmund Banyard (born 1920) was a Londoner. Like Elsie, he was born and grew up in Islington, as did his wife Doris. He had trained for the ministry at Paton College, Nottingham, serving two pastorates, before coming to Hutton and Shenfield. He was minister at Marlpool, Derbyshire 1949–1957, and at Stowmarket 1957–1973, and moved to the Union Church in 1973, not long after Elsie's move to Hutton Free. He remained there until 1987. On one visit to the rectory at Greensted, Edmund and Doris Banyard returned home with some of the herbs which John Garrington grew. Elsie would herself have an occasional meal with the Banyards and would sometimes admit to these friends that she was tired. However, Edmund recalled Elsie as 'a ball of ever renewing energy'. He had one other obvious point of contact with Elsie in that he had become a regular fixture on Anglia Television's late night Christian discussion programme, *The Big Question*, (with Alan Webster, then Dean of Norwich, and Eric Doyle, a Franciscan friar). Banyard appeared on this for over 14 years, continuing the intelligent, thoughtful presentation of Christianity on the television

23. Hutton Free Church, Church Meeting Minutes Book 1968–1975, 22 May 1973, 29 November 1973, 18 December 1973; Church Meeting Minutes Book 1975–1982, 29 April 1976.

which she had herself given and encouraged others to give on the radio.[24]

Edmund Banyard and Elsie Chamberlain clearly saw the formation of the United Reformed Church differently. The church at Stowmarket where Banyard had ministered, at the time of the decision, had been divided on the issue and only came to a sufficiently united mind to enter the United Reformed Church, one year after it was formed. Banyard himself had initially entertained doubts, although he also chose to join the new denomination. Elsie had done her hard thinking at The City Temple. Any hesitation she had felt was by 1973 entirely dispelled. She was then certain of her opposition.

As Elsie became older and more revered, both within her own churches and in the Congregational Federation as a whole, a danger existed that she would be seen as beyond criticism and be placed upon a pedestal. Undoubtedly some did see her in this way yet she herself seems always to have valued friends, like the Banyards and the Slacks, and others in whom she was able to confide her fears and her anxieties. Elsie knew that at times she needed simply to unwind and let all her stresses surface. She was not above seeking the advice of good friends nor was she frightened of taking it.

The Banyards admired Elsie both for her past achievements and for her work at neighbouring Hutton. Edmund understood that she used her 'great gifts' quite 'selflessly'. Yet, knowing her well, he realized that 'she could be forthright' and he expected not always to agree with her. But, he stated, 'that didn't matter' because 'she accepted that there were times when others didn't see the light that was so brilliant for her'! After Elsie's resignation from the ministry at Hutton Free, Banyard took the chair at several church meetings there during 1980. His distinctive gifts were recognized by the United Reformed Church when he was chosen to be the moderator of its general assembly 1988–1989.[25]

In February 1977 Elsie returned to a favourite theme, by actively promoting the Christian ministry as a vocation and urging the church

24. *Reform* (May 1988), pp. 3, 4. Edmund Banyard is also a successful playwright of Christian drama with a number of his plays having been performed notably at the Westminster Theatre, as well as in other venues.

25. Hutton Free Church, Church Meeting Minutes Book 1975–1982, 20 January 1980. *United Reformed Church Year Book 2002* (London: United Reformed Church, 2002), p. 170.

members at Hutton to consider the possibility of entering the ministry in their later years, describing such people as 'worker ministers'.[26] She had made a similar appeal three years earlier in 1974, when president of the Congregational Federation, combining with it the suggestion that Congregationalists should look for suitable church buildings for sale and also for possible manses. Again in May 1976 she had written an article, encouraging men and women to consider training for the Congregational ministry, while one year earlier she had appealed for candidates to take a lay preachers' course.[27]

Annie Chamberlain's Death

In September 1975 Elsie's mother, Annie Chamberlain, died at the great age of 97 years. She had lived almost another 20 years after the death of her husband, Jim. Her own death was a particular sorrow for Elsie who shared so many of her mother's characteristics. Crucially Annie had never wavered in her support for her daughter and, more than anyone, had given Elsie such strong self-belief enabling her, as a Congregationalist and a woman, to break through forbidding social barriers. Elsie spoke of her mother at that time with warmth and love, describing Annie as having been 'simply wonderful', in particular for setting a high priority upon the education of her children.

In the 1980s, after Elsie had moved to Nottingham to live, she bought, with her brother, Ronald, one of the flats in the centre in Castle Gate, where the Congregational Federation has its offices. They named this dwelling place after their mother 'The Annie Chamberlain Flat' and Elsie herself was to occupy this flat for some years.[28] As if the death of her mother in 1975 was not harsh enough, in just over 2 years, Elsie was to suffer another sad personal loss.

John Garrington's Death

Elsie's husband's poor health was one reason why she had sought a church nearer Greensted. In January 1978 John suffered a major heart attack. He was placed on a life support machine in Epping Hospital but

26. Hutton Free Church, Church Meeting Minutes Book 1975–1982, 17 February 1977.

27. *Congregational News* (November–December 1974), p. 3; *Congregational News* (May–June 1975), p. 4, *Congregational News* (May–June 1976), p. 12.

28. Williams, *First Lady of the Pulpit*, p. 89.

died early on Sunday morning, 28 January.[29] Given all the tumultuous events of Elsie's public life, she had always felt strengthened by John's steadiness, cool temper and general bonhomie and, after the recent death of her mother, John had been with her to offer comfort. Now she was without him too. She was truly devastated. One friend observed that she 'lost half of herself when he died'.[30]

After John's death Elsie was obliged to move from the large, comfortable rectory at Greensted, where she had been happy, to the manse at Hutton, a much smaller house. Many items had to be sold and Elsie had to make a new home for herself on her own – without John, and without her mother. For the first time in her life, at the age of 67, Elsie was alone and she felt her loss keenly. John had been able to help the restless and impatient Elsie, who was always such a livewire, and so often in the public eye, to relax. In their home together, at the end of a full day, they would unwind together. He understood her and she felt safe with him. Never a good sleeper, without John, Elsie was to experience solitariness and fear.

Theirs had been a mutually supportive marriage for she had been content, when needed, to be 'the vicar's wife' and he in turn had offered strength, openness and a welcome to her flock and to visitors. When a party of Congregationalists, some 20 or so strong, mistakenly believing that they were expected, appeared unannounced at Greensted rectory one Sunday afternoon, John and Elsie, both surprised, nevertheless welcomed them without any show of awkwardness. John enthusiastically escorted them, all newcomers to him, on a relaxed and informative tour around his beloved ancient church building while Elsie prepared food and drink. The visit, which could so easily have been a disaster, proved a triumph. John's readiness to entertain and the couple's flexibility were crucial. On another occasion at the rectory at Greensted, while playing host to a visiting American couple, whom Elsie herself had only met two or three days earlier, John was more than happy to play his part. He was a gregarious, affable and hospitable man by nature and calling. An improbable union, of two difficult, strong-minded and unusual characters, the marriage had worked supremely well.[31]

29. Williams, *First Lady of the Pulpit*, p. 81.
30. *The Independent*, 20 April 1991.
31. *The Guardian*, 15 April 1991. *The Times*, 12 April 1991. *The Daily Telegraph*, 16 April 1991. John Garrington was a man of 'great charm and deep human understanding', *Congregational News* (March–April 1978), p. 15.

On the Move

Elsie found grief hard to bear. Her remedy, in the months and years to come, was to throw herself 'into service for the Church as never before', although she was then well advanced in age. She attended meetings in London and Nottingham where the Congregational Federation set up its offices, spoke at rallies, conducted services far and wide, and yet somehow found time for her own folk in Hutton, of whom she grew enormously fond. In turn they became protective of her. She also took up the challenge, posed by several small Congregational Federation churches, (echoing her earlier desire to help at Danbury and Little Baddow, near Chelmsford, in the late 1940s) to see if she could revive them and help to reverse their declining fortunes. The most notable of these churches proved to be at Kentish Town, in north London.[32]

After John Garrington's death, Elsie clearly had need of the manse at Hutton. However, this property in Rayleigh Road was legally owned by Hutton and Shenfield Union Church, which had bought the house some years previously and had made it available as a manse for Hutton Free. It remained legally the property of Union and, during the years when Elsie lived with John in the Greensted rectory, Union had looked after it and let it.

Once Elsie had settled into the house, again in use as a manse, Hutton Free asked if it could buy it from Union but selflessly Union decided that the house should be not sold but given to the Free Church. This unexpected act of generosity led to a long running saga of how this could be properly executed in law – i.e. the thorny, legal problem of giving away a trust property. After a considerable amount spent on solicitor's fees, someone at the Union church came up with the perfect solution of just altering the trust in Hutton Free's favour and so the deed was done. This simple, selfless act arose from a unanimous decision, on the part of Hutton and Shenfield Union Church, and reflected and reinforced the excellent relationship between the two churches.[33] The division over the United Reformed Church, which in some areas had grown bitter and left deep scars, had not been allowed to set these two neighbouring Christian fellowships apart from each other.

32. *The Independent*, 20 April 1991.
33. Hutton Free Church, Church Meeting Minutes Book 1975–1982, 21 March 1978.

Other Interests

In February 1979, Elsie raised the possibility of her helping the small church at Kentish Town, in London. She had been concerned previously for a Congregational church in Manchester but, a new minister having started there, her efforts for that cause were no longer required. In fact, this was Walkden Congregational Church where Harold Holdsworth was inducted to the part-time pastorate in March 1979. Elsie took part in that service. In early 1979 Kentish Town's needs were rightly deemed 'urgent'. The church at Hutton was asked to support Elsie in this venture, by releasing her for half a week to Kentish Town, over a period of six months. Elsie anticipated that two or three friends from Hutton might be actively involved, while the 'young people' of Trinity Congregational Church, Brixton, in south London, she assured her folk at Hutton, were willing to help. Elsie expected to be in Kentish Town from Wednesday until noon on Sunday and then in Hutton from Sunday evening to Tuesday night. The great majority of the church members at Hutton, ever loyal to Elsie, gave their blessing, although three abstained and two voted against the proposals.[34]

In July 1979 the name of one member of Hutton Free Church, Mrs Irene Blayney, was put forward to the church meeting for its approval of her decision to offer herself for training for the ministry.[35] Previously Elsie had asked Irene to occupy the Hutton pulpit because she had stated that it was difficult for her to 'pop up and down' from the church 'orchestra' and to leave her other commitments on a Sunday. Irene had therefore preached the grand total of one sermon at Hutton before Elsie recruited her to help at Kentish Town! At that time Irene, like Elsie, had recently been widowed and the two women were naturally drawn to each other for companionship and support.

Resignation from Hutton

In November 1979 Elsie stunned the deacons by stating at their meeting, that she felt that she no longer retained their full support. Without making specific allegations, she said that she believed some

34. Hutton Free Church, Church Meeting Minutes Book 1975–1982, 20 February 1979, 23 March 1979. *Congregational News* (July–August 1979), p. 15.

35. Hutton Free Church, Church Meeting Minutes Book 1975–1982, 25 July 1979.

deacons had been 'disloyal' to her and consequently she had drafted a letter of resignation from Hutton's ministry. On their part the deacons asked her to reconsider her decision and having collected their thoughts, later that month, declared themselves 'unanimous' in their loyalty to her. Elsie thanked the deacons for this support but, after two months' further reflection, in January 1980, she stated that she still wished to hold to her previous decision to resign.[36]

What did she mean by this accusation of disloyalty? Could it be that some deacons had expressed resentment at Elsie's work for Kentish Town and also at her constant travelling to churches and meetings throughout the land? Did they want her to give more time and attention to Hutton Free Church? If so, that would be quite understandable and most ministers might have sympathized with and even shared that desire. Probably most ministers would never have contemplated an involvement in Kentish Town in the first place! However, the standards by which most ministers lived were not for Elsie. As stated previously, she had an inner dynamism which drove her on and, perhaps accentuated after John Garrington's death, her need to immerse herself and use up her energies was overwhelming. Undoubtedly she found some release in Christian service, although eventually the travelling and speaking would take its toll of even her seemingly untiring stamina.

Why then did Elsie resign from Hutton Free Church, after nearly nine happy years in that pastorate? Perhaps some minor criticism may have provided the occasion but realistically one is led to conclude that her spirit sought more freedom, a looser arrangement, guaranteeing her liberty to undertake Christ's work for the churches, when and where she saw fit. The reasons she had originally sought an Essex pastorate were now removed. John's death had released her from the need to be based near Greensted. Perhaps Elsie had sensed that her talents should have a roving commission, which the needs of the Congregational Federation seemed to demand, and that this was neither possible nor fair while she had responsibility for Hutton. A normal pastorate had never proved enough for Elsie. Hutton had given her affection, friendship and respect but once she no longer had to care for John, and, without his constraining influence, she felt able to respond to all those wants she could identify in other

36. Hutton Free Church, Deacons' Meeting Minutes Book 1975–1982, 9 November 1979, 21 November 1979, 3 January 1980.

Congregational churches and which she had long felt keenly. She believed that she might make a difference with her commitment and hope. Her upbringing and her life had taught her not to give in to despair and she maintained that a measure of faith and defiance were sufficient to inspire these apparent 'lost causes'.

Leaving Hutton for the Lost Causes

The disruption of the years prior to, and consequent upon, the formation of the United Reformed Church had left many Congregational churches in a state of shock, their deacons and members saddened, hurt and feeling betrayed. What possible future might these churches have? Should they believe the outpouring of propaganda from the former Congregational moderators and from the Congregational Church in England and Wales's offices in Memorial Hall, London before 1972, that Congregationalism's day had passed? Were they now simply and quietly to wait for that certain death, without making a fuss? That the continuing Congregational churches were an anachronism, an embarrassing survival, which in a few years would quietly die and be forgotten, was a widely held view among those in the United Reformed Church, and those few in other churches who knew of their survival. In truth many Christians, let alone non-churchgoers, were unaware that any Congregationalists survived who had not joined the United Reformed Church. Elsie knew that negative thoughts and doubts abounded, even within those who regularly attended the smaller churches of the Congregational Federation, and she hoped to counter them by sharing her own unbridled optimism, and her confidence in God for the future. Although she was herself elderly in years, if not in spirit, she refused to wait quietly for infirmity and death. She would rather rally her physical and spiritual forces and live to the full. Should she not show the churches of the Congregational Federation how to do the same? She must have reasoned that she could not really be Hutton's minister and take on such a task.

Elsie was loved at Hutton. Her church members knew that she was special and openly spoke of her in the most glowing terms. Possibly Elsie was unaware of this. Certainly it did not influence her. She never gave herself airs and resolutely refused to let praise go to her head. Elsie generated such activity that many of those groups which began in her time, like the toddler's club, the play school, and the old peoples' club, were still going strong twenty years after her departure from the church. At Hutton, just as at Friern Barnet and at Richmond, Elsie's love of music overflowed into her work. She started a church 'orchestra' at Hutton and played the cello in it herself. Negotiating one's way through the musicians in order to reach the pulpit at Hutton could be difficult!

Elsie's sense of fun communicated itself to those who attended the speaker's classes at Hutton. At these she encouraged people to engage in public speaking. Elsie would give each person a subject to speak on, with the result that even the most fearful and reluctant speaker somehow discovered the ability to say a few words, to their own and to others' benefit and amusement. Such groups would surface again in Elsie's later ministry in other churches.

Despite her achievement there and the undoubted high regard in which she was held, by early 1980 Elsie was adamant that she should leave Hutton and seek a different form of service elsewhere. A farewell gathering for her was planned for 29 March and in the spring of 1980, aged 70, the still sprightly Elsie was free to go wherever the Spirit might lead her.[37]

---

37. Hutton Free Church, Deacons' Meeting Minutes Book 1975–1982, 3 January 1980.

Chapter 15

A LOCAL THUNDERSTORM: THE KENTISH
TOWN SITUATION

By December 1978 the deacons and members of Kentish Town
Congregational Church had become convinced that their church
should come to an end. They had all grown old in years and saw little
hope for the future of their fellowship. However, the fate of the church
had become a subject of interest to others in the Congregational
Federation, especially in London and the south-east area, and a
meeting to discuss what to do with Kentish Town was held at Trinity
Congregational Church, Brixton, on Saturday, 13 January 1979. At that
meeting, attended mainly by friends from London Congregational
churches, a further offer of help to the church at Kentish Town was
made and, in consequence, a final decision on the church's future
was put off until the end of March 1979.

The meeting at Brixton had proved lively. If the church's situation
was critical and closure was likely, it was felt that no reason existed to
hold one's views back. The church would not go out with a whimper.
Although the Kentish Town folk had long resigned themselves to their
church's impending fate, others attending strongly urged the opposite
view, that is that more Congregational churches needed to be opened,
and even re-opened, rather than closed and that inner London was
a good place to start. No middle course seemed possible between
these two extremes and some heat was expended in the course of
the meeting, so that the meeting proved inconclusive. With opinions
among concerned individuals in the churches so polarised, David
Watson, the secretary of the Congregational Federation's south-east
area, chose to share his anxieties for Kentish Town with Elsie.

In January 1979 Watson had written to Elsie stating realistically
that he felt there was probably 'no hope' for the church at Kentish
Town. Elsie's reply had refused to accept this counsel of despair
as final. Watson's communication had reported on the meeting at
Brixton and asked Elsie if she was willing to chair a church meeting
at Kentish Town. He had persuaded the members and deacons there

to have one further meeting so as to review the situation. The church secretary also wrote to Elsie, asking her to chair the church meeting in February. He stated that David Watson would also attend. The Kentish Town folk recalled that, on a previous visit some 30 years earlier, Elsie had then stated bluntly that their church was 'more like a club than a church'.[1] On that earlier visit she had left her mark on the church members. She may not herself have remembered the actual words she had used on that occasion, but it is doubtful that Elsie would not have recalled the impressions which that visit had left on her. Had anything occurred in those intervening years to make her think better of the Kentish Town fellowship?

In fact, the earlier visit had occurred not 30, but 22 years previously, when Elsie had conducted the evening service at Kentish Town on 2nd June 1957, as part of the commemoration of the church's 150th anniversary. She had then recently stood down from her year of office as chairman of the Congregational Union of England and Wales in May 1957. At least in 1957 the church had felt it was appropriate to celebrate that anniversary. By 1979 the desire to commemorate anniversaries had completely disappeared.

In that latter year the premises were also being used by a black-led Pentecostal church which had been worshipping there since 1962. Certainly this church would have expressed an interest in purchasing the site, had the Congregational church decided to close and doubtless the Kentish Town deacons would have been aware of this possibility and almost certainly had such a sale in their minds. Had they already sounded out the Pentecostals on this matter? Subsequently Elsie duly attended Kentish Town's next church meeting on 13 February 1979 and, as requested by Watson and also by the Kentish Town church members, she took the chair.

A Crucial Church Meeting

The church secretary explained the situation. The elderly congregation faced rising costs, with much needed repairs to the building, to be met from a small income. At that point in the meeting, events took an astonishing turn. Elsie had not come unprepared. She responded to the church secretary's sombre remarks by making several comments

1. Kentish Town Congregational Church, Church Meeting Minute Book 1967–1979, 16 January 1979.

and by launching a daring initiative. She gave an undertaking that she herself would be responsible for pulpit arrangements for six months, from April 1979, at Kentish Town, and she agreed to visit with 'her own people' the surrounding flats and houses, 'in an endeavour to encourage new people into the Church'. This included her taking personal charge of the women's fellowship meetings. Her offer of help was subject to the approval of her own church at Hutton, the response of which might only be known, after she had had the opportunity to consult the deacons there.

All present at that Kentish Town church meeting in February 1979 accepted Elsie's offer of help. How could they do other? The only concession Elsie made, to the expressed wishes of the members at Kentish Town, was that, if the position remained the same at the north London church in October 1979, 'with few if any, newcomers … She would agree to the closure'.[2] She must have been quietly confident that the situation would change dramatically so that she would not need to honour that undertaking.

The formal nature of the minutes hardly does credit to the unparalleled nature of this occasion. Elsie had decided what she would do before she arrived at Kentish Town. The secretary's depressing account of the church's plight was totally predictable but it was followed by Elsie's revolutionary offer. What could they have made of that? If the young people of Brixton, with their different feel for life and their enthusiasm for Congregationalism, could be depicted as simply not understanding the reality of an older generation's weariness in north London, the same did not apply to Elsie. After all, she was herself an old aged pensioner, exactly of the same generation as these depressed and beaten church members before her! And she had met their inward looking air of self-satisfaction 22 years before and disapproved of it intensely then. Now it had turned to hopelessness, it would no more be to her taste.

She knew what to expect at that meeting. She would at times use the expression, of meetings which had an unpleasant air, 'it smells bad in here', and one feels that this might have been what she sensed at Kentish Town. Certainly to be forewarned was to be forearmed. She had come to the meeting with her mind set on the future. These members and their message of doom belonged to a failed past which

2. Kentish Town Congregational Church, Church Meeting Minute Book 1967–1979, 5 December 1978, p. 13, February 1979.

now had to be abandoned. Her offer to assume control of Kentish Town Congregational Church's affairs amounted to nothing less than a coup d'état, probably as unexpected to David Watson as it was to the Kentish Town church members.

Her arrival at Kentish Town had the effects of a whirlwind. Without any idea of what to expect, the church members must have been thunderstruck and it is likely that they never overcame that sensation. Whatever they expected to happen, at that meeting in February 1979, it was not that Elsie would assume personal control of all church affairs. Yet she was morally justified, if a little high-handed in taking this action. The members and deacons at Kentish Town had stated repeatedly that they did not want to be responsible for the church and that was why they wished to close. She was simply taking them at their word and accepting the responsibility which they were eager to surrender. For them, it seemed, the church's closure was the only option. Would closure have spared their blushes? They had not foreseen the possibility of others coming to the church who might see the situation differently.

Elsie's Campaign

Her takeover of the church's affairs also marked a significant contrast between the Congregational Federation in the 1970s and English Congregationalism prior to 1972. The Congregational Federation, as represented by, and for many personified by Elsie, was not prepared to rubber stamp the fatalism of the earlier Congregational Union and the later Congregational Church in England and Wales. The Congregational Federation had made a difference and was to make a difference, which in part translated into small churches, merely by virtue of their size, not being expendable. That is they were no longer expected or required to close. The Congregational Federation did not see such closures of small churches as inevitable. Elsie had embarked on an exciting enterprise with the Congregational Federation, an adventure, which the submissive attitudes to the spirit of the age of church members like those at Kentish Town would not be allowed to spoil, if she could do anything about it. The Congregational Federation was to know that Elsie's understanding of the church was not the same as that of many of her former colleagues. The fight for Kentish Town Congregational Church was in miniature the fight for the continued existence of the Congregational Federation as a whole. So many of its churches were small, and many were tiny. Either they would learn to survive as small, independent units or they would have to die to be re-born. Kentish Town Congregational Church was going to fight for its life and, with God's help, and with Elsie's energy, it would survive and, if so, it would send out a signal to other Congregational Federation churches and to the world at large. The supporters of the Congregational Federation had not made their stand in 1972 merely to admit defeat abjectly a few years later.

The next church meeting at Kentish Town, the first under the new dispensation, was a test of strength. It was held on 3 May 1979, with Irene Blayney (still at that stage a member of Hutton Free Church) in the chair. It was stated that the church usually closed for the whole of August, as only a small number were expected to attend the services. However Irene, almost certainly briefed by Elsie, had anticipated such negative suggestions and she ruled out this option because, as she admitted, Elsie Chamberlain wanted the church to remain open throughout 1979. By invoking Elsie's name, Irene's decision became incontestable. All present tamely assented. Instead of closing the church for ever or merely for August, and having none or little activity, the church members' attention was then directed to planning for the future, not an exercise which had troubled them overmuch for a long time. The programme of church events for September and October was arranged, including an autumn fair and a harvest festival. As if she had at last realized that the old regime had passed, never to return, the long serving leader of the women's fellowship resigned her office. The change of direction in the church's life was there to stay. The old order at Kentish Town had been confronted and overturned and the church members had been forced to recognize it.[3]

On 26 January 1980 both the fair and the festival were judged to have been successes, with an encouraging response at the autumn harvest from the Brownies. Elsie explained her vision for the church's future which she had already discussed with the deacons. She envisaged that the present buildings, consisting of part of the former church hall and a small, unattractive, prefabricated sanctuary, built after the bomb damage of the Second World War, should be demolished and the entire site re-developed. The new buildings to be erected should include a church, halls with all the required amenities, and some

3. Kentish Town Congregational Church, Church Meeting Minute Book 1967–1979, 3 May 1979.

flats. She had already made contact with various large building firms but stated that the fabric of the old premises was 'crumbling' and constituted a danger. A new beginning was under way.[4]

The six months originally agreed upon, in which Elsie took responsibility for the church at Kentish Town, had come and gone. Elsie remained, without any voice raised, publicly at least, against her. Very clearly she had not gone there to ratify the opinions of any 'club', or established interest group, however long it had held sway. She knew that lasting and effective change at Kentish Town Congregational Church required the passing of this club and the beginning of a new fellowship there.

In 1980 Elsie, appealing for financial assistance at Kentish Town, described the situation in outline as she saw it. 'Some of us felt it was wrong to close another Inner London Church' and so we 'offered to do some work there'. Elsewhere she grieved that so many old London churches had been demolished to make way for supermarkets and housing estates. With property prices constantly rising, 'If a church is ever needed in the neighbourhood no one will be able to afford the land for it', she stated. 'Once they go, they've gone for good'.

She explained that Irene Blayney was then training for the ministry and was helping with the pastoral work. That situation must have reminded Elsie very much of her own days in Liverpool, 40 years earlier, when she had assisted Muriel Paulden in another inner city district. Elsie was simply passing on what she knew both to Irene and to Kentish Town. At that time she was also the chairman of the Congregational Federation's council. The Kentish Town Congregational Church newsletters in 1980 designated Elsie as the 'Minister with Oversight' and gave the title 'Pastor' to Mrs Irene Blayney. By June 1981, Elsie's name had been dropped from the newsletters.[5]

Change at Kentish Town

In 1979 Elsie produced some publicity material to be distributed in the Kentish Town neighbourhood. It announced, 'We are a team

4. Kentish Town Congregational Church, Church Meeting Minutes, 26 January 1980.

5. Correspondence and newsletters held at Kentish Town Congregational Church. R.I. Blayney, *Kentish Town Congregational Church 1804–1991: A Brief History* (London: the author, 1991), pp. 16–17 available from the church.

led by the Revd Elsie Chamberlain. We want to find out if you want a church that is also a community centre'. The treasurer of the Congregational Federation's south-east area, Bill Meyer, sensitive to the financial sacrifices involved on the part of Elsie and her team of helpers, sent an unsolicited cheque for £200 toward the expenses of the work at Kentish Town.[6]

She also asked for volunteers to join the 'mission team in Kentish Town' which, she described, was to explore whether the Congregational church there was 'viable and needed'. The team planned 'a six month campaign camping on or near the premises for half of each week from April through September'. Elsie and Irene found two bedrooms for themselves in Golders Green in the home of an old lady who believed that she should 'help the helpers'. The six months actually began on Easter Day with Elsie preaching and a posy of primroses being given to each woman attending, the flowers coming from the garden of the house in Golders Green. Irene was left in charge when Elsie's many duties called her away and therefore she sought a more formal training and enrolled on the Congregational Federation's course for ministry.

A simple poster was placed on the church's outside notice board reading, 'Do You Have a Problem? Why not come in and talk about it over a cup of tea?' This brought an 'overwhelming' response from those who were homeless, unemployed, poor, or suffering from emotional difficulties, manic depression, schizophrenia, anorexia nervosa, and a variety of other complaints. Friends at Hutton sent blankets, clothing and money and some became regular helpers at Kentish Town's Saturday Club. Many of the Saturday folk began to attend the worship on Sunday mornings and several, in time, were received into church membership. Elsie and Irene also held a healing service on Saturday afternoons in response to the needs. They realized that Christ's help was more effective than their own. This service, although less formally than before, continued after Elsie's move to Devon in 1980.[7]

Unforeseen Developments

On 27 April 1980 a special church meeting at Kentish Town passed a motion unanimously that the trusteeship of the church buildings

6. Material held at Kentish Town Congregational Church.
7. Blayney, *Kentish Town Congregational Church 1804–1991*, pp. 19–28.

should pass to the Congregational Federation Limited. It was also noted that the trusteeship of two adjoining domestic properties – in Upper Holloway, London N19 – would also be transferred to Congregational Federation Limited. These terraced houses (bequeathed to the church several years earlier) had not previously been mentioned in discussions on the church's future and their existence to those outside the 'club' at Kentish Town had been unknown. The church there had only local trustees prior to April 1980. The following month it was reported that one deacon had resigned, as she had recently moved to Abingdon. At this meeting also Elsie announced that ten applications for church membership had been received (Irene Blayney and Elsie herself among them). All ten were women and all ten were accepted. The discovery of the two houses, which the church owned, only served to confirm Elsie's verdict that the church had been acting more like a club, implying that the church was not open to all and that membership was restricted to only a select few. It vindicated her decision not to accept, at face value, the older church members' wish to close down, without first letting in some fresh air and new people from outside the entrenched coterie.

In August 1980 Elsie was still trying to find a satisfactory scheme for the church buildings. The two houses in Upper Holloway were deemed to be in a bad physical condition, a state worsened by widespread damp. The status of these houses, their past use and their neglect, over many years, resulted in the church's seeking advice from a solicitor who had consulted the Land Registry. At this meeting also Irene Blayney, having conducted many services for the church during the past year, asked for leave to take a short rest. On 7 September 1980, it was announced that Bryan Tween would be coming to Kentish Town to preach 'with a view' to becoming the pastor. Tween lived then in North Finchley, had a weekday job and was seeking a church. He had previously been lay pastor of Little Waltham and of Southminster, both in Essex, and was later to accept pastorates within the Congregational Federation at Shalford Green, at Bocking End, Braintree, and at North Walsham, Norfolk to 1992 and also within an Evangelical Fellowship of Congregational Churches, at Dereham, in Norfolk, from 1993 onwards. Kentish Town was also planning to start a newsletter and a young people's social club.[8]

8. Kentish Town Congregational Church, Church Meeting Minutes, 27 April 1980, 24 May 1980, 7 August 1980. *Congregational Year Book 1997* (Nottingham:

On 5 October 1980, at a special church meeting, the church treasurer resigned both from his office and from the diaconate, because he had moved away from the district. At this stage in the church's life Elsie had been in control for two and a half years. Irene Blayney had been a loyal lieutenant, chairing church meetings and conducting services regularly at Kentish Town, since shortly after her first arrival in 1978. Elsie still chaired the occasional church meeting, as on 7 May 1981 but, to all intents and purposes, she had delegated pastoral responsibility to Irene.

At that meeting in May 1981 a tenant at one of the houses in Upper Holloway was reported upon. This man, who was keen to enter the ministry, had been given a six months' trial as assistant pastor, beginning in February 1981. In July, however, he was asked to leave because the church members were unhappy with his work. In September the church members learned that a local council grant of 75 percent might be available for essential repairs to be carried out at the two church owned houses. They were situated in a Housing Action Area designated by Islington Borough Council. Throughout 1982 Elsie gave much time to Kentish Town, although by September 1982 she had become the minister of North Street Congregational Church, Taunton. She was present at church meetings at Kentish Town in May, July, September and November at which repairs to the two houses were reported upon. Once the council grants had been made, the church still had to meet a shortfall of £12,000. This sum was covered by generous interest free loans from the south-east area of the Congregational Federation, from Elsie Chamberlain herself, and from one other relatively new church member.[9]

In November 1982 the church's future was again discussed at a special church meeting. Various options were considered, including the possibility of closure, of joining the United Reformed Church, and of selling to the Calvary Church of Christ, the Pentecostal church which continued to hire the premises for their services, after the Congregationalists had used them on Sundays. All these options,

Congregational Federation, 1997). Blayney, Kentish Town Congregational Church, 19–28. *Congregational Year Book 1995* (Nottingham: Congregational Federation, 1995), p. 104.

9. Kentish Town Congregational Church, Church Meeting Minutes, 5 October 1980, 21 February 1981, 7 May 1981, 12 July 1981, 27 September 1981, 19 May 1982, 21 July 1982, 8 September 1982.

after discussion, were rejected. As if to underline how clean the new broom at Kentish Town was in its sweeping, Elsie reported to the church meeting that, after proper examination, 'many discrepancies' had been discovered in the church's account books. Having taken professional advice, she recommended that no further action should be taken. However, the possibility of selling one of the two houses was mooted. By January 1983 the church had decided to sell this house while the rents of the two flats in the second house were to be raised.[10] The term 'discrepancies' may indicate something more than slipshod amateur practices. The discovery of the two houses and of the errors in the accounts reinforce the sobering judgment that all was not as the deacons and church members in 1979 had presented it to be. Was Elsie's acute observation of a 'club' at Kentish Town in the 1950s simply too kind a ruling? It suggested that her instincts were keen indeed.

In 1984 Barrie Jefferies became a church member and Gail Johnson became the treasurer. Jefferies was to represent the church in conversations with Camden Social Services and he introduced a firm of architects into the discussions on the church's future. This led in time to re-development plans which were finally passed in the autumn of 1989 and to the opening of a completely new church building, on the former site, on the 8 June 1991. The service that day was led by Revd Irene Blayney who, having been lay pastor at Kentish Town since 1979, had been ordained to the ministry in 1984. Despite resigning from Kentish Town in August 1982 (and then withdrawing her resignation), she was to remain there until 1991. In the following year she became the minister of Hutton Free Church in which post she continued until 1997.[11] She had given years of selfless devotion to Kentish Town.

Elsie's unprecedented and courageous intervention in 1979 had made this new building development possible. Her refusal to give up, her dynamism and vision, aided by friends, principally from

10. Kentish Town Congregational Church, *Church Meeting Minutes*, 14, 28 November 1982, 9 January 1983.

11. *Congregational Year Book 2002* (Nottingham: Congregational Federation), p. 140. In April 1991 the elderly couple who lived in the second house in Yerbury Road, Upper Holloway, decided to leave and the house was put on the market for sale. In September 1991, Revd Christopher Damp accepted a call to the pastorate where he remained until 2005 when he moved to Bunyan Meeting, Bedford.

Hutton, combined with the raising of generous loans, had rescued this church, in a changing area of inner London, from a quiet but undignified death. Her dedication and thoroughness also exposed abuses which, in churches large or small, should not be tolerated. What makes this story even more remarkable is that, throughout the whole unusual episode, this indomitable elderly woman minister was simultaneously involved in and fully committed to many other activities.

Chapter 16

PRESIDENTIAL DUTIES AND TRAVELLING, 1973–1980

Six years before her crucial intervention at Kentish Town, in May 1973 Elsie Chamberlain had become the second president of the Congregational Federation, succeeding Lady Stansgate in that office. In her presidential address to the May assembly that year, Elsie spoke of the 'simplicity of our basic belief as Congregationalists' which, she stressed, should provide 'the basis for the unity of all Christendom'. The use of the term 'our' invited her hearers to see themselves as members of one family, that is her family, while simultaneously recalling Jesus' language in The Lord's Prayer. She held that the foundation of Christian unity lay in 'faith in Jesus Christ as Lord and Saviour'. As has already been noted, she argued that Congregationalists should 'stay simple' and be happy to be without worldly influence and power, 'except the power of the Holy Spirit'.[1] This was clearly intended as a rebuke to those in the United Reformed Church, and other like-minded Christians, whom she understood as seeking a measure of prestige and power which had little to do with the gospel of Christ. However, far more than her thoughts on ecumenism and inter-church relations, Elsie's cordial manner and open-heartedness really made the deepest impression upon all. In addition to serving as its president, Elsie was to represent the Congregational Federation on the United Navy, Army and Air Force Board (dealing with chaplains for the forces), and to consult with the BBC over religious broadcasting – both areas where she had a particular interest. She was also one of 14 founder members of the Congregational Federation (Incorporated) and she accepted the post of the Congregational Federation's officer for ecumenical relationships.[2]

In many ways Elsie was ideally suited to the role of Congregational Federation president which was the Congregational Federation's

1. *Congregational News* (July–August 1973), pp. 2, 3.
2. *Congregational News* (May–June 1973), pp. 3, 4, 6; *Congregational News* (July–August 1973), pp. 2, 4.

version of the former role of CUEW chairman which she had held 1956–1957. The position carried with it few defined duties but rather required the officeholder to be prepared to attend churches, anniversaries, area gatherings and rallies, the assemblies of other denominations, and inter-denominational functions, in the name of the Congregational Federation, and bring greetings and encouragement. Elsie's talents and experience uniquely qualified her to gauge just what to say, how to say it, and how to set at their ease the different people she would meet on these occasions. She did not this time try to tell old hands their job, as she was accused of having done when chairman of the Congregational Union of England and Wales. Her ability to inspire meetings and her willingness to speak to both small and large gatherings, at opposite ends of the country, resulted in her being very busy during her time as Congregational Federation president.

At Easter 1973 Elsie addressed the Congregational Federation youth at their rally at Cheltenham. In May 1973 she spoke to the Norfolk Congregational women at their spring rally at the Old Meeting House, Norwich. In June she took part in the induction of Wilfred Potts to the pastorate of West End Congregational Church, Haverhill, Suffolk and also that month was a speaker at the Congregational Federation's south-east area rally at Ardingly in Sussex. There she put 'challenging questions' to the meeting and spoke of 'exciting, encouraging and inspiring responses to the challenge and opportunity of continuing Congregationalism'.[3] In September 1973 Elsie was the main speaker to the Federation of Congregational Women at their meeting at Wilnecote, Staffordshire. In October she filled the same role at a women's rally at Silver End, Witham in Essex.[4]

On the Radio with John Huxtable

On 7 October 1973 Elsie was once again 'on the air' in a Radio Four programme, which marked the first anniversary of the formation of the United Reformed Church. John Huxtable's and Elsie's views were recorded in the studio and then were discussed by a live audience

3. *Congregational News* (September–October 1973), pp. 5, 6, 11.
4. *Congregational News* (November–December 1973), p. 5; *Congregational News* (March–April 1974), p. 12.

of young people from Muswell Hill United Reformed Church, in north London. In the programme, entitled *On Reflection*, she took part in a discussion with Huxtable on 'the way to Christian unity'. Although Huxtable had once been a friend, he had more recently become Elsie's leading adversary, because he had been for some years and remained then the chief advocate of the United Reformed Church. He had been the minister/secretary of the Congregational Church in England and Wales, prior to October 1972, and, one year later, at the time of the broadcast, he was the joint general secretary of the United Reformed Church. As 'the main architect' of the United Reformed Church, he was the man whose policies Elsie and her colleagues in the Congregational Federation had decisively rejected. Would the young people of Muswell Hill, perhaps representative of British opinion in general, see the disagreement about different approaches to church union as an arcane discussion, merely a storm in a small, unimportant teacup? Whatever others thought, Elsie and Huxtable were then in profound disagreement on the course which contemporary Congregationalism should have followed and on the goal which the British churches in general should aim at in the immediate future.

Douglas Brown, the religious correspondent of the BBC, opened the discussion by stating that, in his view, the steam had gone out of the movement for organic unity of the Church and that the future lay in closer relationships at the grass roots. Elsie, in apparent support of this, denounced the pressures for organic unity in 'no uncertain terms'. She was aware, she claimed, that people had tried 'to bend their consciences to meet the needs of something that isn't according to conscience'. Why not, she asked, let 'the little churches keep what may be funny ideas to us but are matters of principle to them'? She defended those who resisted these pressures. 'If funny ideas', the principles of people in little churches, help them 'on the way to God, let them keep them. We have got to go for a church without power and my idea of such a church is one based simply on faith in Jesus Christ as Lord and Saviour – we can all accept that'. She continued, 'I see the way forward as the basis of accepting each other's churchmanship – acceptance of faith in Jesus Christ as the basis of our togetherness. I believe this is the way forward as the basis of our togetherness. I believe this is the way to unity that could include us all provided we do not want to push one another into our kind of mould'. She reiterated that church leaders and committed zealots had no right to force other Christians into 'our kind of mould'.

John Huxtable could not accept this view. He could not allow Elsie's vision of what he called 'an ecclesiastical free-for-all as a responsible structure'. Elsie retorted that even if Huxtable didn't recognize the picture she had put forward, the early church (in the first centuries of the church's life) had done so. He diagnosed 'plain human cussedness' as 'the main problem' facing ecumenists. Elsie responded that she wanted people 'to have a conscience of their own' which seemed to echo her feeling, when associate minister at The City Temple, that the denominational leaders, with their big battalions, were bullying and bamboozling the people in the pews into otherwise unwanted schemes of union.

Did she understand Huxtable's frustration with 'plain human cussedness' (presumably his diagnosis of the ailment afflicting the non-uniters in the Congregational Federation and Elsie, in particular) as an intolerance towards difference and independence? He sincerely yearned for Christians in all churches to share his vision but what if, after heartfelt prayer and reflection, they honestly thought otherwise? Was that honest difference enough to make them cussed in his eyes? By 1973 these two former friends were tragically poles apart.[5]

Presidential Peregrinations

In January 1974, Elsie, as president of the Congregational Federation, attended a seminar on the ministry at Cheltenham. The speakers were Dr W.T. Pennar Davies and Trefor Evans, both Welsh speaking Congregationalists, of Memorial College, Swansea, and members of the Union of Welsh Independents. Elsie closed the seminar with prayers. In May she presided at the induction of John Bourne to the ministry of Bedford Street Congregational Church, Stroud, in Gloucestershire. In April she performed the same function for Gerald Gossage at North Street Congregational Church, Taunton. In 1974 at Cheltenham again, she reported to the Congregational Federation May assembly on the 'talks about talks' on church unity between the Christian denominations. She had attended these, on behalf of the Congregational Federation, with 'a very definite mandate' – that

5. *Congregational News* (November–December 1973), p. 3. *Reform* (October 1973), p. 18.

is, although the Congregational Federation supported the general aim of church unity, it distinguished this from the organic union of denominations, to which it did not subscribe. In August she spoke at Swan Hill Congregational Church, Shrewsbury, to about 150 people gathered from 12 Congregational churches. In September she attended the return of Wavertree Congregational Church, Liverpool, to its repaired church building, having spent two years away from its home after a fire had damaged the premises.[6]

In March 1975 Elsie was the guest speaker at the Dorset and Somerset rally of the Congregational Federation. She repeated her view then that the way forward to church unity was through 'stark simplicity'. At the Easter Congregational Federation youth conference at Penge, in south London, she was again among the speakers. In April she led worship for a packed congregation at the 150th anniversary of Coxheath Congregational Church, in Kent. In May 1975 Elsie was one of 11 Congregational Federation representatives at Chislehurst, Kent, for a planning meeting, which looked forward to the formation of an international Congregational fellowship. Also in May 1975 she became the first president of the Federation of Congregational Women, having, two months earlier, addressed 150 women in Ton Pentre in the Rhondda Valley, in south Wales. At its spring assembly, Elsie, still in her own way a keen ecumenist, proposed that the Congregational Federation should apply to join the British Council of Churches.[7]

All this activity would have exhausted others, younger than her, but the apparently indefatigable Elsie appeared to thrive under the pressure. She wrote that her two years as Congregational Federation president had passed 'with incredible speed'. She planned to spend more time travelling northwards in the coming year and wondered if she might be able to visit more churches. She invited churches in Yorkshire and Cheshire to use her, if they could. In addition she stated that she expected to visit the Rhondda valley, Shrewsbury and the West Country at some time in the coming months and again she was ready and willing to serve churches in those places, if required.[8]

6. *Congregational News* (March–April 1974), pp. 2, 3, 5; *Congregational News* (July–August 1974), pp. 1, 14; *Congregational News* (November–December 1974), p. 10; *Congregational News* (January–February 1975), p. 15.

7. *Congregational News* (May–June 1975), p. 15; *Congregational News* (July–August 1975), pp. 5, 6, 7, 8, 11, 16.

8. *Congregational News* (March–April 1975), p. 1.

Having served as president from May 1973 to May 1975, when David Watson was appointed to succeed her, Elsie found herself still in demand. This may, in part, be explained by the fact that Watson was a layman and, although a lay preacher, he was less likely to be invited to preach at church anniversaries, inductions and ordinations. In addition his was a quieter, more retiring personality than Elsie's and church secretaries may have felt that, although Watson was a competent speaker for an area rally, and undoubtedly he was a committed Congregationalist, Elsie brought authority, colour, drama and warmth to an activity. She was sure to pull in the crowds, in a way which, at that time, few other Christian speakers, however worthy, and in the Congregational Federation or beyond it, could do.

Thus Elsie felt called to give herself in a quest to motivate the Congregational churches. How much these travels drained her we may never know. Certainly she was always at her best with 'ordinary people'. She warmed to them and they loved her. Her engaging smile and confidence enabled even the reticent and awkward to trust her. As president of the Congregational Federation she had welcomed invitations from churches and groups up and down the land. Once she had stood down from office, the invitations still poured in. Should she decline them? She found that she could not and, in truth, she did not wish to.

Elsie's Mileage for God

Elsie attended the first Congregational Federation summer school for ministers in June 1975 at Blackpool. Also that summer she travelled to Mickleby, near Whitby, on the North Yorkshire coast, to speak at the anniversary of the church and then drove to Loddiswell, near Kingsbridge, in the south-west of England, the opposite end of the country, to speak at the annual rally of the South Devon group of Congregational churches.[9] No Congregational Federation rally or meeting seemed complete without her. Her activity was breathtaking. She was simply everywhere, preaching at rallies, anniversaries and ordinations, presiding at inductions, and speaking to young people and to women's groups.

In September 1975 she preached at the ordination of Christopher Gillham at Charlesworth, Derbyshire and at the induction of Victor

---

9. *Congregational News* (September–October 1975), pp. 5, 16, 19.

Cameron at Wivenhoe, Essex. In October 1975 she led worship for the women's guild of Penge Congregational Church, in south London. In February 1976 she preached at the induction of John Watkins at Market Harborough Congregational Church. It was noted that Elsie's 'mileage for God', in these early years of the Congregational Federation, must have set 'a record'. Her appearance at Market Harborough entailed her leaving her husband in hospital in Plymouth and driving 250 miles to Leicestershire. John had been taken ill only the day before. It was so icy, on the Saturday of the induction, that the church's front steps were too dangerous to use, so entry to the building was gained by the side doors. After the service, Elsie bolted a few sandwiches and then motored the 100 or so miles to her own church at Hutton, in order to conduct the Sunday services there. She was not only busy but conscientious and she did not want to let anybody down. In June 1976 she took part in the inductions of Tom Hodgson at Hay Mills, Birmingham, and of Edward Maynard at Latimer, Stepney.[10] In October 1977 she presided at the ordination of Alan Argent in Brixton, and also that month at that of Arthur Boyle at Orsett in Essex.[11]

A Wedding

In June 1975 Elsie conducted the wedding of Janet Morris and Christopher Wootton at Loughborough where the Congregational church was then without a minister. She prepared the couple for marriage by asking them directly, 'This is for life, isn't it?', and by accepting their immediate and reassuringly affirmative reply. The wedding occurred on a Sunday afternoon as part of the normal church service, with the marriage ceremony set between the sermon and the final hymn. However, after preaching the sermon, Elsie announced the final hymn to the quiet consternation of all present. At that point, the bride-to-be leaned forward from the front pew and, betraying no anxiety, reminded the preacher that she had forgotten something!

Elsie had close links with Janet's family for she had been Janet's mother's minister at the Vineyard, Richmond-upon-Thames, and was to inspire Janet's own future ministry. Four years after the wedding,

10. *Congregational News* (November–December 1975), p. 12; *Congregational News* (January–February 1976), p. 10; *Congregational News* (July–August 1976), pp. 14–15; *Congregational News* (September–October 1976), p. 14.

11. *Congregational News* (January–February 1978), pp. 13, 14.

in September 1979, she was to give the charge to the minister and the church when Janet Wootton was herself ordained and inducted to the pastorate of West End Congregational Church, Haverhill, Suffolk.[12]

Elsie the Preacher

When leading worship, Elsie usually wore a long black cassock and preaching bands. This would, of course, save her from the worry of choosing a suitable costume. As we have seen, she was not troubled by fashion. The cassock also enabled her to appear formal when performing a task which many felt should be reserved to men, reasoning that a woman preacher need not flout all established conventions at once. She would have her long hair pulled back neatly but not severely, in order that she should not resemble the archetypal schoolmistress or librarian. This formality of appearance, though not original to Elsie, among women ministers, and though not emulated by all Congregational Federation ministers, was to prove influential, particularly with some younger women.

Elsie's preaching, especially on first acquaintance, could be quite electric. Her disarming manner, lack of side, and good humour enabled her to address a congregation, as if she knew each person intimately and several hearers have described how they felt that she could see inside them as she spoke, leaving them exposed and shriven. She seemed to be directly addressing each individual, as she met their eyes with hers, smiled and drew them to her. This was no formal ecclesiastical exercise. She understood people. Her language eschewed high flown rhetoric and excessive demonstrations of feeling. Rather her preaching, like her character, was straightforward, plain and unadorned. Her own strength of mind, her lack of artifice, her transparent goodness and decency were readily communicated, at once both humbling and accepting her listeners.

Given that her sermons were attractive, in truth, they lacked theological depth. Yet she could hold a congregation in rapt attention and combined reverence with personal and contemporary prayers.[13] Although her preaching was not delivered off the cuff, it was flavoured with immediacy. Her life was too busy, too full, for her

12. Private Correspondence. *Congregational News* (November–December 1979), p. 16.
13. *The Times*, 12 April 1991.

not to include references to her own recent experiences which simply flooded into her thinking. She was happy to share her life with her audience, all friends, new or old, to her. As a preacher she sought not to condemn but to understand, to sympathize and to encourage.

Elsie was God's servant. She had promised to serve him and she did not need to collect worshippers and devotees for herself. She wanted her hearers to know him and his mercy and love and she held out these graces to those who heard her. God's strength enabled her to go on serving his people for as long and as vigorously as she did and, by taking her own experience as a model, she encouraged others to rely on God's strength and forgiveness in their lives. She did not parade her faith before others like some protective badge of identity which shielded her from revealing her true self. Elsie had too strong a character to hide behind any cloak. Yet her faith was genuine and deeply held. It was the mainstay of her life and the possibility of her abandoning that faith never existed.

Churches Unity Commission

In 1973 the United Reformed Church had taken the lead in holding so-called 'talks about talks' with other denominations in this country. These had led to the creation of the Churches Unity Commission. Given the contemporary climate of opinion in the various Christian denominations, with regard to organic church union, in which the United Reformed Church was unmistakably seen as the pacemaker, the Congregational Federation officers felt that they needed to explain why their group of churches was among those bodies willing to participate in the Churches Unity Commission. On 11 November 1974 the Congregational Federation issued a press release, signed by Elsie Chamberlain and ten others. It announced that Elsie and her fellows saw the way forward as working for 'visible unity – but not for organic union'. They argued that 'some ecumenists' eagerness to create a vast integrated structure' contradicted 'the lessons of history' and ignored 'the fact that the Church, being Catholic is properly a mosaic not a monolith'. They feared that 'to contrive mergers while deep differences of interpretation remain unresolved is to sow the seeds for future unease'.[14]

14. A. Dawkins and C. Davey, *The Story of the BCC* (London: British Council of Churches, 1990), pp. 9, 21. *Congregational News* (January–February 1975), p. 3.

In January 1976, in response to a recent call by the Churches Unity Commission for all free church ministers, after a certain date, to be episcopally ordained, Reginald Cleaves, David Watson, and Elsie Chamberlain made a public statement. They declared that they could not in good conscience accept episcopacy but rather commended the churches to seek 'unity in diversity' which they understood to have been the practice of the early church. Such unity, in their view, offered a 'far more practical means of making visible the oneness all Christians know the Church to possess'. Despite the Congregational Federation's relative insignificance, this statement was not ignored by the press. Elsie's stand for 'unity without uniformity' and for 'unity without organic union' was given national publicity in *The Guardian*, as well as being reported on the front pages of the Christian newspapers, *The Methodist Recorder* and *The British Weekly*.[15] Undoubtedly Elsie's personal prominence enabled the Congregational Federation's position to gain greater publicity than otherwise could have been expected.

In late 1976, Elsie was one of four who issued 'Ten New Points on Christian Unity', in response to the Ten Propositions on unity which the Churches Unity Commission had published in January that year. With her fellows she objected to the uniformity which, in their view, was required by the Churches Unity Commission's ten propositions and also to, what they saw as, the imposition of bishops on the free churches. Rather they called for the denominations to extend 'mutual recognition' to one another. Elsie called upon all the Congregational Federation churches to discuss the 'Ten New Points' and to inform her if they found them acceptable. The Churches Unity Commission's ten propositions were eventually taken as the basis for a covenant between the United Reformed Church, the Church of England, Methodists, Moravians and the Churches of Christ.[16]

On behalf of the Congregational Federation Elsie attended the Churches Council for Covenanting in England which began in great optimism in 1978, and which emerged from the Churches Unity Commission. The Churches Council for Covenanting's brief was to draft a form of covenant for the English churches within two years.

15. *Congregational News* (March–April 1976), pp. 2, 3.
16. *Congregational News* (November–December 1976), p. 1; *Congregational News* (January–February 1977), p. 4. Davey and Dawkins, *The Story of the BCC*, pp. 10, 21.

In November 1979 she reported that the attitude of several delegates to the Church of England's General Synod, about the ordination of women, raised serious difficulties for those denominations which already accepted women ministers. Divisions on this thorny doctrinal issue had threatened to halt the move toward covenanting, although the Churches Council for Covenanting resolved that there were grounds for continuing its work.[17]

Congregational Federation Council

By July 1978 Elsie had become the chairman of the Congregational Federation's council. Reginald Cleaves who had acquitted himself well in that office, since the Congregational Federation's inception in 1972, had been forced to take a more prominent and public role than he had desired, through his own conscientious commitment to his principles. Although Elsie was well known, both within and without the Congregational Federation, temperamentally she was not an obvious choice to occupy the chair of any committee. She was impulsive, quick to make judgments and impatient of those with whom she disagreed. At times she could mercilessly browbeat those she considered awkward, stubborn or simply wrong whilst being blind to these same faults in herself. She would not necessarily feel it important to discover the views of all present, nor to ensure that all were happy with a proposed policy.

If the chairman's role, on any committee, entails the organization and preparation for any meeting which he or she is to chair (a task Cleaves had meticulously performed) then Elsie was a poor chairman. She was neither thorough nor ordered. Some even detected her taking the occasional catnap during meetings and Elsie's time management was notoriously bad. More than one meeting, which she chaired, failed to work through its agenda in the time allotted, causing the proceedings to be resumed at a later date, an awkwardness for all, especially those with busy lives. As chairman she tolerated too many asides, too many forays into the interesting but not strictly relevant, so that the meeting could degenerate into a free for all. Yet she was warm-hearted and would encourage the shy, new member of council to contribute and, if the chairman was needed to provide leadership

17. Davey and Dawkins, *The Story of the BCC*, pp. 11, 21. *Congregational News* (November–December 1979), pp. 4, 5.

and direction, then Elsie was more effective than her critics might readily allow.

International Congregational Fellowship

The International Congregational Fellowship held a series of meetings from 9–16 July 1977. The Congregational Federation played host to an international conference of 380 Congregationalists, with representatives from the USA, Australia, New Zealand, Greece, Guyana, England, Wales and other lands, who met in the William Booth Memorial College, Denmark Hill, in south London. Lady Wilson of Rievaulx, whose husband Harold had resigned only one year earlier, as leader of the parliamentary Labour Party, and as Prime Minister, addressed the delegates. She explained that she had known Lady Stansgate for many years and was especially pleased to be among the women ministers present and to be with so many Congregationalists.[18]

Elsie also took a prominent part in the proceedings, speaking on the subject 'Unity in the Spirit' on Monday 11 July, following Lady Wilson's recollections of her childhood in a Congregational manse. Elsie spoke of her 16 years at the BBC, helping both 'simple people' and 'a lot of the great ones, Bishops and all sorts' to clarify their ideas before eight o'clock in the morning. She came to 'know people very well', working with them so early in the day and having breakfast with them. She hoped in similar fashion to be natural and unpretentious with her hearers in Denmark Hill, and warned them not to expect 'the fire and earthquake today'.[19]

She conceded, to the advocates of church unity, that 'the family of God must be united', in response to Jesus' prayer, but she saw the latest plans of the Churches Unity Commission as likely to bring about 'a new division among Christians' – those with bishops and those without. She returned to her old description of herself as 'an ecumaniac born', once again pointing to her Anglican father and Congregational mother, and then to her marriage to an Anglican parson, which all, in her mind, naturally led to her appointment as the Congregational Federation's officer for ecumenical affairs. Yet, she confessed, that she was 'not very interested in positions' as such

18. *Congregational News* (September–October 1977), pp. 2, 3.
19. A reference to Elijah's experiences in 1 Kings 19:9-12.

and was 'not very keen' to sit on the Churches Unity Commission where she was 'a voice in the wilderness' and where her voice was not liked much which, in truth, did hurt her feelings. She described her role there as having 'to battle for Unity in Diversity' and, she stated, 'I battle alone and they're all very clever people, College Professors, Bishops, I think there's an Archbishop too, and they don't know ordinary people like I know people, at least they behave as if they don't'.[20]

In May 1980 Elsie again reported on ecumenical relationships to the Congregational Federation's assembly, stating that 'a lot of water had gone under the bridge – a frightening amount – because the people who got together at first to try to work together towards unity without uniformity were getting more and more uniform'. She was saddened and feared that people would soon face the choice of going into 'a modified form of the Church of England' or of breaking 'with the ecumenical movement'. She did not believe the 'plan for covenanting … was the way to unity'. Rather she held that the Congregational Federation showed the way to unity by its 'inclusiveness', that is by not erecting barriers to exclude any 'who believe in our Lord Jesus Christ'. This positive attitude, she felt, should be communicated by Congregationalists to the churches in their neighbourhoods and, by so doing, the feeling of unity would grow and the world would know more of the gospel.[21] Again we may ponder Kenneth Slack's question to her in the early 1970s, and conclude that, perhaps somewhere deep inside herself, she did hope that the church unity movement would lead all Christians in some way to embrace the insights of the Independents.

In her attitudes to church unity, as expressed throughout the 1970s, Elsie may be accused of being simplistic, of not really listening to arguments put forward at the Churches Unity Commission and Churches Council for Covenanting, without having weighed up all the evidence from different standpoints, stating and restating her own preconceived case. In doing so, did she not simply defend an entrenched and predictable position, repeating the same thin theological gruel? This accusation is not without foundation but

20. *International Congregational Fellowship International Meetings, London, England 1977, The London Witness: Record of Proceedings* (International Congregational Fellowship, 1977), pp. 18–22.
21. *Congregational Federation Assembly: Record of Proceedings* (Nottingham: Congregational Federation 1980), p. 225.

it must be allowed that the minute Congregational Federation, by standing out from the United Reformed Church, was swimming against the tide, in seeking to maintain what was then a deeply unfashionable, if tenable position. The message she had to bring from the Congregational Federation directly challenged the spirit of the times and, in particular, affronted the Churches Unity Commission chairman, John Huxtable, who had moved from his post at the United Reformed Church to lead this inter-denominational body and its successor bodies, which aimed to discover an acceptable formula for organic union. By the same token, if Elsie did not listen to others, did anybody on the Churches Unity Commission or Churches Council for Covenanting seriously pay attention to her and the Congregational Federation, by giving more than lip service to her argument? Without doubt at the Churches Unity Commission and Churches Council for Covenanting meetings, Elsie put forward a view which most in the Congregational Federation would have supported at that time.

Surprisingly, Elsie had confessed that she was overawed by the other representatives of the Churches Unity Commission and Churches Council for Covenanting. She was not easily overawed. She was, after all, very experienced in wider ecclesiastical affairs, having attended the International Congregational Council meetings in the 1950s and 1960s and the inaugural meetings of the World Council of Churches in 1948. Of course, then she had swum with the prevailing current. Thirty years later she was attempting to progress against the tide – far more daunting and demanding. However, she had come to know leading theologians and churchmen and women in all the British denominations, through her ecumenical and international links, and while working for the BBC. Earlier still, when defying the British establishment to become an RAF chaplain, she had become well acquainted with leading parliamentarians. Elsie's record, therefore, shows that she was not easily deterred.

Yet one may understand that she felt unwelcome and hurt at these particular ecumenical gatherings. The Congregational Federation was a tiny rump of what had been, even before 1972, a small body of Christians and her plea for a different approach to unity was easily ignored or dismissed as an elderly woman's eccentricity. She justified her presence at these meetings, in part at least, by claiming to speak for the ordinary Christian, whom she understood, but whom her fellow delegates from other denominations did not. In such circumstances, she must be given credit for her courage and her witness to an unfashionable but consistent message, even though she was marginalized for so doing. Elsie had won the fickle praises of men. Now she suffered their scorn.

In 1981 the proposals for a covenant in England between the Methodists, Moravians, the United Reformed Church and the Church of England failed to gain a sufficient majority in the general synod of the Church of England. The Churches Council for Covenanting disbanded in dismay in 1982.

More Travels

In February 1977 Elsie conducted the ordination service of Ivy Morrison Knights at Old Heath Congregational Church, Colchester.[22] In January 1978, Dr John Crew Tyler was inducted to the pastorate of Vineyard Church, Richmond-upon-Thames and Elsie gave the charge to the church, amid old friends.[23] In the summer of 1978, Elsie preached at the induction of Dr Clifford Hill to Highbury Congregational Church, Cheltenham, and she led the worship at Walkden, Manchester, during the centenary celebrations of the church.[24] In March 1979 the weather was 'terrible' for George Hughes' induction as minister of Harting Congregational Church, West Sussex, but the church was filled to capacity to hear Elsie preach.[25]

In the summer of 1979 she travelled to the United States of America and spent three weeks, covering hundreds of miles, visiting many Congregational churches, eating pot-luck suppers, attending dinners, barbecues and lunch parties. As on her previous visit, she found the worship 'more formal' than in England, with 'more professional music'. At the national assembly of the Congregational Christian Churches of the USA in Claremont College, California, Elsie delivered a 45 minute lecture on 'Congregationalism and Ecumenicity' and took part in two study groups – one on marriage and the other on the world Church. Her views, she discovered, were not always shared by her hosts although she enjoyed the 'lively and exciting time' which she had with them.[26]

22. *Congregational News* (May–June 1977), p. 15.
23. *Congregational News* (May–June 1978), p. 16.
24. *Congregational News* (November–December 1978), p. 19; *Congregational News* (January–February 1979), p. 16.
25. *Congregational News* (July–August 1979), p. 15.
26. *Congregational News* (November–December 1979), pp. 6, 7.

Within five days, in October 1979, Elsie took part in two inductions. On Saturday, 6 October, she presided at Beer, in Devon, to which Tom Cox had moved from Crediton. On Wednesday, 10 October, she gave the charge at the induction of Kenneth Chambers to the pastorate of Victoria Church, Blackpool.[27] In April 1980 Elsie was again the speaker at the Congregational Federation Youth's Easter conference. Seventy-six young people from 21 churches gathered at Hutton Free, Elsie's former church in Essex. The theme of her five talks was 'Love is'. Among other events, the young people were also taken on a visit to Greensted parish church. They had not found a venue for their conference until the eleventh hour when Elsie had suggested Hutton. This shows the continuing regard for her at her former church. She had just resigned its ministry, with many at Hutton not understanding her decision. Yet the church members were persuaded at little notice to open their homes to these visitors and provide for them, on Elsie's recommendation.[28]

In June 1980 Elsie gave the Dr Shergold Memorial Address to the Congregational lay preachers' annual conference also at Hutton.[29] In July 1980 Elsie attended the 400th anniversary celebrations at the Old Meeting House, Colegate, Norwich, and spoke on 'Congregationalism at the present'.[30] In June 1980 she attended the Congregational Federation's south west area women's rally at Idle, Devon. Two weeks later she conducted the morning and evening services at the new Congregational cause in Bournemouth, on the occasion of that church's first anniversary.[31] In 1980 she offered her help to the restoration of the Pennymoor building at Poughill, also in Devon, where young people were assisting in the church's development.[32]

Where Next?

In April 1980 Elsie Chamberlain had left her pastorate at Hutton. By training Irene Blayney 'on the job' and installing her as pastor at Kentish Town in 1979, Elsie had prepared the way for the loosening

27. *Congregational News* (January–February 1980), p. 15.
28. *Congregational News* (January–February 1980), p. 11; *Congregational News* (September–October 1980), p. 15.
29. *Congregational News* (May–June 1980), p. 13.
30. *Congregational News* (May–June 1980), p. 30.
31. *Congregational News* (September–October 1980), p. 18.
32. *Congregational News* (September–October 1980), p. 19.

of her ties there also. In May 1980 at the Congregational Federation assembly in Bristol Elsie announced that she intended to take 'a sabbatical' but was 'prepared to visit any churches that cannot keep going or are about to close'. Others may ask if that is really a sabbatical or is it just doing your work somewhere else? Nevertheless, Elsie knew that she had a talent for rescuing church fellowships, especially those which others might be tempted to write off as beyond saving. Certainly the Congregational Federation presented her with a challenge for it had many small churches in town and country, up and down the land. Elsie announced that she was 'available for service' for the remainder of 1980 from July onwards, although in truth she was then also thinking about a new pastorate. She declared that she was prepared to visit any church and stay for one day or one month. She was then still living in the manse at Hutton.[33]

In September 1980, Long Compton Congregational Church, Warwickshire, was visited by Elsie and Irene Blayney who spent a week in the village, delivered leaflets and visited every house, ending their time there with an open meeting at the church, on the first Thursday in October. Church attendances had been dwindling for some time and the open meeting brought out several new ideas – a young people's group, a musicians group, a Bible study meeting and others.[34]

However, Elsie was not to be without a church of her own for very long for in late 1980, she accepted the pastorates of the Congregational churches at Chulmleigh in Devon and in North Street, Taunton, in Somerset.[35] Yet this compulsion to help struggling causes had not left her and she would find many opportunities to make telling interventions in the years to come. While serving as Congregational Federation president, she had come to know at first hand the dire needs of some Congregational Federation churches, often with dis-spirited congregations. She announced to the assembled delegates in May 1980, 'I know a church that refuses to change its ways one wit (sic!) in order to bring in more people; I know two other churches that together could become a community centre but they are ... jealous of each other.'[36] Such obvious weaknesses provoked and stimulated

---

33. *Congregational News* (July–August 1980), p. 6.
34. *Congregational News* (January–February 1981), p. 4.
35. *Congregational News* (March–April 1981), p. 4.
36. *Congregational Federation Assembly: Record of Proceeedings*, p. 241.

her to action. Not for her the inertia of old age, the gentle lapse into physical frailty or senility. If the Congregational Federation churches must change to live, perhaps radically, she was ready to initiate the change and to act the part of midwife at the re-birth, albeit a very experienced, and rather elderly, midwife.

Thus Elsie discovered and developed a new calling. At the age of 70 years, when her contemporaries had been retired for some time, she was ready and willing to give the kiss of life to ailing congregations, to become a one woman flying hospital service, a paramedic for churches, who brought succour and a cure, if possible, to sickening, weary and neglected flocks. She had not founded the Congregational Federation but, having cast in her lot with it, she would do her considerable best to maintain it and to save its churches. Making no concessions to age, she showed no signs of flagging.

Chapter 17

GOING WEST, 1980

In 1980 Elsie Chamberlain began two new ministries in the west of England, at Chulmleigh, in Devon, and at Taunton, in Somerset. The two churches are situated over 40 miles apart and this unusual pastorate required Elsie to make the journey between them at least twice a week, because she intended to spend half her time with one church and half with the other. Taunton is an historic town, with a castle dating from the twelfth and thirteenth centuries, which is noted as the site of the 'Bloody Assizes' of the notorious Judge Jeffreys, following the failure of the Duke of Monmouth's rebellion against the Roman Catholic King James II in 1685, after which many of his forlorn supporters were condemned to death. Chulmleigh is an old market town, situated on the hills of north Devon, with a parish church dating from the fifteenth century. Despite their obviously attractive settings, these churches were to offer Elsie no soft options in her later years. She certainly did not see herself as settling down to a comfortable sinecure by which, in exchange for her stipend, she undertook the minimum of duties in two idyllic backwaters.

Indeed, if Chulmleigh might be seen as a tiny Nonconformist community in a small country settlement, superficially seeming to demand little from her, Taunton's needs were evidently greater. Taunton is a busy county town, prone to traffic jams, with its fair share of the usual problems found in any comparably sized commercial community – unemployment, restless youth, a sense of hopelessness, the poor, the elderly and lonely etc. Elsie may have felt that both churches had settled down too much, were stuck in a rut and needed positive ideas and effective change. She did not feel sorry for herself, although her husband had only died two years before, and his loss remained a bitter blow. She saw these churches as needing her unique kind of revival. She intended to shake them up a bit, to make waves and to help them to grow. That is what she had always done. She could promise the church members excitement and stimulation but not rest. Perhaps they suspected that they were to experience an overhaul but it is doubtful that they could have had much inkling of how thorough it would be.

Elsie's previous ministerial experience had been chiefly in urban or commuter settings. Although her pioneering work, as the first woman chaplain in the RAF, took her far from London, her time at the BBC ensured that she was based in the capital. Truth to tell in 1980 Elsie was still actively involved with the Congregational church at Kentish Town where, since the previous year, she had played a pivotal role in rescuing the church from its expected closure, and she continued that involvement until, at least, May 1981 when she was back again in north London, chairing the church meeting there.[1] She was essentially a Londoner, born and bred, at her ease in the big city, amid the noise and crowds, and she enjoyed responding to the unceasing demands of the capital's ever-changing population. However, it would be foolish to infer that before 1980 Elsie knew little about the West Country. She had, after all, been visiting the area at regular intervals as she and her husband had owned a house, overlooking Kit Hill, near Callington in Cornwall, north west of Plymouth, for several years and, although Elsie clearly felt a call to the two churches, her fondness for and knowledge of Somerset and Devon must have weighed in her decision to go west.

In 1980 Elsie was also much involved in work for the Congregational Federation nationally. She was still the chairman of the Congregational Federation's council and in addition she was the Congregational Federation's officer for ecumenical relationships. She was also deeply affected by the death of Reginald Cleaves in hospital in Leicester in July that year. He had not only been the prime mover behind both the Congregational Federation and that earlier body which had steered it into being, the Congregational Association, but he had also been among its most prudent counsellors and, although he had been unwell for some time, his death was largely unexpected and removed his quiet strength and wisdom from her and her Congregational Federation colleagues. They would miss his qualities in the months and years to come. In the following spring Elsie would launch a memorial fund for Cleaves, to provide a suitable remembrance at the new Congregational Centre in Nottingham.[2]

1. Kentish Town Congregational Church, Church Meeting Minutes, 7 May 1981.
2. *Congregational News* (September–October 1980), p. 1; *Congregational News* (July–August 1981), p. 4. A portrait of Reginald Cleaves by Roy Porter was later unveiled at the Congregational Federation's base in Nottingham.

The Move to the West

Elsie's move to the West Country was the result of a series of decisions in the summer of 1980. The minister of North Street since April 1974 had been Gerald Gossage, at whose induction service Elsie had herself presided. After five and a half years he had resigned his pastorate there and had moved to become the minister of Hanham Road Congregational Church, Kingswood, Bristol in September 1979. After learning that she was seeking a pastorate, on 24 July 1980 the deacons of North Street decided to invite Elsie to preach, with a view to her becoming their minister and, one week later, the church meeting unanimously endorsed this invitation. On 27 August it was reported that Elsie had replied, accepting the invitation. She had by then already agreed to be the part-time minister of Chulmleigh Congregational Church where she succeeded a series of pastors who from 1970 to 1979 had given only qualified oversight to the church. She had also had first hand experience of the church at Chulmleigh because she had first preached there in 1958 when it was without a minister. Therefore, if appointed at Taunton, she would have only a part-time ministry there. Elsie had also explained to the North Street deacons that she would not wish to live in the manse alone and had asked them if she might offer accommodation to another person. She cared no more for being alone than she did for being idle. She stated frankly that she would see her appointment at Taunton as 'caretaking' and as 'comparatively short term'. On the same day the deacons' meeting at Chulmleigh learned that Elsie had offered to live in the manse there and conduct services at the church during the winter months.[3]

Initially then it appears that Elsie may not have intended to stay very long in either of these churches. A one year pastorate was mentioned in October at Taunton and in 1988 she wrote of having initially offered six months' service to Chulmleigh. As it transpired, she would remain at Chulmleigh as minister for nearly three years (although she was a significant presence there much longer) and at

3. *Congregational News* (July–August 1974), p. 14; *Congregational News* (January–February 1980), p. 15. L. Fisher, *History of Chulmleigh Congregational Church* (Chulmleigh: the author, 1997), p. 10. North Street Congregational Church, Church Meeting Minutes Book 1966–1983, 31 July 1980; Deacons' Meeting Minutes Book 1972–1980, 24 July, 27 August, 1980, Chulmleigh Congregational Church Deacons' Meeting Minutes Book 1969–1983, 27 August 1980.

North Street for six, far longer than she had originally intended, but how could she have set a firm date for her departure at that early stage? Until she had begun her ministry in these two places she would not really have understood the problems nor known how best they might be tackled. Only after having become acquainted with the people, could she have set realistic targets for her work.

On 23 October 1980 the North Street deacons passed a proposal to offer Elsie a part-time ministry at their church. One deacon abstained. The church meeting discussed this recommendation from the deacons later that same evening. If appointed, she was to have half the minister's stipend plus expenses (a total of approximately

Figure 17.1 Elsie at Chulmleigh. Photograph by Ian Anderson L.M.P.A. Reproduced with his permission.

£2,000 per annum). She expected to conduct morning worship each Sunday and evening worship and communion on the third Sunday of each month. She would normally be in Chulmleigh on Sunday evenings and on Mondays, Tuesdays and Wednesdays. Then she would travel to Taunton to spend Thursdays, Fridays, Saturdays and Sunday mornings there. The appointment was expected to be for about a year and it would start in December. Thirty-one church members voted for Elsie to be their minister on these terms, three were against the motion and, again as at the deacons' meeting, one abstained.[4]

Before October 1972 Taunton had other Congregational churches besides North Street but Paul's Meeting and Bishop's Hull, each proudly dating their foundations to 1662, had chosen to join the new United Reformed Church. North Street had originally been formed in 1843, by a group which had seceded from Paul's Meeting, but it had enjoyed friendly contacts with its parent church and other local Congregationalists for many years. They had joined together in founding Taunton School, in the mid-nineteenth century, and, even after the awkward disruptions of 1972, the ministers of these churches had succeeded in maintaining good relations.

Chulmleigh

In the summer of 1980 Ted and Mary Wilson, personal members of the Congregational Federation, from Solihull in the West Midlands, paid their first visit to the Congregational church at Chulmleigh on a Sunday and found that the town 'was at tea'. Although there was 'not a soul about', they reported, 'the place did not feel deserted'. Rather they were 'delighted' with it and momentarily thought that they had been transported back in time to the 1920s when some places they had known in Warwickshire and Worcestershire had been 'like that, particularly on Sundays'. To the Wilsons, on this visit, in holiday mood and, therefore, perhaps looking through rose-coloured spectacles, Chulmleigh was 'forever England'.

They were directed to the Congregational chapel and, finding that they were early but the door was open, they entered. Inside they sensed the atmosphere of this small but ancient building, decorated with heraldic designs, representing 'the man who gave the land', John

4. North St Deacons' Meeting Minutes, 23 October 1980; Church Meeting, 23 October 1980.

Bowring, a local merchant, and 'the man who built the chapel', Lewis Stucley. They admired the minstrels' gallery, the antique Bible box, the fine pulpit with its effective sounding board, and the white dove, seemingly 'lost in the clouds'. In these prayerful surroundings, they were impressed by the ease with which they were able to sit quietly and 'consider him'. They found the chapel 'splendidly maintained' and 'clean', with its brass shining, having 'the patina of age' but with 'no trace of mustiness' and concluded that it was 'greatly loved'. The Wilsons felt blessed by their experience and nominated the chapel at Chulmleigh as a place of pilgrimage for modern Congregationalists.[5]

The Congregational church at Chulmleigh has long claimed that it was founded as early as 1633 (some nine years before the English Civil War allowed the Independents to gather their churches openly and almost 30 years before the Great Ejection of 1662), a claim which Elsie herself reiterated, although this early date has been disputed. Lewis Stucley was a notable Devon Congregationalist who was ejected from his parish living in Exeter in 1662 and who preached in several places in the county, until his death in 1687. His link to Chulmleigh may then be genuine, and lends some credibility to its claim for early Congregational associations, but the Congregational historian, T.G. Crippen, noted in the 1920s that John Moore of Tiverton had given ten shillings to the building of the meeting place at 'Chimleigh', some 48 years after 1662, and 77 years after 1633, in 1710. More recently, Charles Surman questioned why licences were issued to meeting places, in the houses of John Bowring and Digory Cock (another local Dissenter), in 1672, if there was already an existing place of worship in the town. Surman concluded that the claim for a foundation of the church in 1633 was 'very doubtful'. Recent local researchers have suggested 1662 as a probable foundation date. These academic details, however interesting for historians, should not detract from the charm of the present chapel which dates from the early eighteenth century, probably from 1710, but admittedly is resonant with antiquity and must have accorded admirably with the simple, dignified worship of the Dissenters who met there.[6]

5. *Congregational News* (September–October 1980), pp. 4–5.

6. J.G. Cording, *A Short History of the Congregational Church, Chulmleigh, Devon* (Chulmleigh: the author, 1933), p. 7. H. Holland, *A Short History of Chulmleigh Congregational Church Devon 1633–1983* (Chulmleigh: the author, 1983), Preface, p. 1. T.G. Crippen, 'John Moore of Tiverton' in *Transactions of the Congregational Historical Society Vol IX* (London: Congregational Historical

Elsie herself felt something of the same sentiment as the Wilsons, describing it in 1988 as 'The lovely old chapel at Chulmleigh'. She stated then that she had originally offered her ministry to the church members there for six months and that she had 'always been an espouser ... of problem churches'. She explained further that she did not 'believe in churches closing down and buildings being sold. It looks like a lack of faith in the future.' As a result 'several times', she continued, she had intervened 'to bring a little weight to bear on the side of renewal'.[7] In 1981 she had spoken with conviction of the need of the village churches in Devon which on Sundays, she stated, were 'mostly preached to by Plymouth Brethren ... and it's not quite Congregationalism, believe you me!'[8] It seems, therefore, that Chulmleigh and other churches which she had served in her latter years, but probably not North Street, Taunton and Hutton, should be understood as Elsie's renewal projects where her 'little weight' had been tellingly applied. Certainly Kentish Town should be seen in that light and she was to identify several others during her foray into the West Country. Having resolutely set her hands to the plough, Elsie would not look back.

Early Days in Somerset and Devon

Elsie was present at the deacons' meeting at Chulmleigh on 12 November, 1980 and made the suggestion that she should hold a 'speakers class', in order to encourage people to 'talk up the church' and to attract more people to attend the Sunday services. She had held similar classes at Hutton where she had succeeded in encouraging participants to gain confidence in public speaking. Did she use them also to spot potential lay preachers or ministers? In January 1981 Elsie announced that she would be holding speakers classes twice monthly at North Street, Taunton, also. She had found a winning formula

Society, 1924–26), pp. 186. Fisher, *History of Chulmleigh*, A Memorandum on the dating of the Chapel is kept at the chapel. See also, Charles Surman's manuscript note on the flyleaf of Cording's history in Dr Williams's Library, London. For Stucley, see, A.G. Matthews, *Calamy Revised* (Oxford: Oxford University Press, 1934), p. 469.

7. J. Hibbs, *The Country Chapel* (Newton Abbot: David & Charles, 1988), p. 9.

8. *International Congregational Fellowship 2nd International Meetings, Bangor, Gwynedd, North Wales, 1981, The Bangor Challenge: Record of Proceedings* (International Congregational Fellowship), p. 28.

and would see how it might work in these different settings. The deacons at Chulmleigh noted that the local Comprehensive College was to have a carol service on 19 December in the church.[9] Elsie was beginning to make her presence felt in the community. At Taunton the induction and service of welcome for the new minister at North Street was held on Saturday, 6 December 1980.[10]

Elsie was determined that her two churches should make a greater impact on the local communities. North Street Congregational Church is set back from the road, partially hidden by the buildings to the front, although it is situated in a busy shopping area at the hub of the town. It is, therefore, possible for the thousands who pass every day to walk by the church's entrance without noticing it. Elsie decided that the church needed to have a more visible presence. Consequently she would often stand where the path leading to the church buildings met the pavement, in her ministerial garb, to engage in friendly chatter with Taunton's passing population. By February 1981 a new notice board had been erected outside North Street and leaflets had been printed, for distribution by recruits from the congregation. A box, to carry leaflets detailing the church's activities and encouraging enquiries, was to be fixed to the church gate so that passers by could help themselves to these. Also in February Elsie began her practice at the church meetings of airing what she called the minister's concern. That month she brought the church members' attention to the fact that not all the members were present regularly at Sunday worship. She appealed for those with their own transport to offer lifts to those without cars.[11]

At Chulmleigh in March 1981 Elsie was settling into the manse, busily decorating the bedrooms. Characteristically she also had plans to develop the musical side of the church's life and invited all those with instruments to form 'an instrumental party'. Later she would hold 'an instrument evening once a fortnight' and she formed a choir to practise singing hymns on Monday evenings. Her encouragement of music in the town also included her giving violin lessons to the

9. Chulmleigh Congregational Church Deacons' Meeting Minutes, 12 November 1980. North St Congregational Church, Church Meeting Minutes, 29 January 1981.

10. North St Deacons' Meeting Minutes, 20 November 1980, *Congregational News* (March–April 1981), p. 4.

11. North St Deacons' Meeting Minutes 1981–1994, 12 February, 26 February 1981.

children. In her entry in *Who's Who* Elsie listed only one recreation, music. She announced that she intended that the church should hold services during Holy Week, a departure from tradition for rural Nonconformists in Devon![12]

The annual general meeting at North Street, in March 1981, noted that the church members shared a feeling of confidence in the future although, one month later, Elsie informed the deacons that 'more enthusiasm' was required from them. They discussed the possible removal of some pews from the rear of the church to make room for serving coffee and for greeting 'new friends'. Nobody dared suggest that new friends would not come! That same day the minister's concern at the church meeting was how best such newcomers might be welcomed. On the recommendation of the deacons, the meeting agreed to move forward the time of the morning services, in the summer months, from 11 to 10 am. To reinforce the welcoming fellowship at the church, the meeting agreed also to serve coffee at the rear of the building after the service.

The early start began in May on a three months' trial. It was explained that worshippers were enabled to enjoy a cup of coffee for 15 minutes and could become better acquainted with each other. Afterwards, if desired, they still would have time for a day out with their families. In June the church meeting minutes record that the 10 am start had been well received and that 'a good number' had stayed for the coffee. However, more volunteers were wanted to offer lifts in their cars and teachers were needed in the Sunday School – a sure sign that the children's work was progressing.[13]

Steady Progress

In the summer of 1981 Elsie responded to an enquiring Congregationalist who had complained that he knew very little of any ecumenical ventures involving churches in the Congregational Federation. She stated that her Chulmleigh church had 'a permanent two-way arrangement' with the local Methodists, in which the Congregationalists united with the Methodists for the Sunday

12. Chulmleigh Congregational Church Deacons' Meeting Minutes, 22 March, 7 September 1981. *Who Was Who 1991–1995* (London: A & C Black, 1996), pp. 91–92.

13. North St Church Meeting Minutes, 25 March, 23 April, 28 May, 25 June 1981; Deacons' Meeting Minutes, 23 April 1981.

morning service and, in their turn, the Methodists joined the Congregationalists on a Sunday evening. Whatever the ecumenical merits of this scheme may have been, it did mean, of course, that Elsie who would be present in Chulmleigh on a Sunday evening but not in the morning, would always be preaching to a united congregation, and also presumably to a fuller one. She continued to explain that on Good Friday, 1981 over forty members of 'a gathered choir' sang part of Handel's *Messiah* at the Congregational chapel and repeated their performance at the parish church on Easter Day. She confessed that she herself had been the conductor. We may be in no doubt that she had also been the moving spirit behind this venture.

She commented on one interesting development at 'her Taunton church'. Here she had gathered four ministerial volunteers – Baptist, Church of England, Roman Catholic and United Reformed Church – to share in a 'Spouters' Corner', as she called it, which took place on the forecourt of the Congregational church.[14] Was it similar to the early morning gatherings she had arranged in The City Temple in the early 1970s? She did not state how successful this venture at Taunton had been, although it does not appear to have been repeated. Yet she was determined that her church should make an impression upon those who walked down North Street. She had not gone to Taunton to acquiesce in the locals ignoring the church's presence.

By September 1981 North Street's deacons had decided that the provision of coffee on a Sunday morning had proved worthwhile and they also felt that the earlier time for the morning service had been justified, so much so that they recommended that the time remain at 10 am throughout the coming winter. In addition, they commented favourably on the keeping of children in the church, for the whole of the service. Contrary to the fears of some, the children had behaved well. The church members, later that month, heard from the minister that the church needed to be 'a family' which should 'open its arms and have love to spare'. In her view the Taunton church needed 'prayer, love and a readiness to try new approaches'. Only then would it have a future but, without these gifts, she prophesied that it had nothing to look forward to. Had she met resistance to her initiatives for positive change? Such solemn language suggests so. The members recognized that Elsie had brought vitality and stimulation to the church and in October 1981 they remarked upon the success of

14. *Congregational News* (September–October 1981), pp. 7–8.

the children's work, reflected in the 'Amazing growth of the Sunday Club', reminiscent of similar comments made in Friern Barnet and Richmond-upon-Thames. They noted as well that in December the church would have reached a 'landmark' as Elsie would have been their minister for one year.[15] In January 1982 Elsie shared her monthly 'minister's concern' with the Taunton church meeting, asking that members might consider encouraging their friends and neighbours who do not attend any place of worship to come with them to North Street.[16]

Henstridge

In late April 1982 she reported to the church that she had organized a party of volunteers to attempt 'to uplift' the Congregational church at Henstridge, a village also in Somerset, some 40 miles from Taunton. This 'spring-cleaning' at Henstridge had actually occurred, only a few days before the North Street church meeting, and it was explained that the Henstridge church needed help because it consisted of only one church member and 30 children. In her earlier appeal, Elsie had asked for volunteers to visit the Henstridge villagers in their homes and also to clean the church buildings. She stated that the Congregational church there was the only Free church in the village. 'We shall visit everyone to see who is interested', she announced, 'and then clean the church and hall and hold a family rally on Sunday morning'. Those who offered their help were told that they needed 'a sleeping-bag, a scrubbing-brush and the joy of the Lord'.[17] The first two were clearly required for physical needs and the latter was essential for conveying Christian good news, through the distribution of pamphlets and personal visits, to the neighbourhood. This essentially practical recipe which Elsie recommended to the helpers at Henstridge seems to sum up her own simple approach to church work and, of course, she specialized in the last of her three ingredients. She brought with her 'the joy of the Lord'.

The spring-cleaning at Henstridge resulted in 52 people attending a general meeting on the Wednesday and in an encouraging 49 coming

15. North St Deacons' Meeting Minutes, 10 September 1981; Church Meeting Minutes, 24 September, 22 October.

16. North St Church Meeting Minutes, 28 January 1982.

17. *Congregational News* (March–April 1982), p. 3. North St Church Meeting Minutes, 22 April 1982.

to the morning worship there on the following Sunday. In July 1982 the news from Henstridge was still described as 'heartening' although the official statistics do not reflect that optimism. The official returns for 1981–1982 state that the church at Henstridge had 5 members, 4 adherents and 16 children and that only one service was held each month, at 2.45 pm on a Sunday afternoon. In 1983 the figures indicate no change in these categories although the word 'closed' follows the church's name in the year book and no service details are recorded. In 1984 the returns indicate only 2 members, 8 adherents and 20 children, with a weekly service on Sunday at 11.00 am, but now Ronald Stockley was noted as the pastor. Stockley, who had been the pastor at the Congregational Church at Stalbridge, near Sturminster Newton, in Dorset since 1980, later was described as having settled at Henstridge in 1982. He was still there in 1986 when he had acquired Geoffrey Trimby as the assistant pastor. That year the returns still state only 2 members (presumably in addition to the two pastors) but the number of children had increased to 30. In 1990–1991 the membership had halved to one and, in the following year, G. Davies was the pastor but the church then had no members (although it still served 20 children). In 1994 the church at Henstridge ceased to appear in the *Congregational Year Book*.[18] Elsie's valiant efforts at Henstridge appear not to have had the results that she desired in the long term, but should she not have made them? Cynics will say that the closure was predictable and that Elsie and her volunteers should have realized this and resigned themselves to the uncomfortable fact. The eventual outcome does suggest that she should have saved her energies but the Church of Christ was not founded by cynics. In every case local factors, as well as national trends, have their impact.

18. *Congregational Year Book 1981–1982* (Nottingham: Congregational Federation, 1982), p. 92; *Congregational Year Book 1983* (Nottingham: Congregational Federation, 1983), p. 96; *Congregational Year Book 1984* (Nottingham: Congregational Federation, 1984), p. 94; *Congregational Year Book 1985* (Nottingham: Congregational Federation, 1985), p. 98; *Congregational Year Book 1985–1986* (Nottingham: Congregational Federation, 1986), p. 60; *Congregational Year Book 1986–1987* (Nottingham: Congregational Federation, 1987), p. 60; *Congregational Year Book 1987–1988* (Nottingham: Congregational Federation, 1988), pp. 60, 61; *Congregational Year Book 1988–1989* (Nottingham: Congregational Federation, 1989), p. 62; *Congregational Year Book 1989–1990* (Nottingham: Congregational Federation, 1990), p. 63; *Congregational Year Book 1990–1991* (Nottingham: Congregational Federation, 1991), p. 61; *Congregational Year Book 1991–1992* (Nottingham: Congregational Federation, 1992), p. 64.

Certainly her experience at Kentish Town would have justified her in not accepting at face value the depressing conclusions which some might have preferred.

Elsie's desire to save not 'lost causes' but 'problem churches', as she called them, was also revealed at this time in her concern for the Congregational church at Stawell, near Bridgwater, in Somerset, and for her involvement with the re-opened church at Pennymoor, Poughill, near Tiverton, in Devon. In May 1982 Elsie expressed her gratitude for 'the large gathering' at Pennymoor which gave encouragement to all those who had worked hard to re-open the building for regular worship.[19]

Developments at Chulmleigh

In the spring of 1982, Elsie happened upon an original way of supplementing the restoration fund at Chulmleigh. Somewhat sacrificially she decided to offer accommodation in her manse there to visitors whom she described as 'do it yourself ones', by which she presumably meant self-catering visitors, at £7 per person per week. She also commented that Chulmleigh was an 'excellent spot' for a retired minister or a lay pastor 'with plenty of enthusiasm', thus, by praising its virtues, she cast her net wide to catch a potential successor. She stated that the church had one Sunday service at 6 pm, as well as a family service, and, most remarkable of all, that the congregation had trebled during the past year. A Sunday afternoon school was planned to begin in the coming February. The church also boasted an 'orchestra' and a choir for 'special music' which, she proudly stated, had performed Handel's *Messiah* last Easter and was then preparing Stainer's *Crucifixion* for Easter that year.[20] Arguably her repertoire, or what she considered the works which a village choir could cope with, was a little limited.

In October 1982 Elsie told her deacons at Chulmleigh that she intended to leave the church in the following year but that she had high hopes of finding a suitable minister to succeed her. In November she asked her Taunton church members to give support to Chulmleigh during its 350th anniversary celebrations, planned

19. *Congregational News* (September–October 1980), p. 19. North St Church Meeting Minutes, 22 April 1982. Hibbs, *The Country Chapel*, p. 9.
20. *Congregational News* (March–April 1982), p. 3.

for 1983. She was hoping then to attract Cliff Richard to come to Chulmleigh to sing but, if he was not able to accept, then the choir would at least perform *The Messiah* in July 1983. In February 1983 Elsie told the deacons at Chulmleigh that she expected to leave them in August that year but she had good news. Elaine Marsh, an experienced Congregational minister from Minneapolis, Minnesota, in the United States of America, would be coming to take her place (had she asked the church meeting's agreement to this first?). Initially Elaine had been asked to come for two years but prudently she had committed herself to only one year at Chulmleigh. The contrast for Elaine could hardly have been greater, moving from a church in Minneapolis of 2,000 members to a small Devon chapel.[21]

Not Quite Leaving Chulmleigh – A Constant Good Friend

Elsie did not easily relinquish her pastoral concern for the folk at Chulmleigh. On leaving their ministry in August 1983, she gave two stationery books to the church for the recording of the minutes of the deacons' meeting and for those of the church meeting. In September 1983, although she was no longer the minister and Elaine Marsh was then present chairing the meeting (and probably occupying the manse), the deacons reported that Elsie had given a new bath to the manse and it was ready to be installed. At that same meeting the suggestion was made that Elsie should be asked to accept the title of 'Minister Emeritus' of the church. The choir had made known its keenness to continue so Elsie had agreed to lead it once a month, travelling over from Taunton, as no other conductor or accompanist had come forward. One month later Elsie had consented to accept the title of minister emeritus and she also had written to state that an interest free loan would be available shortly to the church, for the purpose of buying a new property in Church Close, to replace the existing manse. The old five bed-roomed manse was then put up for sale and Elsie, Elaine Marsh and two others were to form a small committee to oversee the sale. Elsie was determined that the old manse should go and set her heart on the church purchasing a new one. The deacons agreed to accept the loan with gratitude. In Elaine's

21. Chulmleigh Deacons' Meeting Minutes, 25 October 1982, 13 February 1983. North St Church Meeting Minutes, 25 November 1982. Hibbs, *The Country Chapel*, p. 9.

time at Chulmleigh, when Elsie stayed overnight, she would sleep downstairs in the manse's dining room, in a chair which 'let out', while Elaine herself used a bedroom. Somewhat eerily Elaine felt an unpleasant presence in the living room which was later explained by the discovery that the sewer, which flowed under the house, had developed a leak and an unpleasant odour had escaped.

Elsie was back in Chulmleigh in November 1983 leading worship in the church. In December, Elaine Marsh took the chair at the deacons' meeting but Elsie was among those attending and she opened the meeting in prayer. Elsie was also present at the church and deacons' meetings in January and February 1984, although Elaine Marsh chaired on both occasions. However in May, Elaine informed the deacons that she was returning to the USA in July, thus bringing to a close the year of ministry which she had originally agreed to give to Chulmleigh. At this same meeting it was stated that Elsie was again endeavouring to find a minister for the church but also that she had herself consented to preach at the church in the autumn.[22]

At the annual general meeting in July 1984, Elsie was in the chair. It was stated that, although Elaine Marsh had become their minister in August 1983, Elsie had 'continued to be a constant good friend to our church'. The members decided that more communion cups and hymn books were needed – a sure sign that the congregation was growing – and Elsie volunteered to obtain them. Several church and deacons' meetings in late 1984 were chaired by Elsie. In October, she encouraged people to train as lay preachers and in November she revealed her eagerness to lead 'a candlelight get together' at 6 pm on Christmas Day. In September 1984, she had asked the lay preachers at North Street, Taunton to make a regular commitment to conduct the services at Chulmleigh on the first Sunday of every month. In December 1984 Elsie told the church that Elaine Marsh was returning in April 1985 from America for six months. In July 1985, Elsie had called a brief deacons' meeting, prior to the church's annual general meeting, at which she announced that Elaine Marsh had offered her services as minister to the church at Chulmleigh for a further two years, commencing in January 1986. The deacons were very happy at

22. Chulmleigh Church Meeting Minutes 1983 onwards, 26 October, 15 December 1983, 19 January, 16 February, 15 March 1984; Deacons' Meeting Minutes Book 1983–1997, 15 and 26 September, 1 December 1983, 19 January, 16 February, 21 May 1984.

this news. Elsewhere it was explained that Elaine had already spent two spells of time serving the church and her return merely made the point that, 'She loves the Chulmleigh people and they love her'. The same words applied to Elsie herself.

In November 1985, Elsie was again present at the church and deacons' meetings. She was to conduct 'Carols by Candlelight' on Christmas Day and she was still available to lead worship in the summer of 1986, notably a Sunday evening of singing the old favourite hymns, associated with the nineteenth century American evangelists, Moody and Sankey. Elsie's repeated involvement with Chulmleigh suggests that, although she had formally resigned the pastorate there in 1983, while she remained in the south-west, serving North Street Congregational Church, Taunton, she made herself open to help the Congregationalists at Chulmleigh whenever possible.[23]

In January 1987, Elaine Marsh and her friend, Alice Huston, made known their decision that they had put their home in Minneapolis on the market, intending to settle permanently in England. Elsie observed with satisfaction that Elaine not only came to Chulmleigh 'and saw and conquered' but that she herself had been 'conquered'. Influenced by Elsie, she had undoubtedly come to love Chulmleigh and its people and the West Country. Elsie was then still helping Chulmleigh on occasions and, in May 1987, she conducted services there on two successive Sundays.[24]

Elaine Marsh

Elaine Marsh had first met Elsie at the William Booth Memorial College, Denmark Hill, in south London at the International Congregational Fellowship meeting in 1977. Elaine was serving as the chaplain to the meetings and opened the conference with worship. On the platform were Mary Wilson, Margaret Stansgate and Elsie Chamberlain. The time for tea followed and some of the ladies, preferring not to walk across the campus to the tea rooms, took it

23. Chulmleigh Church Meeting Minutes, 5 July, 12 August, 14 October, 9 December 1984, 14 July, 24 November 1985; Deacons' Meeting Minutes, 29 November 1984, 14 July, 5 November 1985, 10 July 1986. North St Church Meeting Minutes, 27 September 1984. *Congregational Quarterly* vol. 3, no. 3 (September 1985), p. 23.

24. Chulmleigh Deacons' Meeting Minutes, 20 January 1987; Church Meeting Minutes, 24 November 1987, Hibbs, *The Country Chapel*, p. 9.

together backstage. As a result of this and other sociable contacts during the conference, the two became friends. For many years Elaine had been minister at Plymouth Church, Minneapolis, and as the date for her retirement was approaching, Elsie had asked her to consider coming to the United Kingdom to care for one of the Congregational Federation's churches. Elaine was due to retire in 1983. At the ICF committee meeting in Wisconsin, Elaine renewed her friendship with Elsie who attended with Jean Young and Felicity Cleaves. Elaine expected the English ladies to be 'rather proper' and so she decided to wear a skirt. However, all the English ladies, including Elsie, wore trousers and Elaine felt that she should not be the odd woman out so she changed into trousers.

On her return to England, Elsie kept up her correspondence with Elaine and on seeing her at the ICF meetings at Bangor in 1981 she had asked again, 'Why are you not serving a church in the UK yet?' Elaine had not then retired but she did agree to come to Chulmleigh to take over from Elsie when she left the pastorate. Elaine stated that she would come for a year while her friend, Alice, with whom she had lived for many years, remained in the USA to look after their house. Elaine's arrival on 1 July 1983 coincided with Chulmleigh Congregational Church's celebration of their 350th anniversary.

After spending a little time at Elsie's house in Cornwall, Elaine and Alice, who had joined her, felt that they knew Elsie much better. Indeed, Elaine's opinion of Elsie was to rise so markedly that she came to regard her as one of the most exceptional people she had ever met. Elaine recalled a story which literally conveys much of Elsie's no frills attitude. At an ordination service, in which she was to play a leading role, she looked down and noticed that her dress worryingly was really neither long enough nor formal enough. The remedy was obvious. She simply reached down and ripped the hem, smoothing it down with her hand. She explained that under her cassock the hem line was obscured.

While Elaine was at Chulmleigh, Elsie would drive over 'once in a while' from Taunton in her Volvo and Elaine could see that folk at Chulmleigh almost worshipped her. The success of the Sunday evening service there was helped by Elsie having no competition at that time from the Methodist and the parish churches. Even Roman Catholics joined the regulars, and some from these other churches, who worshipped at the Congregational chapel on a Sunday evening. The fellowship in the church grew in many ways – a Christmas bazaar in the town hall, a Maundy Thursday pancake supper – but, although larger numbers of people attended church events and the Sunday worship, many resisted making the full commitment to become church members. One of the Anglican women who often attended those functions, which Elsie led and inspired, was the widowed mother of a parson in London. He reported that his mother had guiltily confessed that she had gone, and wanted to continue going to the chapel to see and hear Elsie. She agonized that she was betraying her son and her own Anglicanism by enjoying so much these services with the Nonconformists. With a bemused air, he related to Congregational friends in London that she had even asked his permission to attend Elsie's activities in the chapel!

In 1984 Elsie reflected on her three and a half years' experience of West Country churchmanship. She had found that customarily 'the men leave the women to 'do the religious thing' especially in the villages' and she had observed that 'there are Church of England women outside the big towns who still look down on their Free Church neighbours, some of whom are given an inferiority complex by this old-fashioned attitude'.[25] If that attitude had ever existed in Chulmleigh, Elsie and Elaine had both done their level best to break it down, with some success. At the end of her first year in Devon, Elaine faced the necessity of returning to the USA for her friend had suffered a stroke in her absence. However, Alice's doctor advised her that she was well enough to come to England for a few weeks' holiday before they travelled home together.

Meanwhile Elsie had become concerned for the Congregational church at Dulverton, in Somerset, some 16 or 17 miles from Chulmleigh. The Dulverton church was then experiencing some difficulties. In 1984 Elsie asked Elaine to preach at Dulverton once a month, on a regular basis, and she agreed. Elaine discovered that now she could not easily leave these English West Country churches for she was even visited in the USA by friends from Chulmleigh and Dulverton – a measure of the positive impression she had made. When the time came for Elaine to end her monthly commitment to Dulverton, the church members there had a minister coming to serve them in six months, but decided to ask Elaine to continue as their minister until his arrival. In the autumn of 1984, Elaine returned from the USA to Dulverton as minister there for six months but, at that time,

25. *Free Church Chronicle*, no 3, vol XXXIX (Autumn 1984), p. 2.

Chulmleigh had no minister so she served them also. Consequently, Elaine preached on a Sunday morning in Dulverton and in the evening at Chulmleigh. In 1985, at the end of this six months' period, she agreed to return to Chulmleigh as their minister. Her companion, Alice, was to retire from her job in Minneapolis, enabling the two friends to set up home there. Elaine's promise to Elsie of a year's ministry at Chulmleigh Congregational Church led to her giving well over nine years to that church, from which she finally retired in 1992, when she moved to Dulverton which she had also served.

North Street Taunton

In April 1982 the church meeting noted that improvements to the kitchen were needed. By September a new sink and a new water heater had been installed and, in passing, the members were grateful for the increase in giving to the Sunday collections. By May 1983, the church kitchen had been re-decorated and new units had been acquired and fitted. In December 1982 the minister had shared her concern that the church at North Street, being set in the centre of Taunton, should do more for the town.

In May 1982 Elsie brought to the deacons' meeting her keen desire to have John Murray, a United Reformed Church minister who had retired to Taunton, helping with the work at North Street. She was ready to take £500 less per annum in her stipend, if the church could raise another £500 and give Murray a total of £1,000 per annum. She hoped that he would preach on Sunday evenings and assume other duties. To their credit, the deacons did not want to pay Elsie less but agreed in principle that John Murray's help would be an asset to the church. However, in June it was reported that Murray had replied, stating that he was not willing to share the ministry officially, but was prepared to assist with Sunday preaching when required.

Murray, formerly a Congregationalist, was not the only United Reformed Church minister who regularly gave support to North Street. Another frequent visitor was his friend, Owen Butler, also a former Congregationalist, who led worship regularly at North Street and, with Murray, met the minister for prayer and discussion. The records suggest that Murray's contribution to the church's life was far in excess of his restrained offer of June 1982. At the annual general meeting of the church in March 1983, Elsie thanked Murray for his valuable support throughout the past year. In April he informed the church meeting of the work of those lay missioners who were seeking to make effective contact with people on the fringes of the church. He believed that this might be a fruitful avenue for North Street to explore in its outreach. In February 1984, Murray was chairing the church meeting in the absence of the minister and he was thanked again, at the annual general meeting in March 1985, for his help throughout the previous year.[26]

Owen Butler was an old friend of Elsie's. They had known each other since he had been a student for the ministry at New College, London (where Murray had also trained) in the 1930s, before either of them had been ordained. His friend and fellow student at New College knew her family in Islington and they would have tea together. Butler's first pastorate from 1939 to 1951 was at Northampton and he had recruited Elsie to preach at his church there. After serving Congregational churches in Harrow and Hastings, he had given oversight to the United Reformed Church at Minehead 1977–1983, on the Somerset coast, and had then retired to Taunton.[27] He found Elsie to be a devoted, capable and enthusiastic friend to the church at North Street.

Miscellaneous Concerns

Other matters occupied Elsie's Taunton ministry. In December 1982 she was troubled about the elderly who would be alone at Christmas, singling out one old lady who needed a family to invite her to spend some time during the holiday with them. Elsie noted that the congregation was not good at saying 'Amen' to the prayers in worship. In June 1983 the church planned a new layout for its magazine and in April 1984 Elsie returned to two favourite themes, that of the church's publicity which, in her view, should be better and the welcoming of newcomers to the fellowship. The theft of church keys by an unwelcome intruder caused a degree of anxiety in May 1984.

A measure of the church's modest success at this time was that the Bible study meeting had grown so large that it was deemed necessary

26. North St Deacons' Meeting Minutes, 13 May, 10 June, 1982, 4 June 1983; Church Meeting Minutes, 22 April, 23 September, 16 December 1982, 17 March 1983, 23 February 1984, 25 March 1985. *United Reformed Church Year Book 1984–1985* (London: United Reformed Church, 1984).

27. *United Reformed Church Year Book 2003* (London: United Reformed Church, 2003), p. 191.

to divide into two groups. By October 1985 Elsie was encouraging the North Street folk to attend the Congregational Federation's rallies in the south-west area in greater numbers, especially when these were held in the smaller churches, close to her heart, where a good attendance would give a fillip to the local church people. In November 1985, Elsie felt that a suitable way to mark her fifth anniversary as minister at Taunton would be to invite all couples whom she had married there, and the parents of those children whom she had baptised, to attend one particular Sunday evening service and to stay for coffee afterwards.[28]

Property Considerations at North Street

In late December 1983 the church meeting learned of proposals to alter the property at the back of the church. The local social services department had indicated that they would favour the provision of a crèche for the children of shoppers in this space or alternatively the building of warden controlled flats for the mentally handicapped. The church members were also told that proposals for a music school had been made and that the voluntary sector in Taunton was in need of offices. Returning to this theme of redevelopment in March 1984, at the annual general meeting, Elsie expressed her hope that the church halls might in time be replaced by flats for the elderly. Repairs to the church property, especially to the drive, were discussed at the church meeting in May 1984.

Some frustration was clearly felt by the church in its efforts to find a viable scheme for the redevelopment of the property to its rear. In July 1984, the church members were told that the number of flats which could adequately be built in the available space would be insufficient to justify the expense involved. In January 1985 Elsie met the Member of Parliament for Taunton, the distinguished Conservative politician, Sir Edward du Cann, in an attempt to enlist his help for the desired redevelopment. He promised to do what he could.[29]

In the summer of 1985 it was revealed that the town council, wishing to enhance the appearance of the centre of Taunton, intended

28. North St Church Meeting Minutes, 9 December 1982, 23 June 1983, 12 April, 24 May, 27 September 1984; Deacons' Meeting Minutes, 7 October, 11 November 1985.
29. For Sir Edward du Cann, see *Who's Who* (London: A & C Black, 2002), p. 606.

to floodlight some of the churches, including North Street. In April 1986, she reported that she had spoken to a planning officer from the local council, enquiring whether it might be possible to build a bungalow in the church garden and gain formal approval for this. The officer had replied positively, stating that such a structure might be deemed to add to the safety of the church which is a listed building. Were the manse in Ashley Road to be put on the market, its price at that time was estimated to be in the region of £40,000– £50,000.[30]

In March 1986, an extraordinary church meeting had been held at which the minister stressed the need for a sound church roof. She stated that the sale of the manse and the building of a bungalow in the church garden would release enough money to enable the necessary roof repairs to be completed. Estimates suggested that a sum of £13,000 was required for the roof. Elsie also spoke of the alterations which were due to be carried out in the near future at the back of the church by the Manpower Services Unit. The church would be expected to fund some of this work and she stated that she wished to pay for part of the expenses herself, that is for the materials needed and the necessary heating, providing the church agreed to accept the estimate for the roof repairs and that this work commenced quickly. This offer was accepted by a clear majority. By May the order for the roof repairs had been placed and by June the work had started and was expected to be finished in three or four weeks.[31]

30. North St Deacons' Meeting Minutes, 10 February, 28 April 1986; Church Meeting Minutes, 22 December 1983, 23 February, 15 March, 26 April, 26 July 1984, 24 January 1985, 24 March 1986. *Congregational Quarterly* vol 3, no 3 (September 1985), p. 23.
31. North St Church Meeting Minutes, 24 March, 22 May, 23 June 1986.

Chapter 18

MINISTRY IN NOTTINGHAM, 1984–1991

Having acquired the former Castle Gate Congregational Church and hall premises in Nottingham from the United Reformed Church (intending to use them as offices, student rooms, and for church purposes), the Congregational Federation held a service of thanksgiving in September 1981. Those arriving early were amazed to discover Elsie, as practical and unstuffy as ever, on her knees washing the floor. Elsie hoped that the new centre in Nottingham would be 'a place where we can learn more about the faith and find new inspiration for the work that is to be done'. The formal opening of the Congregational Centre in Castle Gate occurred a year later in September 1982 when Elsie, speaking last, struck an uncharacteristically solemn note, by reminding the assembly that 'the fulfilment of the dream depends on the reality of our faith'. In truth she had herself given generously towards the cost of setting up the centre. She became a regular visitor to the Castle Gate buildings for Congregational Federation council and committee meetings. In late 1982 she addressed the Federation of Congregational Women, in the East Midlands area there, taking the theme that 'the Kingdom of God is within you' and urging those present to communicate the gospel to people outside the churches.[1]

In September 1983 the minister spoke to the deacons at North Street about the new church which was then being founded in Castle Gate, Nottingham, to which building the offices of the Congregational Federation had been moved. She had been invited to lead worship in Nottingham on two Sundays each month and, keen to accept, she sought the approval of the deacons for this arrangement. John Murray was willing to deputise for her in Taunton. Knowing the determined nature of their minister and that resisting her will was pointless, the

1. *Congregational News* (November–December 1981), p. 2; *Congregational News* (November–December 1982), p. 2; *Congregational News* (January–February 1983), p. 2, *The Bangor Challenge*, p. 28.

deacons gave their formal assent. In November she reported on these developments to the church meeting. She informed the meeting that she would be leading worship in Nottingham on alternate Sunday mornings for the next three months. In her absence from Taunton the members learned that the reliable Murray had 'graciously' agreed to conduct the services at North Street.[2] Elsie had been enthusiastic about the founding of the church in Castle Gate from its beginnings.

One must suspect that the curious invitation to Elsie to preach on two Sundays each month in Nottingham, as she reported it to the deacons at North Street, could not have been issued without her prior knowledge. Indeed it seems likely that she had herself first indicated her willingness to accept such an invitation, to a member or members of the new church in Castle Gate, Nottingham before the invitation was issued. Who else would suggest to a 73 year old woman, even one with such apparently inexhaustible energy as Elsie, that she should commit herself to a punishing regime of weekly travelling across the country? Who else would think that serious pastoral work in two churches so far from each other could realistically be accomplished?

As a result of Elsie's ministry in Nottingham, she would often travel the 185 miles between the East Midlands and Taunton on Sundays, so that she would conduct the morning service in Nottingham and the evening service in Taunton, an unenviable prospect for anyone in the prime of life but a gruelling task for a woman in her 70s. On one occasion, as has already been stated, when her own vehicle was misbehaving, Elsie was grateful for a lift from Nottingham to Taunton in the car of her friends, Millicent and Kenneth Slack. This routine of travelling between the two towns continued for two and a half years. Although Elsie was an experienced driver, opinions differ as to her prowess behind the wheel!

Not until January 1984, however, did the church at Castle Gate hold its first church meeting. At this, the members unsurprisingly were unanimous in their invitation to Elsie to become their minister although it was stated that she was to occupy this position 'in an honorary capacity'. Elsie was present in Nottingham at this church meeting which in a more settled fellowship might be considered improper but this church was in its infancy. In truth this was a missionary situation and Elsie had been involved in gathering this

2. North St Deacons' Meeting Minutes, 8 September, 1983; Church Meeting Minutes, 24 November 1983.

church almost from its beginnings. She was therefore able to give an immediate answer to the church – again unusual for a minister when invited to serve a pastorate – and she accepted.[3]

Ministry in Nottingham

At the first church meeting of the Congregational Centre church since her appointment as its minister, in February 1984, Elsie reported that her friend, Viscountess Stansgate, the first president of the Congregational Federation, then aged 86, had asked if she could become an associate church member of the new fellowship. Living in London, she would not be able to attend in person very often. The meeting agreed to her request. The church saw a small but steady flow of new members throughout 1984 and 1985 (in the latter year it had 12 members). Indeed the church made every attempt to increase its membership, approaching a number of people to consider making a commitment to the church. In January 1986, nine new members were recorded as having joined the church during the past year, making a total of 21. At the annual general meeting, Elsie commented that she wanted to maintain the church's reputation as 'a very friendly Church … a place of friendship, helpfulness and inspiration' and she hoped that in 1986 it would become 'a place of study'. She stated that she may be resident in Nottingham for the winter of 1986, instead of commuting between Somerset and Nottingham as she had been doing for two years then. Was she aware that the demands she had made on her health were beginning to take their toll? In January 1986 the Congregational Federation was noted for having expressed 'its joy' at the centre church's growth and in Elsie's final year of ministry the church returned a figure of 29 members.

In March 1985, enquiries about their using the Castle Gate church were made by Methodists in central Nottingham who were seeking a temporary home while their former place of worship was being demolished and replaced. They expected to be without their own premises for approximately one year. Elsie and John Wilcox, by then a leading member of the Congregational church in Nottingham, had met some delegates from the Methodists and discussed the possibility of joint services and shared accommodation (perhaps a united Sunday morning service and a Methodist service on Sunday evenings). The

3. Nottingham Centre Church Meeting Minutes, 15 January 1984.

Congregationalists were keen to welcome the Methodists for any period of time but in June 1985 the Methodists had still not made any firm decision and in September they felt unable to commit themselves until the new year. Eventually they found it possible to continue using part of their own building, although their minister did occupy an office in the Congregational complex in Castle Gate.

Elsie arranged to give a series of lectures at the church on biblical subjects in the five weeks before Christmas 1985 – these were later judged to be 'a highlight of the year'. One church member was keen to set up a group for depressives or perhaps leukaemia sufferers at the centre. Elsie agreed to meet a local psychotherapist to see if she could advise on the practicability of such a scheme.[4] In September 1987, a care watch centre was to be set up for Nottingham in the premises. It was intended that this would work along lines first developed within Congregational churches by John Pellow at his church in Tower Hamlets, in east London. Pellow, an unusual minister, who had written television scripts for many years, had since his ordination in 1957 only served one pastorate, Coverdale and Ebenezer, in Stepney. He was to act as an adviser to the Nottingham scheme. One year later a young theology graduate, Deborah Reynolds, was appointed to manage the Care Trust in Nottingham. Although she had completed her training for the ministry and was accepted by the church as the assistant minister from the outset, she was not ordained immediately. She was employed at the centre in Castle Gate where her title was the Nottingham Care Watch Officer. In the following January, it was stated that a service of induction and ordination for Deborah should be arranged. This occurred in April 1988.[5]

Later Years

Elsie returned to broadcasting while at Nottingham with the local radio station for which she made some Sunday morning programmes

4. Nottingham Centre Church Meeting Minutes, 19 February 1984, 11 January, 13 March, 27 June, 12 September, 13 November 1985, 19 January, 20 March 1986. *Congregational Year Book 1985* (Nottingham: Congregational Federation, 1985), p. 88; *Congregational Year Book 1990–1991* (Nottingham: Congregational Federation, 1991), p. 54.

5. Nottingham Centre Church Meeting Minutes, 22 September 1987, 20 September 1988, 10 January 1989. *Congregational Year Book 1958* (London: Congregational Union of England and Wales, 1958), p. 397.

in 1989 and she continued writing radio scripts until her death. In 1988 she was the proud guest of honour at the 60th anniversary of the BBC's daily service, broadcast from All Souls, Langham Place, London. At this time she was interviewed on BBC Radio Four's programme, *Women's Hour*, after which she stated candidly that she had enjoyed more the pre-broadcast conversation, outside the studio, with the programme's researcher, than that which had unfolded on the air. In September 1989 she proposed that the church held 'prayer services for shoppers' on Thursdays at 2.30 pm beginning in October. Elsie also was keen for the church to perform some of her musical favourites and in April 1990 the church members were described as being 'stretched' by the demands of Stainer's *Crucifixion*, while it was noted that they would soon be asked to put on Handel's *Messiah* – the two musical standards of Elsie's ministry. In February 1990 the church meeting learned that Deborah Reynolds was to marry and leave the Nottingham Care Watch group and that she would be moving to Birmingham. At this time also the Congregational Federation was considering the appointment of a warden to Cleaves Hall, the adjoining building to the church, thus relieving Elsie of her unofficial work there and allowing her to return to the manse 'if she wished'. Elsie did occupy the manse, which was situated in The Park, but she felt some pastoral responsibility for the Castle Gate residents (mostly students at the various colleges in the town who stayed in the Cleaves Hall rooms).

Having decided to buy with her brother, Ronald, one of the self-contained flats in the Castle Gate block, in memory of their mother, Elsie had naturally taken upon herself the role of an unpaid warden of Cleaves Hall. Three months later no warden had been appointed, although the centre church members had become concerned about 'the pressures on the Minister', and welcomed the church secretary's initiative 'to persuade her to spend two days per week away' from the premises in Castle Gate. This clearly was a difficult and exhausting time in Elsie's life and she made some curious decisions.

The centre of Nottingham can be a noisy place throughout the night and Elsie is remembered as having telephoned friends in Taunton, late one evening, to ask if anyone was sleeping in their spare bed. She was finding it difficult at that time to sleep in the flat in Castle Gate and, on learning that the spare bed was available, she drove through the night, arriving at 3 am. The bell rang and there stood Elsie in a plastic mackintosh, holding a cup of tea. She had been so keen to leave Nottingham that she had forgotten to pack a dressing gown![6]

At Nottingham Elsie was no autocrat in the church. She would routinely discuss her proposals with the church officers and she would take advice. She used candles once in worship and wanted to have them as a regular part of the Sunday service but, when advised to put them aside, she did so. She would listen to the church members at the church meeting and act accordingly, not forcing her desires down their throats. The members were encouraged to air their views although Elsie liked the meetings to reach agreement. However, the observant members noticed that Elsie, for all her experience, would be just as nervous before the small congregation at Nottingham as she might be before a huge audience. She was a loyal colleague and, at most of her churches, she made generous and significant financial contributions, usually anonymously.

Leaving Taunton

In the mid-1980s Elsie seems to have been aware that she needed to slow down a little, although her work-load was still considerable. She had given up her position as chairman of the council of the Congregational Federation in 1985 – a post she had held since 1978 – and in February 1986 she confided to the Taunton deacons that she feared she could not continue at North Street for another winter. She was clearly preparing them for her departure which would occur later that year. Elsie was actively looking for a successor at this time and she informed the deacons that she intended to leave the church 'on 8th June' when she would preach her last sermon at the church. She admitted that she had two people in mind whom she thought might be suitable to take over the ministry at North Street on a part-time basis. However, in this she was to suffer disappointment and in May 1986 John Murray was asked and agreed to lead the church during the gap ahead, with the title of 'interim moderator', a term then borrowed, somewhat ironically, from the United Reformed Church. In June that year Elsie was treated to a farewell luncheon at which a presentation was made to her. Also that month, Murray met the Congregational Federation's minister for pastoral settlements, Bill Bentham, to discuss the pastoral situation. Bentham had advised Murray that the church

6. Nottingham Centre Church Minutes, 20 June, 19 September 1989, 14 February, 28 April, 9 May 1990.

might yet be able to afford a full time minister, with a recommended stipend of £5,000 per annum, plus expenses of £400. In the light of this advice, the church decided to 'consider its options'. Subsequently in March 1987, Ray Avent was invited to become the minister at North Street, an invitation which he was led to accept.[7]

Following Elsie was always going to be difficult but the new minister on the whole found his inheritance at North Street beneficial, although he prudently announced to the church at the outset that he would not try to be another Elsie Chamberlain! However, like Elsie, he was greatly helped by John Murray and Owen Butler who continued for some years to be of assistance both to the church and the minister, freely giving time, wisdom and experience.

Elsie's Taunton Ministry

Elsie is recalled at Taunton as having brought energy and enthusiasm to the church, although she was also noted for her plain speaking. On her pastoral visits she always made herself at home and put people at their ease, although if she thought anyone was in the wrong then she would tell them. She was popular with everybody in the church. As the choir-mistress, she encouraged the choir in all its undertakings. Her predecessor as minister of the church, Gerald Gossage, had left it in a fairly healthy condition and she further enhanced its reputation as a family church, so that all came to feel that they belonged. Certainly Elsie made great efforts to attract more people to attend the worship and her name came to be widely known around the town. On one occasion when the church held a sale of work only a handful of people initially turned up, so Elsie took herself off to the pavement to draw passers by into the building – and they came. In her time at North Street it became customary during any church sale to put some stalls outside in the drive, especially in the summer, and this proved successful and continued after she had left. She was proud that in 1985 her Taunton church, with less than 100 members, gave £646 on one Sunday for relief work in Ethiopia and she held this up as an example of what fellowships across the country could do, if sufficiently motivated.[8] Elsie began the practice of the church

7. North St Deacons' Meeting Minutes, 10 February, 28 April 1986; Church Meeting Minutes, 22 December 1983, 23 February, 15 March, 26 April, 26 July 1984, 24 January 1985, 24 March, 22 May, 23 June 1986, 19 March 1987.

8. *Free Church Chronicle* no 1, vol XL (Spring 1985), p. 2.

members singing hymns on occasions, during the week and on a Sunday, in the church drive. Although she did not start a band at Taunton, as she had elsewhere, nevertheless she would regularly encourage those with musical instruments to play them in church.

She was not content with the architectural settings and internal design of the church. At one point she had considered moving the worship area upstairs and putting in a false floor but the professional advice received was strongly against this. The building's foundations simply would not stand the strain. North Street Congregational Church, it seemed, had been built in a hurry. Elsie was keen to have a central aisle to aid funerals and weddings but the Fire Service vetoed the alterations which might make this possible. One particular wedding, which she conducted at North Street, proved to be trying for her as children were allowed to run up and down too freely. She simply stopped the service and said to the congregation, 'Until you all behave I shall go no further'. In conversation with one of her friends in the church, she later confessed, 'You know, dear, I really prefer funerals. I know they'll be happy'!

Elsie's stated preference not to live on her own resulted in her having some young nurses living with her in the North Street manse. It was convenient for them because the hospital is situated nearby. However she sometimes took risks which others then judged 'frightening' and would later properly be frowned upon by professionals in the social services. A young man came to church one Sunday and declared that he had nowhere to stay. Consequently Elsie took him home with her, even though she had the nurses in the house. Understandably, they were not happy with the situation and made their feelings known. When later Elsie moved home from Taunton to Nottingham this same young man followed her there. Her Taunton church members were not alone in worrying for her and in believing that it had not been sensible for her to take him in as she did. Friends at Nottingham shared this same concern when they saw her take difficult people into her flat there. Some of her visitors seemed awkward, threatening and even violent and Elsie was, in the view of these friends, often deceived with fanciful stories and cheated out of her money.

Elsie was a painstaking pastor. On one occasion, the death of a church member necessitated a telephone call to the minister whom, it was believed, would be found in Chulmleigh. However, it was discovered that she was not in Devon but rather was in London, some

180 miles away, yet, having learned of the death and the widow's needs, Elsie drove back to Taunton, arriving after 11.30pm. As a widow herself, she understood the desolation of grief. She spoke of her husband, John, frequently to her Taunton friends, recalling with affection all that they had done together. In 1981 she stated that during the past three years 'through circumstances that I greatly regret', that is John's death, she had been able to devote her time to the Lord's work 'and it has given me as much joy to make up for the sorrow as one could expect of life'.[9] Was that one of the reasons why she drove herself so hard and dedicated herself to so much work at an advanced age?

During her Taunton ministry, the usually hale and hearty Elsie suffered some bouts of ill-health. In February 1982, her arthritis was so painful and distressing that she was bedridden – she had suffered arthritis since her younger years and, of course, it had contributed to her retiring from her RAF chaplaincy. In March 1983 she had influenza so badly that she confessed to spending at least one night 'in the depths of melancholy', for her a rare and uncharacteristic admission. On this occasion she was comforted to receive a greetings card from the church members which they had all signed. Only one month after Elsie had left her ministry at Taunton, the members there were still concerned for her health. It was reported to the church meeting that she was 'very poorly' in health and was in hospital in Nottingham undergoing tests. In December 1986, Elsie's participation in the official opening of Cleaves Hall in Nottingham (adjoining the former Castle Gate church) was recorded. She had chosen to exhort and 'stir up' the assembly and was against the settling down which she diagnosed as the disease of the church. She wanted Christians to trust the Holy Spirit to guide and enliven them. However, prior to the gathering, Elsie had been in hospital undergoing tests and she had only been discharged so that she might take part in these opening celebrations.[10] Delegates to the British Council of Churches in the 1980s could not fail to notice that Elsie was very badly stricken with arthritis. Yet some still admired her willingness to maintain

9. *The Bangor Challenge*, p. 32.

10. North Street Congregational Church Magazine, February 1982, March 1983. North St Church Meeting Minutes, 24 July 1986. Much of the information above derives from the church members. *Congregational Quarterly* vol 4, no 4 (December 1986), p. 16.

her witness to her principles, even if doing so set her apart from the majority of her fellows.

Membership Figures

Elsie Chamberlain began her ministry at Chulmleigh in 1980. In the previous year the church had 18 members, 9 adherents, one lay preacher and no children. It held one service per week, at 6.30pm on a Sunday. In 1980 the church membership had fallen to 15 and the downward trend seemed likely to continue. That was the situation when Elsie arrived. By 1983 the trend had been reversed. The membership had grown to 21. There were 10 adherents, 13 children and the service had been moved half an hour earlier to 6 pm. Sadly the lay preacher no longer was listed in the returned statistics. In 1984, the year after Elsie had officially left the ministry at Chulmleigh, the membership stood at an even more impressive 24, although no children were listed as attending the church. At that time Elsie's friend and successor, Elaine Marsh, was the minister and in her time the church membership grew to 31 in 1985, and to 35 in 1986 when 18 children were recorded.[11] Elaine recalled having 40 regularly attending the church and a women's group of 22. These returns suggest that the dramatic effort undertaken in the town in the 1980s by both women did not go unrewarded.

The figures at Taunton do not tell quite the same story. In 1979 the membership at North Street stood at 94, with 16 adherents, 10 children and no lay preacher. Two services were held on Sundays. One year later, also before Elsie's arrival, the members had increased by two to 96, the adherents were 24 in number, as also were the children. In 1983 there were 95 members, 30 adherents and 30 children. One year later, however, the membership had fallen to 77 but the numbers of adherents and of children alike had risen to 60. In 1985 the membership still stood at 77 but the church had acquired 85 adherents while the children remained steady at 60. Elsie herself

11. *Congregational Year Book 1979–1980* (Nottingham: Congregational Federation, 1980), p. 93; *Congregational Year Book 1980–1981* (Nottingham: Congregational Federation, 1981), p. 97; *Congregational Year Book 1983* (Nottingham: Congregational Federation, 1983), p. 96; *Congregational Year Book 1984* (Nottingham: Congregational Federation, 1984), p. 96; *Congregational Year Book 1985*, p. 98; *Congregational Year Book 1985–1986* (Nottingham: Congregational Federation, 1986), p. 59.

commented at the church meeting in July that year that many among the large number of adherents at North Street should really become church members. In Elsie's last year at the church at Taunton the membership had grown to 80 but, in 1987, Ray Avent's first year at North Street, it fell to 54, growing to 59 in 1989, while the numbers of children fell to 20.[12]

We may conclude from these figures – especially those relating to adherents –that Elsie was particularly good at attracting the occasional passers by, even the regular visitors, and their children, whom she called the newcomers so often in the church meetings, to worship at North Street. But, like others who lacked her special charisma, she was not able to overcome their deep seated reservations and convert such attenders into committed church members in either town, although she had more success in this respect in Chulmleigh than in Taunton. Scholars have recognized the phenomenon of 'believing but not belonging' as a characteristic of the age. After Elsie's departure from Taunton, the huge number of adherents, even exceeding that of the church members, seems to have lost interest and melted away. How deeply did her Christian faith touch their hearts and minds?

Clearly Elsie had a positive impact on both churches and on their respective communities. One woman, even with all her willing input of dynamism, could not on her own reverse national trends. Yet she could hardly be blamed for trying! Certainly she brought the people in both churches out of any quiet resignation that decline was inevitable and should, therefore, not be challenged. Challenge was meat and drink to Elsie and her best efforts did yield dividends but would they be permanent? Was Elsie just a flash in the pan, bright, colourful, but bound to fizzle out sooner or later and leave no lasting benefit? Was she perhaps a rare breed of English eccentric, if of a peculiar ecclesiastical variety? The church people in Taunton and Chulmleigh would not agree with this harsh assessment but what of the townsfolk in general?

---

12. *Congregational Year Book 1979–1980*, p. 96; *Congregational Year Book 1980–1981*, p. 99; *Congregational Year Book 1983*, p. 98; *Congregational Year Book 1984*, p. 96; *Congregational Year Book 1985*, p. 100; *Congregational Year Book 1985–1986*, p. 61; *Congregational Year Book 1987–1988* (Nottingham: Congregational Federation, 1988), p. 61; *Congregational Year Book 1989–1990* (Nottingham: Congregational Federation, 1990), p. 64. North St Church Meeting Minutes, 22 July 1985.

The International Congregational Fellowship: Bangor 1981

In early July 1981, at Bangor, in north Wales, the International Congregational Fellowship held its second formal meeting. Elsie attended among the delegates from the Congregational Federation and was chosen as the representative from England to be introduced to the mayor at the formal welcome. Later in open discussion Elsie turned to the topical theme of Christian unity, one of her preoccupations. She asked:

> Would you say that we would do more to move towards a sense of unity if ... we could offer to people the simplicity of our Congregational basis without demanding any change in their structures? We all believe in Jesus Christ and ... when his presence is with us there is the church, can we not claim to the world that we are one in Christ and let them go on with their own administrations and structures and bishops if they want them? Isn't this the way towards unity, we'll never do it in detail as they are doing it now?

Another of her preoccupations surfaced at Bangor when Elsie spoke of her wish that church members would trust the Holy Spirit more. She expressed frustration that Christians so often made excuses in order to avoid tackling a challenging but necessary task. If they were to trust the Holy Spirit, they would discover 'this excitement of the Christian life' which was for her 'the exciting part of service'. She offered a criticism of those Christians who 'were tied to material things', pointing to her own previous church 'where I loved my folk for nine years, and still love them' – probably a reference to Hutton Free Church. But 'they were all on the up and up, they were all earning more money – at least most of them', she said. She saw such materialism and the desire for 'social success' and 'money-making' as a loss of the 'tremendous freedom we have been given' and 'very sad'. She cautioned her listeners, 'We must be careful of the demands of modern life which get in the way of our freedom'.[13]

The National Free Church Women's Council

Elsie had long been an active encourager of women's work in the churches. She felt that the National Free Church Women's Council,

---

13. *The Bangor Challenge*, pp. 9, 27, 32, 34.

in particular, failed to publicize its doings well enough so that its achievements went largely unnoticed. Elsie was elected president of the National Free Church Women's Council, assuming that office in 1984 at the congress of the Free Church Federal Council at Eastbourne in Sussex and serving until the following year. On the assembly platform with her were the retiring Free Church Federal Council moderator, her old friend and sparring partner, Kenneth Slack, and Howard Williams, the incoming moderator who was the minister of Bloomsbury Central Baptist Church, London. She confided to a friend later, in one of her favourite sayings, that at the Free Church Federal Council 'we can assemble in unity and not be disagreeable'.

Her presidential address was entitled 'Dissent and Freedom', both of which she believed were not valued sufficiently by contemporary free churchmen and women. She commented on the setting up of yet another committee to examine the purpose and future of the Free Church Federal Council, stating that 'on the whole men call for committees and commissions and conferences while the women get on with the job'. However, she did confess to having sat on a few committees herself and that she relished the prospect – 'I enjoy the cut and thrust of it'. Yet she prayed that the churches of England should 'always ... remain organisationally divided' because she could not bear to think of the time it would take 'to construct a constitution to include all of us'. All the administration involved in such a scheme she dismissed as 'ridiculous', an adjective she applied also to 'the covenant' for unity which had by then failed, although she believed that the hours spent, by the denominational delegates in each others' company, were worthwhile because we came to 'believe in one another and forget that we had previously used our different structures as barriers'. Rather she invited her listeners to 'delight in the variety of religious experience and liturgy and worship – yes, and of theology and doctrine and organisation and constitution – all a spur to our deeper thought'.

She then turned her attention to Christian attitudes to a variety of social and political issues – teenage sex, video 'nasties', drug abuse, prostitution, aid to under-developed countries, international peace, unemployment, poverty and greed. She anticipated that she would be called 'simplistic' for her refusal to turn a blind eye and for her hope that some way may be found to tackle these difficult issues. Yet she maintained that the freedom of the free churches, and of Christians in general, and Christian women in particular, should be used in their being 'constructively different'. During Elsie's year of office the Free Church women had undertaken to raise enough money to fund the sinking of two wells in the drought stricken parts of Africa. By the spring of 1985 the sum raised was £6,000 and she had hopes of more than doubling that in order to pay for ten wells. She retained her faith in the conscience of Free Church women, remarking that where that conscience was awake 'there is a great power working'.

In 1985 the new Free Church Federal Council moderator, the historian and leading Welsh Congregationalist, R. Tudur Jones, paid tribute to his predecessor, Howard Williams, and to Elsie Chamberlain, as the retiring president of the Women's Council, whom, he stated, had 'discharged the responsibilities of her office with her customary energy and good humour'. Her successor as women's president, Dorothy Alexander, also thanked Elsie for her 'guidance and example'. She continued, 'Elsie has thrown herself into the work of the Women's Council with characteristic wholehearted zeal. While she ministers to her own two churches – so widely spaced geographically'– (Taunton and Nottingham) 'she has not spared herself; but has travelled all over the country to visit and inspire the Women's Councils who have invited her to their meetings.' She spoke of Elsie's influence after one such visit. 'I know, myself, from her visit to us at Cheltenham, that women leave her conferences stimulated and with greater determination, not only to carry on their existing work, but also to be ready to see other needs'.

Elsie's vehement support for the ministry of women in the churches had not slowed, as she had aged. The issue, so close to her heart since childhood, was associated for her with her mother, with Muriel Paulden, with Maude Royden, and her old friend Lady Stansgate. Elsie felt so strongly on this issue that before the Methodist Church approved the ordination of women, she refused to write or speak on behalf of the Methodists because she believed that they discriminated unfairly against their deaconesses. She dismissed with contempt the arguments put forward by those within the Church of England who opposed the ordination of women stating, in an interview not long before her death, 'The doctrine against women priests is hooey, based partly on selective scripture, partly on the Old Testament view of the uncleanness of women at certain times. All in all it makes a pretty funny theological background'. *The Times* noted that 'she certainly felt called to be an invigorating influence sweeping through male-dominated ecclesiasticism with tornado-like force'.[14]

In March 1985 she spoke of the future of the Free Church Federal Council, explaining that a working party had been considering that subject since September 1983. She pointed out that the women's department of the Free Church Federal Council had 47 active local women's councils, of which 21 were responsible for residential homes. As president of the National Free Church Women's Council, Elsie had attended one of the Queen's garden parties at Buckingham Palace and had also been present for a long weekend at Canterbury, at the invitation of the Archbishop of Canterbury who wished to meet representatives of all the main British denominations, including Cardinal Hume, several Roman Catholic bishops, and other leading church men and women.[15]

Other Activities

In early 1982 Elsie led the prayers of dedication at the opening of the new church building at Belper, in Derbyshire, calling the whole project 'a remarkable achievement'. In March 1982 she was the speaker at the Federation of Congregational Women's meeting at Penge which took as its theme a celebration of the Bible. In the summer of that year she gave the address to the Stratford and District Free Church Council at Long Compton, in Warwickshire. She attended the ordination of Leslie Morrison at Victoria Congregational Church, Blackpool in September 1982, and led the prayers. Two weeks later she was with old friends as the presiding minister at Morrison's induction to her former charge in Essex, Hutton Free Church, where he remained until 1987. In April 1983 she gave the charge to the ministers, Elizabeth and Ron Bending, at their induction to the ministry of Corfe Castle Congregational Church, in Dorset. This couple had served as pastors of Chulmleigh Congregational Church 1962–1970.[16]

14. *Free Church Chronicle* no 4, vol XXXVIII (Winter 1983), p. 24; *Free Church Chronicle* no 2, vol XXXIX (Summer 1984), pp. 8–11; *Free Church Chronicle* no 1, vol XL (Spring 1985), pp. 2–3; *Free Church Chronicle* no 2, vol XL (Summer 1985), pp. 2–3. *Congregational Quarterly* vol 9, no 2 (Summer 1991), pp. 12–14. *The Daily Telegraph*, 16 April 1991. *The Times*, 12 April 1991.

15. *Congregational Quarterly* vol 3, no 2 (March 1985), p. 3.

16. *Congregational News* (January–February), pp. 2, 11; *Congregational News* (March–April), p. 2; *Congregational News* (September–October 1982), p. 2;

Elsie took seriously her responsibilities as the Congregational Federation's officer for ecumenical relationships, attending conferences of the British Council of Churches, and encouraging Congregationalists in larger and smaller churches to become involved with other churches and with their local communities. During the 1980s she was busy with, among her many other duties, a variety of inter-denominational activities. In March 1984 she reported on the failure of the covenant for unity which had emerged eventually from the work of the English Churches Unity Commission. She stated that this failure had spurred ecumenical efforts at the local level which was, she claimed for the Congregational Federation, 'how it should be'. She praised the Bishop of Taunton's recent address to the Congregational Federation's southwest area in which he had stressed that 'Unity is a harmony, not unison'. She certainly did not see free church ministries as defective, needing to be set right by episcopal ordination. In March 1986 Elsie praised the new approach to ecumenical relations demonstrated in the 'Not Strangers But Pilgrims' programme, which had been launched by the Archbishop of York in November 1985. In March 1988 she was present at an ecumenical gathering at Swanwick which she found 'hopeful'. The delegates included Roman Catholics who met there on equal terms with other Christians in order to plan a new ecumenical instrument to replace the British Council of Churches.[17]

In the Spring of 1985, Elsie was one of 60 who attended the Congregational Federation's ministers and pastors school at Swanage in Dorset which she found 'stimulating'. That summer she shared in the funeral service for Ronald Newman at Old Coulsdon Congregational Church, near Purley, south of London. He had served as minister there for 32 years, since the church's founding in 1953. In the mid 1980s Elsie was instrumental in helping one dissatisfied elder in the United Reformed Church to rediscover his former Congregationalism, as a personal member of the Congregational Federation. In the autumn of 1989 Elsie again addressed the subject

Congregational News (January–February), p. 2, *Congregational News* (May–June 1983), p. 3. L. Fisher History of *Chulmleigh Congregational Church* (Chulmleigh: the author, 1997), p. 10.

17. *Congregational Quarterly* vol 1, no 1 (November 1983), pp. 26–28; *Congregational Quarterly* vol 2, no 1 (March 1984), p. 10; *Congregational Quarterly* vol 4, no 1 (March 1986), p. 43; *Congregational Quarterly* vol 6, no 1 (March 1988), p. 20. *Free Church Chronicle* no 4, vol XXXIX (Winter 1984), pp. 3–4.

of women in the church. She claimed that the greater number of women in the churches is partially explained by the fact that women live longer than men and she ventured to suggest that men and boys would come to church more if they were given jobs to do, such as painting or gardening. She felt that churches should provide games for men like pool and snooker as well as be friendly to them.[18] Close friends noticed that Elsie herself related more easily to women than she did to men and, in the opinion of one woman minister, she was simply too forceful a personality for most men to cope with.

Elsie's Death

As we have seen, Elsie did not know how to retire although she did eventually slow down under pressure. She was forced to face the inevitable and cut back a little on the many commitments she had previously taken for granted. After 1986 she was minister of only one church, in the Congregational Centre at Nottingham. She continued her involvement in the church's activities and would make herself available at all the Congregational Federation's functions, assemblies, rallies, ministers' conferences, and at the training weekends for students and tutors alike, with as much vigour as she could muster. However, her health was causing concern and a non-malignant lymphoma, necessitating radium treatment, was initially diagnosed. At Christmas 1990 Elsie did not send cards to her friends but instead she telephoned them. The sensitive among them realized that she was more unwell than she admitted. In early 1991 Elsie was admitted to the University Hospital, Nottingham, and, after making a partial recovery, she was discharged. She stayed at the home of Paddy and Henry Morris, enjoying the company and hospitality of these old friends, whom she had known since her time in Richmond-upon-Thames, but was re-admitted to hospital one week before her death on 10 April 1991, aged 81 years.

The BBC summarized Elsie's achievement in these terms. 'For many, she was the symbol of the place women were beginning to occupy in the public ministry of the churches in the post war years. A Congregational Minister, making history in 1946 as the first woman chaplain to the Forces; making history, too, as the first woman

18. *Congregational Quarterly* vol 3, no 2 (June), pp. 18–19, *Congregational Quarterly* vol 3, no 3 (September–October 1985), 16 (Autumn 1989), vol 7, no 3, 5.

presenter of the *Daily Service* on BBC Radio, where she worked in religious broadcasting for almost thirty years.'[19]

The funeral and thanksgiving service was held at the Congregational Centre in Nottingham on Thursday, 18 April. It was led by Graham M. Adams, the general secretary of the Congregational Federation, and the address was given by John Parker, the chairman of the Congregational Federation's council. Dorothy Twiss, an RAF chaplain, read the lesson from 2 Timothy 4. 1-8, and between 200 and 250 people attended, including a representative from the women's branch of the Free Church Federal Council. In his tribute, Parker recalled her occasional impatience at council meetings with those who rambled or digressed – 'Oh, do get on with it', she would say – but also her hard work and humility – in working in the cafeteria and bookshop at Nottingham, changing the sheets in the bedrooms, and washing the steps outside the building there. He also spoke of her desire to spread the Christian faith and her urging Congregationalists to engage in 'gossiping the gospel'. Elsie's body was cremated and her ashes were buried in the garden of remembrance, next to those of her husband, John Garrington, at Greensted, in Essex, where he had been the rector and where life for them both had been fulfilling.

Four months later an equally well attended memorial service was held at The City Temple in London, on 31 August 1991. At this, Janet Wootton (the daughter of Paddy and Henry Morris) officiated, assisted by Irene Blayney and Leslie Morrison. The Baptist minister and scholar, Edwin Robertson, Elsie's friend and colleague from her time with the BBC, gave the address and the Right Honourable Tony Benn MP recalled the unique difficulties, surrounding her appointment as an RAF chaplain, and her unfailing courage in these daunting circumstances. Ernest Rea, then head of religious broadcasting at the BBC, and Jacqueline Petrie, a United Reformed Church minister and the next woman chaplain appointed by the RAF after Elsie (she served as a full-time chaplain 1989–1998), led the prayers while Trixie Norcott, Elsie's friend, played the organ. Her nephew, Geoffrey Chamberlain, read from the Jerusalem Bible and the choir of her old school, Channing School for Girls, sang. In addition, refreshments were prepared and served by members of her former church, Hutton Free Church, Essex.[20]

19. J. Williams, *First Lady of the Pulpit: A Biography of Elsie Chamberlain* (Lewes, Sussex: Book Guild, 1993), p. 71.

20. Williams, *First Lady of the Pulpit*, p. 91. For Benn and Rea, see *Who's Who* (London: A & C Black, 2002).

Chapter 19

EPILOGUE

A number of more permanent tributes were deemed appropriate by church members and others whose lives she had affected, especially in her last three churches. The walls of the chapel at Chulmleigh have long been adorned by several plaques and the church members there decided, one month after Elsie's death, that they wanted to commemorate her by adding another in marble and brass. Particular friends may wonder whether Elsie herself would entirely approve of this commemoration, yet she knew the sincerity of these West Country people's feelings. The plaque is situated on the wall to the left of the chapel entrance and it reads:

> We remember The Rev Elsie Chamberlain 1910–1991
> Congregational Leader
> Minister of this Church 1980–1983
> Minister Emeritus
> 'She hath done what she could', Mark 14. 8.[1]

The Congregational church members at Castle Gate, Nottingham also chose to honour their friend and first minister but in a different way. At the church meeting in September 1991 they decided to consult, with the Congregational Federation, about commissioning a portrait of Elsie to be hung on the wall of the sanctuary there. Some years earlier a portrait of Reginald Cleaves had been painted by Roy Porter and this had been hung in the church building in Nottingham. Porter was again commissioned and his painting of Elsie was duly placed there.[2] Although Elsie, and the modest Cleaves too, may have been embarrassed at the thought of their likenesses hanging

---

1. Chulmleigh Church Meeting Minutes, 19 May 1991.
2. Nottingham Centre Church Meeting Minutes, 10 September 1991. The issues of veneration of the saints and iconography, in a Congregational church in particular, seem not to have been considered before these portraits were hung, although in the same space there were historical portraits of eighteenth and nineteenth century ministers and other worthies.

in the church (they did not seek to become objects of worship), it is not inappropriate that these portraits should grace the walls somewhere at Castle Gate where the Congregational Federation has its offices. Three years before her death Elsie had written, 'I am proud of my own now small denomination, that has chosen to remain Congregational and independent'.[3] That pride was mutual. Her fellow Congregationalists, not all uncritically, held her in the highest esteem and felt for her a deep gratitude and love. Visitors to Castle Gate may gaze on her likeness but miss her greeting, 'Welcome, good people'.

Also at Nottingham the acquisition of the adjoining property to Cleaves Hall, (two away from the church building, in Castle Gate) and its refurbishment as offices and meeting rooms, resulted in its being named the Elsie Chamberlain House. On 11 October 1997 this was formally opened, at the Congregational Federation's autumn assembly, by Tony Benn. Among the many guests in Nottingham on this occasion was Elsie's daughter and biographer, Janette Williams.[4]

At North Street, Taunton the church did not forget Elsie either. A room which opens directly to the outside, at the back of the premises, was set aside for use as a charity shop, run by the church members, during Ray Avent's ministry there. This was then called 'The Elsie Chamberlain Shop'. In 2001 this was refurbished and converted into 'Chamberlains', an attractive coffee shop during the daytime, run by the church. At weekends this shop has been used as a youth cyber café, run by Taunton Youth for Christ, in conjunction with the church. In addition, just inside the entrance to Chamberlains, was placed a picture of Elsie, with a brief explanation of the café's name.

Elsie as Minister

It would be unfair and misleading to suggest that Elsie Chamberlain regarded herself as superior to and more enlightened than those to whom she ministered. She did not look down upon or stand aloof from those she served. After all, she was not afraid to get her hands dirty and would often help with menial chores, joining in and adding to the camaraderie of such occasions. If then she was not Lady Bountiful, whose largesse was freely distributed to the deserving poor, was there nevertheless some element of condescension in Elsie's

3. Hibbs, *The Country Chapel*, p. 9.
4. *The Congregationalist* no 2 (February 1998), p. 1.

ministry? After all, she was a tall, confident, middle class lady who carried herself well, had a fine bearing, an open smiling face, winning ways and a strong presence, and she came to do good, often to those from less well-off backgrounds.

To those who did not know her, Elsie could seem austere, even aloof, yet she did not keep people at a distance and made friends easily. Indeed, she made deep friendships wherever she went, maintaining them across denominational divides – with Kenneth and Millicent Slack, with Rachel Storr, with several bishops, and with many others. Elsie arranged for friends from New Zealand who had a healing ministry to see Kenneth Slack, during his last illness, and she herself visited him and prayed with him. She was deeply loved by many and delighted to love in return. She had no time nor reason to cultivate a condescending manner. She was always too busy for that. Perhaps she was also too busy for detailed self-examination, and she was not noted for her reflection on issues which others found more complex than she did (indeed she could be impatient with such thinkers).

Some of her church members may have come dangerously close to adoring Elsie, as Elaine Marsh had noticed at Chulmleigh and others had seen at Hutton, yet Elsie did not require adoration, if indeed she was conscious of it, and many outstanding ministers have had their admiring 'worshippers' in the past. Certainly Elsie was aware of her natural authority and of her powers of persuasion and she used them in her ministry, in her attempts to revive dying churches, and in her readiness to befriend all. Her laughter too was genuine and infectious. It broke down defences and opened doors. Lacking pretension herself, she recognized few, if any, social barriers.

Elsie's lack of vanity was demonstrated in one episode when she was robing before a service in the minister's vestry, in the company of a young male colleague who wanted to comb his tangled hair free from its wind-blown state, before moving into the chapel. They were to take part in an ordination service. The young minister asked if she had a mirror and she replied, 'Whatever for?' Her long hair (dark brown when she was younger and greyer with age) was plaited and tied neatly behind her head in a style she maintained for many years. That style suited her and she simply had no need for a mirror and could not imagine that others had different needs. Although she

5. *The Bangor Challenge*, p. 32.

had once been a dress designer, and had made her own clothes, and some for Janette when she was young, she saw no reason to wear fine clothes nor to preen herself. She was easily content. During one service at Taunton Elsie had slipped as she descended from the pulpit. The church members knew that her shoes which she had bought in a charity shop were simply too big for her. She would not waste money on new shoes if she could buy them more reasonably.

Elsie was usually a good cook but she could be distracted by seemingly more important duties. Staying in the Chulmleigh manse one Sunday when Elaine Marsh was ministering there, she put a pie with a meringue topping in the oven and forgot about it with the result that it was badly overdone. On realizing what she had done, she left the Methodist church hurriedly and rushed back to the house but she was too late and the pie was baked hard. On another occasion Elsie charred the potatoes when two visiting friends from the Congregational Federation were invited to dinner. She also complained that she could not make the beautiful, jam sponge cakes at which others in her churches excelled.[5] At Taunton Elsie revealed her frugal approach to housekeeping when she chastized those who, to her thinking, were extravagant in their making of the sandwiches for church teas. Following her mother's advice, Elsie insisted that the bread only needed butter at the edges. It should not be spread all over the bread. She had grown up in a different age!

We may also ask how saintly Elsie was. If she was good, as indeed she was, how good was she? Did she strive for inward peace and spiritual perfection? Given her larger than life presence and early fame, was she truly humble? Certainly she was dedicated to her people and to the God to whom she had given her heart at a young age. She was always willing to share her own good cheer, although she would not flatter nor deceive, in order to gain an advantage and her bluntness could verge on downright rudeness. Did she really say the truth in love? Yet her bright and dazzling goodness was neither mannered nor affected in any way but simply came straight from the person she was. She had the old fashioned but understated Christian virtues of loyalty, diligence and reliability. She would not boast and, although she had a sense of humour, she had little time for frivolity and none for conceit and self-importance. Her word was her bond and her ceaseless industry and total dedication to the cause

6. *Reform* (May 1991), p. 18.

were exemplary. Following her training with Muriel Paulden, she was ever the evangelist. Her mind never stopped wrestling with the problem of communicating the gospel and in this she had succeeded for much of her life uncommonly well.

Conclusion

Elsie was not an original thinker. Her intellect was keen but not outstanding. Her gifts lay in her being so much a normal person, with quite extraordinary energy and confidence, but lacking all artifice, that when she spoke she was trusted. She brought to her listeners not only challenge and excitement but a measure of comfort and reassurance. By speaking plainly she articulated their fears and misgivings, their hopes and beliefs. Her style was perfectly suited for everyman, the man or woman in the street whom she encountered outside The City Temple early on a weekday morning, or in North Street, Taunton, whilst doing the shopping. She gave these people a taste of her vibrant personality, a glimpse of her Christian graciousness and, if they wanted more, they would and often did come to church. If later they fell away, then it is likely that they never forgot this tall, fascinating and prepossessing woman who told them of her faith and of her saviour. Being no scholar, she prepared a simple, essential address for Sunday worship, often with few notes, and delivered it with vitality because it came from her heart and came often with her heart.

She did not trouble herself overmuch with doctrinal niceties and towards the end of her life she confessed to a friend that she thought that her own theological views had moved in a heterodox direction, away from strict Trinitarian correctness. Perhaps in this she was simply returning to the ideas current in her youth for, when she was growing up, the dominant trend in Congregationalism had been more liberal in theology and closer to Unitarianism than it was later and, of course, as a girl she had attended a Unitarian school. Yet there is no denying her genuine passion for God which was only matched, but not exceeded, by her passion for God's people. She could neither tolerate complacency nor understand worldly resignation on the part of Christians, taking seriously the injunction not to conform to the ways of this world. She demanded that Christians should be active in their witness to the faith and she clearly led by example.

Elsie's long ministry consistently revealed that she would be neither intimidated nor profoundly overawed. As a woman she had overcome prejudice in being ordained and in gaining acceptance as a minister. She had made history in confronting and overcoming the obstacles to her marriage and to her service as an RAF chaplain. Her broadcasting which, in the opinion of many, brought her into full bloom and gave her deep happiness, honed her ability to communicate to and hold the attention of a mass audience, which probably included many who shunned all things religious. Her varied pastoral experiences demonstrated a singular ability to discover beneath the humdrum and mediocre, so often naturally overlooked, the promise of renewal. Even more exceptionally she was able to convert that promise into reality. She believed in people and helped them to excel beyond the limited assumptions made about them by the world, so that they came to believe in themselves and in their God-given possibilities. Essentially humble and in many ways ordinary herself, she did not despise the ordinary and commonplace but looked beyond them and, therefore, discovered a surprising potential for growth and development, treasures in earthen vessels.

As John Marsh, the former principal of Mansfield College, Oxford wrote in 1991, 'To meet and to know Elsie was a liberalising joy. She was a radiant person with a joyful faith'.[6] To those who knew her, whose lives were graced by her wonderful capacity for love, and in her wholehearted acceptance of so many assorted waifs and strays in the churches and beyond, she reflected the love and acceptance of Christ himself. This is where her true genius lay. Elsie was a dynamo, involved in so many activities, making Herculean efforts herself and enabling others to join her and to discover and release their talents and gifts in a joint enterprise and a marvellous adventure. Alongside her impressive physical strength, which lasted almost to the end, she conveyed great power of character and spirit. In truth she was simply unstoppable and wondrous to behold.

BIBLIOGRAPHY

Primary Material

Manuscript and Other Archive Records: The minute books etc., are all retained at the churches mentioned. I am grateful to the ministers, deacons and members of these churches for enabling me to consult their records and also to learn from their memories.

BBC Archive: Religious Scripts on Microfilm
    Contributors' Talks, File I 1945–1962 Revd Elsie Chamberlain

Christ Church Friern Barnet: ministerial committee records
    church meeting minutes
    deacons' meeting minutes

Chulmleigh Congregational Church: church meeting minutes
    deacons' meeting minutes
    memorandum on the dating of the chapel

Fen Place News-Letter (August 1964, April, October 1968) held at The Congregational Library, Gordon Square, London.

'A Festival of Congregationalism', programme in The Congregational Library, Gordon Square, London.

Hutton Free Church: church meeting minutes
    deacons' meeting minutes

Kentish Town Congregational Church: church meeting minutes
    church newsletter
    correspondence and other material

North St Congregational Church, Taunton: church meeting minutes
    deacons' meeting minutes
    church magazine
    information from church members

Nottingham Centre Church: church meeting minutes

C.E. Surman: Index of Congregational Ministers, held at Dr Williams's Library, London.
    Manuscript note on the flyleaf of Cording's history of Chulmleigh CC in Dr Williams's Library, 14 Gordon Square, London, WC1H OAR.

Vineyard Congregational Church, Richmond-upon-Thames:
    church meeting minutes
    deacons' meeting minutes

Secondary Material

Books and Articles

Austin, A.W., *The Surrey Congregational Union 1862–1965* (Banbury, Oxon: the author, nd).

Baker T.F.T. (ed.), *Victoria History of the Counties of England: Middlesex, Vol. VI* (London: published for the Institute of Historical Research by Oxford University Press, 1980).

Benn, Tony *Office Without Power: Diaries 1968–72* (London: Hutchinson, 1988).

Benn, Tony MP, Lord Carrington, Lord Deedes and Mary Soames, 'Churchill Remembered. Recollections'. *Transactions of the Royal Historical Society* (sixth series, XI; London: Royal Historical Society, 2001).

Blayney, R.I., *Kentish Town Congregational Church 1804–1991: A Brief History* (London: the author, 1991).

Calder, R.F.G. (ed.), *Proceedings of the Seventh International Congregational Council* (London: Independent Press, 1953).

Carpenter, E. *Archbishop Fisher – His Life and Times* (Norwich: Canterbury Press, 1991).

Chadwick, O., *Hensley Henson: A Study in the Friction between Church and State* (Oxford: Clarendon Press, 1983).

Chamberlain E.D., 'Impressions of the Conference' *Congregational Quarterly, Vol. XXVII* (London: Congregational Union of England and Wales, 1949).

– *White to Harvest* (London: Independent Press, 1956).

– *Lift Up Your Hearts* (London: Max Parrish, 1959).

– *Calm Delight* (London: Hodder & Stoughton, 1960).

Cherry B., and N. Pevsner, *The Buildings of England. London 2: South* (London: Penguin, 1983).

– *The Buildings of England London 4: North* (London: Penguin, 1998).

Clare, A., *The City Temple 1640–1940* (London: Independent Press, 1940).

Cleaves R.W., *Congregationalism 1960–1976: The Story of the Federation* (Swansea: John Penry Press, 1977).

Crippen, T.G., 'John Moore of Tiverton' in A. Peel (ed.), *Transactions of the Congregational Historical Society, Vol. IX* (London: Congregational Historical Society, 1924–26), pp. 180–90.

Cockburn, J.S., H.P.F. King, and K.G.T. McDonnell (eds), *Victoria History of the Counties of England: Middlesex, Vol. I* (Westminster: Archibald Constable, 1911).

Coltman, C., 'Post-Reformation: The Free Churches', in A.M. Royden, *The Church and Woman* (London: J. Clarke & Co., 1924).

Congregational Federation Assembly: Record of Proceedings (Nottingham: Congregational Federation, 1980).

Congregational Union of England and Wales Spring Assembly – Official Programme (London: Congregational Union of England and Wales, 1941).

Cording, J.G., *A Short History of the Congregational Church, Chulmleigh, Devon* (Chulmleigh: the author, 1933).

Davies, H., *Worship and Theology in England – The Ecumenical Century 1900–65* (Princeton, NJ: Princeton University Press).

Dixon, L., *Seven Score Years and Ten: The Story of Islington Chapel during One Hundred and Fifty Years 1788–1938* (London: E.O. Beck, nd.).

Dougall, R., *In and Out of the Box* (London: Collins, Harvill Press, 1975).

Elders, E.A., *The Kirk on the Green: The Story of Richmond's Presbyterian Congregation 1876–1976* (Richmond, Surrey: Richmond Green United Reformed Church, 1976).

Goodall, N., *A History of the London Missionary Society 1895–1945* (London: Oxford University Press, 1954).

Fagley, F.L. (ed.), *Proceedings of the Sixth International Congregational Council* (London: Independent Press, 1949).

Field-Bibb, J. *Women Towards Priesthood: Ministerial Politics and Feminist Praxis* (Cambridge: Cambridge University Press, 1991).

Fisher, L., *History of Chulmleigh Congregational Church* (Chulmleigh: the author, 1997).

Fletcher, S., *Maude Royden: A Life* (Oxford: Basil Blackwell, 1989).

Harwood, E., and A. Saint, *Exploring England's Heritage: London* (London: English Heritage, 1991).

Hearnshaw, F.J.C., *The Centenary History of King's College, London 1828–1928* (London: Harrap, 1929).

Hendry, K., *Don't Ask Me Why 60 Years a Woman Minister* (London: United Reformed Church, 1991).

Herklots, H.G.G., *Looking at Evanston: A Study of the Second Assembly of the World Council of Churches* (London: SCM Press, 1954).

Hibbs, J., *The Country Chapel* (Newton Abbot: David & Charles, 1988).

Holland, H., *A Short History of Chulmleigh Congregational Church Devon 1633–1983* (Chulmleigh: the author, 1983).

Huelin, G., *King's College, London 1828–1978* (London: King's College, University of London, 1978).

Hunkins Hallinan, H. (ed.), *In Her Own Right* (London: Harrap, 1968).

Huxtable, J., *As It Seemed To Me* (London: United Reformed Church, 1990).

International Congregational Fellowship International Meetings, London, England 1977, The London Witness: Record of Proceedings (np: International Congregational Fellowship, 1977).

International Congregational Fellowship 2nd International Meetings, Bangor, Gwynedd, North Wales, 1981 The Bangor Challenge: Record of Proceedings (np: International Congregational Fellowship, 1981).

Iremonger, F.A., *William Temple Archbishop of Canterbury His life and Letters* (London: Oxford University Press, 1948).

Jones, R.T., *Congregationalism in England, 1662–1962* (London: Independent Press, 1962).

Kay, E., *Pragmatic Premier: An Intimate Portrait of Harold Wilson* (London: Leslie Frewin, 1967).

Kaye, E., 'A Turning-Point in the Ministry of Women: the Ordination of the First Woman to the Christian Ministry in September 1917', in W.J. Sheils and D. Wood (eds), *Women in the Church* (Oxford: Basil Blackwell, 1990).

— *Mansfield College, Oxford: Its Origin, History and Significance* (Oxford: Oxford University Press, 1996).

— 'Constance Coltman — A Forgotten Pioneer', in *Journal of the United Reformed Church History Society* vol. 4, no. 2 (May 1988).

— 'From "Woman Minister" to "Minister"?' In *Journal of the United Reformed Church History Society* vol. 6, no. 10 (July 2002).

Kaye, E., J. Lees and K. Thorpe, *Daughters of Dissent* (London: United Reformed Church, 2004).

Livingstone, E.A. (ed.), 'Women, ordination of' in *The Oxford Dictionary of the Christian Church* (Oxford: Oxford University Press, 3rd edn 1997).

Malden H.E. (ed.), *Victoria History of the Counties of England: Surrey, Vol. III* (Westminster: Archibald Constable, 1911).

Macarthur, A., 'The Background to the Formation of the United Reformed Church', in *Journal of the United Reformed Church History Society* vol. 4, no. 1 (October 1987).

McLachlan, H., *English Education Under the Test Acts* (Manchester: Manchester University Press, 1931).

Matthews, A.G., *Calamy Revised* (Oxford: Clarendon Press, 1934).

Matthews, W.R., *Memories and Meanings* (London: Hodder & Stoughton, 1969).

Mearns, A., *The London Congregational Directory* (London: Alexander & Shepheard, 1889).

Micklem, C., 'Erik Routley 1917–1982', in R.A. Leaver and J.H. Litton, *Duty and Delight: Routley Remembered* (Norwich: Canterbury Press, 1985).

Newton, J.F., *River of Years* (Philadelphia, PA: J.B. Lippincott & Co., 1946).

Oxford Dictionary of National Biography (Oxford: Oxford University Press, 2004).

Oldfield, A., *The Story of the London Women's League of the London Congregational Union 1909–1959* (London: Independent Press, 1959).

Paulden, M.O., 'How to use a Down-town Church', *Congregational Quarterly, Vol. I* (London: Congregational Union of England and Wales, 1923).

Peel, A., *The Congregational Two Hundred* (London: Independent Press, 1948).

— *The Noble Army of Congregational Martyrs* (London: Independent Press, 1948).

Powell W.R. (ed.), *Victoria History of the Counties of England: Essex, Vol. IV* (London: published for the Institute of Historical Research by Oxford University Press, 1956).

P(reston), G.H., *Vineyard Congregational Church Richmond 1830–1980* (Richmond, Surrey, the author, no date).

Purcell, W., *Fisher of Lambeth A Portrait from Life* (London: Hodder & Stoughton, 1969).

Read, L.H., 'Impressions of the Conference', *Congregational Quarterly, Vol. XXVII* (London: Congregational Union of England and Wales, 1949).

Robinson, W.G., *A History of The Lancashire Congregational Union 1806–1956* (Manchester: Lancashire Congregational Union, 1955).

Routley, E., *The Story of Congregationalism* (London: Independent Press, 1961).

Royden, A.M., *The Church and Woman* (London: J. Clarke & Co., 1924).

Saunders, E.M., *A Progress: Channing School 1885–1985* (Saxmundham, Suffolk: John Catt, 1984).

Slack, K., *Matthew, Mark, Luke and Acts* (London: A. & R. Mowbray, 1968).

— *The City Temple: A Hundred Years* (London: the Elders' Meeting, The City Temple, 1974).

Smith, L., *Harold Wilson: The Authentic Portrait* (London: Hodder & Stoughton, 1964).

Spears, R., *Record of Unitarian Worthies* (London: E.T. Whitfield, 1876).

— *Memorable Unitarians Being a Series of Brief Biographical Sketches* (London: British and Foreign Unitarian Association, 1906).

Stansgate, M., *My Exit Visa: An Autobiography* (London: Hutchinson, 1992).

Taylor, J., and C. Binfield (eds), *Who They Were in the Reformed Churches of England and Wales 1901–2000* (Donington: Shaun Tyas for the United Reformed Church History Society, 2007).

Taylor, J.H., *LCU Story 1873–1972* (Southampton: Hobbs the Printers Limited, 1972).

Temple, P., *Islington Chapels* (London: Royal Commission on Historical Monuments England, 1992).

Travell, J., *Doctor of Souls: Leslie D. Weatherhead 1893–1976* (London: Lutterworth Press, 1999).

Visser 't. Hooft, W.A. (ed.), *The First Assembly of the World Council of Churches* (London: SCM Press Ltd, 1949).

— *The Evanston Report: The Second Assembly of the World Council of Churches 1954* (London: SCM Press Ltd, 1955).

Wand, J.W.C., *Aspects of the Cross* (London: Independent Press, 1956).

— *Aspects of Advent* (London: Independent Press, 1957).

— *Changeful Page: The Autobiography of William Wand* (London: Hodder & Stoughton, 1965).

Watson, D., *Angel of Jesus: Muriel Paulden of Liverpool 8* (Wimborne, Dorset: the author, 1994).

Weatherhead, L., *The Significance of Silence* (London: Epworth Press, 1945).

Waugh, R., *The Life of Benjamin Waugh* (London: T. Fisher Unwin, 1913).

Who's Who 2001 (London: A & C Black, 2001).

Who's Who 2002 (London: A & C Black, 2002).

Who Was Who 1941–1950 (London: A & C Black, 1980).

Who Was Who 1951–1960 (London: A & C Black, 1961).

Who Was Who 1961–1970 (London: A & C Black, 1971).

Who Was Who 1981–1990 (London: A & C Black, 1991).

Who Was Who 1991–1995 (London: A & C Black, 1996).

Williams, J., *First Lady of the Pulpit A Biography of Elsie Chamberlain* (Lewes, Sussex: Book Guild, 1993).

Wolfe, K.M., *The Churches and the British Broadcasting Corporation 1922–1956* (London: SCM Press, 1984).

Periodicals

The Baptist Handbook (1970)

British Weekly

The Christian World

The Congregationalist

Congregational Monthly

Congregational News — started in early 1972 as a duplicated typescript and from November 1972 was printed and issued bi-monthly until the mid 1980s.

Congregational Quarterly 1923–1952

Congregational Quarterly, published by the Congregational Federation from the mid 1980s to the late 1990s.

Congregational Year Book, published by the Congregational Union and after 1972 the same name was used by the Congregational Federation.

Evangelical Fellowship of Congregational Churches Year Book (1992–1993)

Free Church Chronicle

Reform

United Reformed Church Year Book

INDEX